A How-to Guide for Teaching English Language Learners

A How-to Guide for Teaching English Language Learners

In the Primary Classroom

Pat Barrett Dragan

HEINEMANN
Portsmouth, NH

Heinemann

A division of Reed Elsevier Inc.
361 Hanover Street
Portsmouth, NH 03801–3912
www.heinemann.com

Offices and agents throughout the world

The author and publisher wish to thank those who have generously given
permission to reprint borrowed material:

"In the Museum" from *Everything Glistens and Everything Sings: New
and Selected Poems* by Charlotte Zolotow. Copyright © 1987 by Charlotte
Zolotow. Reprinted by permission of Harcourt, Inc.

Library of Congress Cataloging-in-Publication Data
Barrett Dragan, Patricia.
      A how-to guide for teaching English language learners : in the primary
classroom / Pat Barrett Dragan.
            p.   cm.
      Includes references and index.
      ISBN 0-325-00700-4 (alk. paper)
      1. English language—Study and teaching (Primary)—Foreign speakers.
I. Title.

PE1128.A2B314   2005
372.652′1044—dc22   2005016361

Editor: Lois Bridges
Production editor: Sonja S. Chapman
Cover design: Night & Day Design
Compositor: Publishers' Design and Production Services, Inc.
Manufacturing: Jamie Carter
Cover photograph: Alfonso Alvarez, grade 1, and Tatiana Alvarez, grade 5,
      taken by Pat Barrett Dragan

Printed in the United States of America on acid-free paper
09 08 07 06 05 ML 1 2 3 4 5

This book is for my family, especially for George,
who lights up my life.

CONTENTS

viii

Contents

A great part of my joy in writing this book comes to me because of the children I teach. I would like to give a giant thank-you to my students at Martin Elementary School in South San Francisco. They have eagerly shared their ideas with me, as well as their dreams and achievements and their excitement about learning. I have woven some of their words, thoughts, writing, drawings, and photographs into this text. This back-and-forth interaction with my first graders, as well as with former students now in higher grades, makes this book possible.

I want to thank Heinemann and the wonderful people there for working to make this book the best it could be. I especially thank Sonja Chapman, my production editor; Amy Rowe, editorial assistant; Brita Mess, permissions; Doria Turner, promotions coordinator; Pat Carls, marketing manager; and Eric Chalek, copywriter.

Most of all I want to thank my dear editor and friend, Lois Bridges. Having Lois as my editor has been one of life's special gifts. She is brilliant and insightful, unstinting in her help, and a beautiful, caring person.

I'd like to say a big thank you to Phil Erskine, who once again rescued me from diabolical problems with my computer, and kept everything up and running.

Thanks go to Stephen Cary, Heinemann author, who gave an important ESL lesson in my classroom, and author-illustrator Ashley Bryan, who inspired us with his stories and graciously agreed to be photographed with me. Dr. Ryan James, now teaching English in Budapest, shared his wonderful new ESL materials. Gloria Norton and

Dr. Bev Hock pulled for me, as always, as did Dick Sperisen and Pete Newton. Gabe Kerschner of Wild Things, Weimar, California, was a good sport about posing for a photo with Izog the alligator, one of the animals he has rescued.

I send special thanks to Kay Goines, my literature mentor, who has influenced me profoundly and taught me so much. The wondrous things I learned from Kay are now so much a part of the fabric of my being that I find it difficult to separate them. If, in error, I have used her words or ideas without acknowledgment, I do apologize. Kay always says, when thanked for sharing her beliefs and her bountiful knowledge, "Take the ribbon and run." I have taken the ribbon, and I'm still running . . .

My family has been most patient during the writing of this book. My sister Sherry has helped me in so many special ways. My mother gave me wonderful pep talks and was understanding about the shortness of visits. My brother Jim and his wife Debi pitched in and gave me great support as well. Marsha Oviatt has been an invaluable listener, with many helpful ideas and responses.

And most of all, my husband George unfailingly supported all my efforts, with his usual great sense of humor and wise feedback. George has helped me so much by valuing my work, and giving me always the gift of time. I am so grateful, even though he now wants to give me back the kitchen.

*You must never tell a thing. You must illustrate it. We learn through
the eye and not the noggin.*

—Will Rogers

The Beginning

A few years into my teaching career, after teaching on both the East
Coast and the West Coast, I transferred to a school filled with children
who spoke several different languages. This was a new challenge for me.
I found it difficult to communicate with my students, most of whom
were Hispanic. I frequently drew pictures, acted things out, and asked
some first graders to translate for me to help other children understand
what was going on. As the year wore on, this job apparently became
burdensome for one child, who said, when asked to translate, "Is your
problem. Not gonna do it." It dawned on me then that this six-year-
old had a more clear-sighted idea of the situation than I did. I decided
to get some help.

That summer I sat with twenty-five educators in a warm, crowded
room in Morelia, Michoacan, waiting for some much-needed teacher
training. The other teachers were talking animatedly in Spanish as they
waited for class to start. It was obvious that many were friends, sharing
experiences and catching up on summer news. I was the only one who

*The children and
I make books
together.*

skipped the festivities and sat alone and silent, trying to ignore nerves, an upset stomach, and a giant feeling of inadequacy.

It had seemed a good idea, when I'd gone to live with a family in Mexico for two months and attend language school, to add a Songs and Games for Children elective to my beginning Spanish course. Now, with no way of understanding much, and unsupported in this class by a beginning Spanish curriculum, I was overwhelmed by feelings of loneliness and helplessness, as well as mortification. I had always felt able to express myself well in my own language. It was a blow to my confidence to be suddenly tongue-tied and mute as I sat with elementary teacher peers. I wanted to say, "Tell me about your teaching and how you learned Spanish. How do you help the English learners in your classroom?" I even wished I could let my fellow teachers know that I was a functioning educator as they were, that I could be articulate in my own language, and that I loved working with the second language speakers in my first-grade class. But I could say very little, and I didn't have the nerve to try. How I missed Orlando, my six-year-old translator!

There was no improvement to my situation when the course began that day. The instructor dictated the Spanish words and directions to Mexican songs and games, page after page. The rest of the class wrote furiously. There was no notice of me or awareness of my plight. I realize now that it can be difficult to spot such communication problems.

I also know now that even when teachers are aware of problems, some do not know how to deal with them.

For me, communication-challenged and in what I felt to be a crisis situation, other strategies were in order. I strove to peek at the papers of teachers on either side of me and was rewarded not with help, but with the annoyed shuffling of pages and covering up of work. Tears were just below the surface for me now. I certainly had no idea at the time that this was one of the most important experiences I would ever have as an educator. At this point I had very clear firsthand knowledge of just how my first-grade English learners might feel in a classroom where everyone else seemed to be able to communicate in English and the teacher and most of the children didn't speak their language.

I have thought of that horrible three hours (and the other indelible seven class sessions) countless times over my teaching career, and I have to admit that I have benefited more from that trial than any other single course or occurrence. Those nightmare experiences informed my teaching from deep down inside me in ways nothing else could have done. Since that time, I believe I have had a superheightened awareness of the plights and needs of the English learners in my classroom. Number one on my list of goals has been to create a caring, comfortable community in which each and every child has language and culture support and has a chance to flourish, grow, and succeed.

Fortunately for me, in my unhappy situation, my teacher changed her mode of instruction. (If she hadn't done so, I would never have lasted through the eight class meetings!) She moved from static pen-and-pencil exercises to hands-on class sessions in which we sang, moved to the rhythms of the songs, and played the games she had been dictating. And I was finally able to participate, even though I had to guess a lot and my involvement was at a minimal level.

Also fortunately for me, I was truly rescued by a kind act of my host family. On that first miserable day of class, the family I lived with could see that I was upset about something. When Marta, the family member closest to my own age and a new friend, heard what had happened to me, she was outraged. She went to the telephone and made a long-distance call to her sister-in-law in Mexico City. Socorro was a primary school teacher and knew many songs and games played by Mexican children. Marta and her sister-in-law made a Spanish audiocassette together, with simple directions for me in English. They also typed the written text in Spanish. Thanks to the help of people who cared, when

I returned home, I too was able to teach my primary students songs and games in Spanish.

The help I received from these two wonderful new friends in Mexico is as big a part of my memory as my difficult language experience. The two things must go together. Where there is struggle, there must be help to accompany it. Having people stand up for me gave me hope that I *could* succeed and the confidence and courage to keep struggling to learn. As an Arab proverb states, "He who has help, has hope. He who has hope has everything."

Ultimately, in part because of the encouragement I received when I desperately needed it, I went on to earn a bilingual credential and a master's degree in bilingual/cross-cultural education. I taught in a bilingual program until it was no longer an available option in my school district.

This book is about ways I work with my primary-grade students to give them hope—to help them acquire English language as well as academic content and to help them succeed as learners in my classroom. Like many teachers across the country, I use an ESL program my district has purchased for me. I also supplement this program and integrate curriculum wherever I can. I strive to teach joyfully and meaningfully and to create an atmosphere of excitement about learning. In our year together, the children have a lot to teach me too. As one of my wise first-grade children actually said this year, "We're here for each other."

CHAPTER 1

Looking Through the Eyes of
Second Language Learners

I want to learn English! I want to learn everything!

—Alejandro

Each August or September by the time the opening bell rings, I have a pretty good idea of who my students will be. I met many of them on the playground the previous year at recess and had contact with others in the lunchroom and during our classroom visits. I have studied school pictures and know everyone's name, and I've made some notes about the languages the children speak at home. I try to learn as much as I can about my children before school begins. Of course there are always surprises, as we acquire new class members throughout the year.

In greeting my new students, I strive to be welcoming, bending down to speak to each child, calling children by name, and using some familiar language, if possible. I have some cheat sheets on my wall near the classroom door, giving me phonetic greetings in Korean, Hindi, Samoan, Tagalog, Portuguese, Indonesian, and a few other languages. I find the phrase book section at the back of Dorling Kindersley's Eyewitness Travel Guides to be the best source of essential phrases and pronunciation tips. Fortunately, I can now converse in Spanish, although the children give me tips and help all year.

I make sure to have some culturally familiar books and photos in the room from countries represented by children in each new class. Some good choices are books with photos of children from several countries, such as *Children Just Like Me* by Barnabas and Anabel Kindersley (1995) and *Children from Australia to Zimbabwe: A Photographic Journey Around the World* by Mayo Ajemera et al. (2001). Old calendars—sold at a discount after the year begins—are an easy way to acquire photos. *National Geographic* magazines are wonderful photo resources too. I also like to have some folk art from other places in the world, such as a few masks, small carvings, and toys. I find that toys are universally appealing. I like them myself.

Gestures, Facial Expressions, and Modeling

I realized as I watched myself at the beginning of the school year that I gesture and model everything I do. I have many children in my class who will not have any idea what I am talking about unless I hold up the paper, book, or project; demonstrate; and use an overhead projector, the whiteboard, or other learning tools. I always remind myself that I have students who may look as if they are understanding me, but with little command of English, they could not possibly know what I mean if I don't *show* them and we don't try things out together. We are learning and doing. As my principal, Mario Penman, says, *model, model, model.*

I remind myself to speak clearly and a little more slowly and to give more wait time when I call on English learners. This added time relieves pressure and leaves a space that the learner is sometimes compelled to fill by speaking and trying to express himself. Waiting sometimes elicits some language that would not have emerged in a classroom climate with a fast and furious pace.

I make sure I call on children who are raising their hands and appear eager to speak. It is very important that English learners are *never* pressured to talk or respond orally.

The Right Name

One of the most important things I do at the beginning of the year to help students become comfortable in the classroom is work on saying children's names correctly. There have been cases when it took me countless repetitions and even an audiocassette for practice, but I believe it is a crucial step for helping children feel that they belong in my classroom.

I relate strongly to this problem of getting a child's name right and also feel it is very important to use the name the child prefers. As a third grader, I almost lost my name when there were three of us named Patty in class and the teacher arbitrarily renamed two of us. I still remember that disorienting moment of panic I experienced when she told us we couldn't all keep our names. I recall her annoyance at having to deal with three girls with the same name—and being scratched by one of the other Patricias and hit by the third because I was the lucky one who got to keep my name and my identity. (Perhaps when the teacher was making her decisions about what to call us, she realized I was not planning to answer to anything else but Patty.) A wonderful book dealing with this sensitive problem is *My Name Is María Isabel* by Alma Flor Ada (1995).

Sometimes children just aren't sure what they want to be called in the classroom. For example, they may be torn between the pronunciations of their name in English and in their home language. I try to let them know that they don't have to decide right away. They can think this over. I'll ask again in a few days if I haven't received a response from a child. I believe that children benefit from the lack of pressure here. It helps them make decisions they are satisfied with. They are free to change their minds as well. Even native English speakers have this name dilemma sometimes. One of my first graders went from being called Tommy to Tom and then to Thomas in a single year. Now in high school, he is back to being called Tommy. I would still be called Patty if it hadn't been for the arbitrary decision of a well-meaning middle school teacher in a new school situation and my failure to assert myself.

Making Children Feel Welcome

Even children who do not speak English or who speak with limited proficiency will soon be able to find their nametags in the pocket chart at our class meeting area as well as on bulletin boards and cubbyholes. Having children's names up around the room is a great way to say, "Welcome! I am expecting you!" I also have a bulletin board up with multicultural photos of children's faces and the title "Children Come in All the Colors of the Earth." As we get to know each other, we can fill

Figure 1–1

*Evolving Bulletin
Board Display:
Children Come in
All the Colors of
the Earth with text
from the picture
book* I Love My
Love with an A *by
Diana Ross.*

in the board with our own names and photos. We will talk about how we are all citizens of planet Earth. (See Figure 1–1.)

Children who do not speak English may spend a lot of time looking around the room, touching things, and taking things in. This is one way to make sense of a new place or situation. With this in mind, I keep out lots of things to look at and handle: a carved fish from Mexico, a wooden mask from Fiji, stacking marushka dolls from Russia, a queca (musical instrument) from Peru, painted wooden eggs from Poland, a galimoto (wire sculpture toy) from Africa, and so on. The children and I add to this little collection throughout the year. None of these items is expensive, and making them available is both a diversion and a way of showing acceptance for everyone in the room. Later on we'll have fun matching objects to places on the classroom map.

Terms to Use for Students Learning English

As the U.S. Census of 2000 shows, one child in five (or 9.8 million children) speaks a language other than English at home. And 6.8 million of these children speak Spanish with their families. Since children frequently speak more than one language, and many speak multiple languages, the term *second language learner* is sometimes inaccurate. The term *English language learner* is not precise either, since all primary students are English learners. However, I will use the terms *second language learner*, *English language learner*, and *English learner* to refer to children in my room who are not yet proficient in English. I would rather use these positive-sounding labels than some other possibilities.

Cultural Diversity

I believe it is important to do some research on the cultural backgrounds of my students if I am to understand them and teach them well. I need to ask their former teachers for information, check office records, and frequently do some research at the library and on the Internet. I can't rely on just what I see when I open my classroom door. I need to prepare.

For example, one of my former first graders, Roxane, spoke only German, had learned just a few words in English, and looked Japanese. Two years later, when Roxane's little sister Natasha came to my class, I couldn't help noticing she had a totally different body build and personality, spoke mostly English, and looked German. Since confusion can arise when trying to match students with their cultural backgrounds on the spot, and on the basis of how they look, it definitely helps to find out as much as possible ahead of time. The kindergarten teacher filled me in on Roxane's background, and her parents shared a lot of important information when we met early in the school year. Later, when Natasha was in my class, I was ready for her.

Misunderstood Cultural Differences

I once knew a child from Nicaragua who was a newcomer to our school. One of the first things I noticed about her was the way she waved good-bye: she held her hand with the palm facing her and moved her fingers up and down. I had never seen this before, but I had read about it in an article on cultural diversity. Our ESL teacher at the time was very savvy, but she was a bit baffled—as I had been—by this manner of waving good-bye. The teacher's conclusion was that perhaps the new student was somewhat immature. When I mentioned the article I had read and that this was probably a cultural difference, we both had a more accurate and complete picture of this child.

Cultural Differences: An Important Key to Behavior

I recently taught a student from Indonesia who just did not respond to our classroom rules and chose to ignore them most of the time. Even though I do not speak Indonesian, I expected to be able to make myself understood by *showing* Salim what I expected, modeling for him, miming, and repeating brief instructions. I also assigned him two buddies to model for him and show him what he should be doing. After each effort, I waited for some follow-through on his part, but it never came. These strategies usually work for me, but not this time. Salim would nod his head, repeat some of my words, and appear to agree with me. Then he would go his merry way.

I finally decided that there had to be some cultural components operating here. I mentioned this dilemma to my friend Alison Maloney, who had spent quite a lot of time in Indonesia when she was teaching primary-grade children on Christmas Island, 190 miles from Jakarta. Alison, now the former seminars manager at Heinemann, still remembers quite a bit of the Indonesian language and knows a great deal about the culture.

Alison explained that many Asian parents begin formal discipline around the time students start school. And in Indonesia, Salim would have had access to a large extended family, with grandparents and even great-grandparents around to model for him. Here in America, both of Salim's parents worked long hours and did not seem to be in agreement about what should be expected of their son. (Of course, parental inconsistency is always a problem!) Most interesting to me, Alison felt that this child was probably acting up more because he was "between" cultures.

All of this information rang true. I *knew* there had to be more going on than just a child refusing to behave. When I did some research on the Internet, articles I found supported my hypothesis that child discipline customs in Indonesia are quite different than those in America.

Now that I had some idea of what was going on in this child's world, and what that world expected of him, I felt that I could more easily understand him and work with him. However, before I could deal with this situation, Salim and his parents moved to another locale some distance away.

The main thing *I* learned from this experience was that cultural expectations may well be the key to what is going on with a child and that to understand that student and effect some changes, we need to know about both the student's traditional culture and his current way of life.

Home Language Proficiency

I try to be sensitive to children's heritage and learning styles. I have noticed that at times students who come to class with little or no English language may also lack proficiency in their home language. And sometimes children enter first or second grade never having been to school before, with little awareness of the world beyond a small village or ranch. Part of my job is to help children, especially those with little academic experience, become comfortable and learn how to *do school*. I also want to help them learn English quickly and easily in the most positive and nurturing ways that I can.

Differences in Learning Success

I noticed that two English learners in my class last year made distinctly different progress in their acquisition of reading and other skills although they had similar backgrounds and second language abilities and both had lived on small ranches in Mexico.

When I investigated further, I realized that there was one great difference in these children's experiences: Roberto had attended school for more than a year in Mexico. He had learned how to read in Spanish and had acquired many other skills. He could rely on these skills and prior knowledge and successes to help him make sense of new learning challenges. Fernanda, however, had spent very little time in school. She had misbehaved so badly, according to her stepmother, that she was sent home repeatedly and finally never went back. Fernanda had not acquired much knowledge as a result of her brief time in school while Roberto had accumulated some solid learning. He could rely on his experiences in learning to read in Spanish when he tackled reading in English.

I lament the demise of first language support in our schools. For children like Fernanda, who have very little educational background and speak little or no English, some instruction in basic skills in Spanish would absolutely make the difference between success and failure. Children learn faster, better, and more enthusiastically if they are able to apply *all* the skills at their disposal. The chance to learn curriculum content in their first language certainly speeds up their learning in content areas, as well as in English, and makes school success possible.

Building Community: We Need to *See* Ourselves Together

I always have a photo taken of all of us on the first day of school. Usually I set up our group and arrange for an upper-grade teacher on break to drop by and take some quick snapshots. I make enlarged black-and-white photocopies of the best photo as soon as possible so that each child has one right away. We use these photos in many ways, as I will explain later in the text. Using a digital camera is another way to get quick photos of your new class.

Another thing I like to do with a special beginning-of-the-year photo is take it to a camera store and have it put on a sweatshirt or a T-shirt. I keep this plan a secret and then wear the photo sweatshirt on Back-to-School Night. My kids really love this surprise, and their parents do too.

Integrating Music, Literature, Language, and Art

I like to begin teaching an integrated language, music, writing, and art theme the first week of school. The topics are self-concept and self-esteem. This activity melds the children's ideas about things they like, in their own words, with images they make of themselves.

To prepare for this theme I share related music and literature. I have a wonderful CD, *Free to Be . . . You and Me* by Marlo Thomas and Friends, with several songs to inspire poise and self-confidence. There are many songs and books on this theme. Here are a few of them.

Musical Recordings

Magical Miracle Me by John Archambalt and David Plummer (2000) (There is an accompanying sixteen-page picture book of the same title.)

*I'm a Can-Do Kid and Other Self-Esteem Building Songs and
   Activities* by John Archambalt and David Plummer (1999)
   (book and CD)

Books

Ruby the Copycat by Peggy Rathmann (1997) (also available in
   Spanish: *Ruby, mono ve, mono hace*)
I Like Me! by Nancy L. Carlson (1990)
ABC I Like Me! by Nancy L. Carlson (1999)
I'm Gonna Like Me: Letting Off a Little Self-Esteem by Jamie
   Lee Curtis (2002)

Things We Like—An Early Language Assessment

To get ready for an easy art and writing project on the theme of things
we like, I fold or draw a 1½-inch border on 8½-by-11-inch copy paper.
I print the sentence frame "I like _____" on three sides (using dots
so that children can trace the letters). There is a special space for the
children to write their names on the bottom portion of the border. (See
the Appendix, page 200, for a reproducible copy of this project; see Figure 1–2 for Azeneth's self-portrait.)

I'd like to thank colleagues Jan Switick and Leslie Anderson for
adaptations to this sentence-frame idea. I had planned to use a more
involved sentence pattern for the border and to ask the children to pick
three words to describe themselves. This would have been more difficult
for beginning English learners, if not impossible, and would not have
yielded as much information about children's use of language.

Because children will fill the center rectangular space with other
things if we do the borders first, we begin with the central self-portrait
portion of the lesson and then create our written borders after. This also
gives time for children to think about what they like while they are
drawing. This project may be done in one class session or two.

Directing the Crayon Self-Portrait

I show children a couple of art prints with self-portraits of the head and
shoulders. We converse about the things they notice, and I pass out small

Figure 1–2
Self-Portrait with Azeneth's "I like" Sentences.

shatterproof mirrors. Students examine themselves carefully and I often note that many check out their teeth. As I have suggested, they also look at their skin, eye, and hair color so that they can mix crayon colors to match.

To begin our close-up drawings, I show children the rectangle on their papers and ask them to place their papers on the desks portrait-style. The rectangle is now placed so that the long sides go up and down vertically. (The other direction, with the long sides of the rectangle placed horizontally, is called landscape-style.)

Now I ask children to make a dot up near the top of the rectangle and one near the bottom, using a light-colored crayon. Directional words, such as *top* and *bottom,* can be tricky for language learners, so I always make a big point of modeling this by making these dots on my own paper. We join the dots to make an oval or facelike shape, and then we talk about the parts of our faces, feel them, and look at them in the mirrors. I ask children to put one hand on top of their heads and one under their chins and then to move them toward the center. Everyone is surprised to find out that the eyes are in the middle, about halfway down the face. Children draw eyes their way, using crayons. We divide the space between the eyes and the chin in half to find the nose, and in half again to find a place for the mouth.

We name other body parts too, such as the neck and shoulders and ears, and include them in the drawings. The intent here is not to get students to create portraits that all look the same. We are simply practicing vocabulary as we draw. I show my budding artists rudimentary ways to draw some facial features and they create their own.

For example, when Betsy says, "How do you make a nose?" I show her a few sample noses on the whiteboard, and children add their ideas too. We look at everyone's nose. Betsy is on her own now, free to create the nose she has or the one she wishes she had.

Filling in the Sentence-Frame Border

After drawing their self-portraits, children have a chance to talk about and brainstorm things they like. (You may want to do this second part of the activity the next day.) I read some related picture books, such as *I Like Me!* by Nancy Carlson (1990). Individual children then dictate to me three special things they like. I print their words in pencil in the borders, and they trace over these "I like" sentence frames with a black marking pen. If children want to write the words by themselves, I encourage them to do so.

This activity gives me a lot of information about students' language capabilities. When Azeneth says, "I like the school come" (see Figure 1–2), I know that she is having difficulty with the sentence structure of English. I see by Alejandro's words—"I like truck. I like cars."—that he is inconsistent in the way he forms plurals in English. And I notice that Alex can fairly fluently rattle off three sentences about things he likes: "I like new shoes to run fast," "I like to do something," and "I like to play and run a lot."

To finish their creative combination of writing and art, the children can outline their crayon portraits with black crayon or with the pens. Kids may fill in the background area around their drawings with any colors they choose.

Taking Inventory of Our Success

We accomplished a great deal with this beginning lesson. To wrap things up, the children and I try to think of *all* the things we did: First of all, we now have creative, original work and writing from each child that we can admire and put up on our classroom walls. We have completed our self-portraits and know about mixing skin tones with crayons. We have practiced drawing body parts such as eyes and noses, hair and ears. Children who did not have this English vocabulary may pick it up at this time. These portraits may be placed next to each other on a whiteboard or bulletin board: an array of faces from our classroom in the first week of school! We come together on the rug to talk about the portraits, make guesses as to which one was done by which artist, make riddles, comment on artistic styles, and so on. I date these pieces, which will later be saved in the students' portfolios.

There is a lot of information to be gained from looking closely at these pieces of art: how confident children are in using crayons, the amount of detail included, relative sizes of facial features, whether directions were followed, the amount of creativity shown, color preferences, and so on. I gain a pretty good idea of children's comfort level with English as well.

Throughout the year, now that we know how to create self-portraits, we can do them other ways: We can draw ourselves on money, on postage stamps, and on top of elaborate trophies. We can depict ourselves as famous people in newspaper stories we ourselves create and even portray ourselves winning Olympic medals, Nobel prizes, and other astounding awards. We can integrate these lessons with drama and act out gestures and facial expressions too.

Assessments and Follow-Up Activities

These "I like" self-portraits are great projects to date and save; then you can repeat the activity at the end of the school year. Children will be astonished by the difference in what they can achieve in just one grade.

As a follow-up to making our personal drawings, it's fun to play with face making. This helps children develop vocabulary too. Ruth Krauss says in her book *A Hole Is to Dig* (1989), "A face is so you can make faces!" So we make *lots* of faces. Then we give names to the emotions we are feeling when we make them.

As we become adept at creating expressions, by both acting them out and drawing them, we create our own mural of facial expressions. Each child practices making faces and then draws a personal favorite. Then we cut them or tear them out and place them on a piece of colored butcher paper to make a class mural. I encourage children to choose or invent a name such as silly, mad, or playful, for their personal cartoons. I write these words in pen near the correct face. Children are, of course, free to add these words themselves.

Our mural becomes a vocabulary resource. It also sensitizes all of us to the importance of reading the faces (and body language) of others, and it emphasizes that this skill is one way to learn how others might feel.

Understanding My Students' Worlds

As soon as possible in the school year, I meet with children individually to chat, to draw, and to share. I photograph each child (usually reading or showing off something the child wants to be photographed doing) and put up the photos so that we are all represented in the room right away. I also have a board with photos of my family and my life, including my own first-grade picture.

The first week of school, as children are getting settled and comfortable in the classroom, I get them started working on autobiographical booklets—stapled sheets of paper with colored construction paper covers. Children can draw and "write" whatever they wish about themselves and their families or dictate their stories to me. An alternative to this is to provide simple text for students to use as starters for their writing:

- Here I am. I am ____ years old. My birthday is _____.

- Here I am with my family: _____.

- My favorite game is _____.

- My favorite toy is _____.

- My best friend is _____.

- My favorite food is _____.

- My favorite color is _____.

- My favorite music is _____.

- My favorite movie is _____.

- My favorite thing to do is _____.

Jump-Starting Children with Good Stories and Art

I share a few picture books to help get students started on their own memoirs and personal drawings. A few good choices to read are *Family Pictures/Cuadros de familia* by Carmen Lomas Garza (1990), *Would You Rather?* by John Burningham (2003), and Amy Schwartz's book *What James Likes Best* (2003). Children may wish to use this latter title with their own name in it, as one of my children did: *What Fernanda Likes Best*. And of course many students come up with their own titles, such as *Patty's Favorite Things* and *Edwin's Important Book*. How I would have loved making a book like this when I was younger!

Before children start their booklets, I stress the drawing aspect of their work. Even if they do not know how to write, or write in English, they can convey so much through their art. And of course, I want them to try to write things "their way." We practice this as a group, emphasizing the fact that when we make marks, we decide what they mean, and we are really writing. I let the children know that when we do this, we are writing just the way people learned to write long ago, by trying out names and marks and making symbols that mean something to us.

Individual Interviews

As children work on their own personal booklets, I call them over one by one to talk with me. I ask questions, such as those listed earlier. I also ask each child personally, "Is there anything you want to know about school? Or are there things you want to know about me or about the other children?" I spend a little longer with English learners. I have a few things on the table to fiddle with so that we will have something to do if we're conversationally challenged. Several things serve this purpose well: some sheets of paper, colored pens or pencils, the snow globe a child brought me from Disneyland, my floating dolphin encased in plastic with syrupy-looking waves. Other options are small squishy balls and some toys that click and snap as you manipulate them. It is better to have just a couple of items or it might be difficult to keep a focus on the one-to-one interview.

As we fiddle and doodle and try to communicate with each other, I make some notes on my interview sheet for each child. I keep these pages in a labeled binder in alphabetical order by first name. Although it is most crucial to have these brief assessment interviews with children who are new to English, I find it important to do it for all the students in my class, so I squeeze them in between other activities. Figure 1–3 shows a sample interview sheet (see Appendix, page 201, for a blank interview grid).

I add anecdotal notes to these pages throughout the year as I watch and listen to children and notice their facial expressions and body language and their struggles and successes in acquiring English.

This interview process described may be too difficult for some children. Late in the school year I got a new student from Amman, Jordan, who had no prior experience with English. I asked her to sit with me (motioning, as well as speaking, so she would understand). My goal was just to have a brief personal time with her, so she would know that I cared about her and would help her all I could.

I asked Sarah whether she had a sister. I drew a picture of Sarah, and labeled it with her name. She seemed delighted. I drew a smaller girl, and looked at Sarah inquiringly. She shook her head "no." I repeated the process, drawing a larger girl, and she nodded "yes." I pointed to the drawing of Sarah and said her name. I pointed to the drawing of the larger girl and she told me her sister's name. I said, "Arabic" and wrote a word or two. Sarah labeled the drawing with her sister's name. In this way, together we were able to compose a picture of her family with everyone's name.

This process also helped me show Sarah how to take home her overnight book and return it. I drew her leaving school with the book, taking it to her house, and bringing it back. After just a few minutes I felt that this child and I had begun the bonding process. We understood each other, had a special bit of time together, and best of all, we began to forge a relationship.

I saved this paper as Sarah's interview. At a later time, the previous interview format would be easier for Sarah and me to use.

Figure 1–3
Sample Interview Grid.

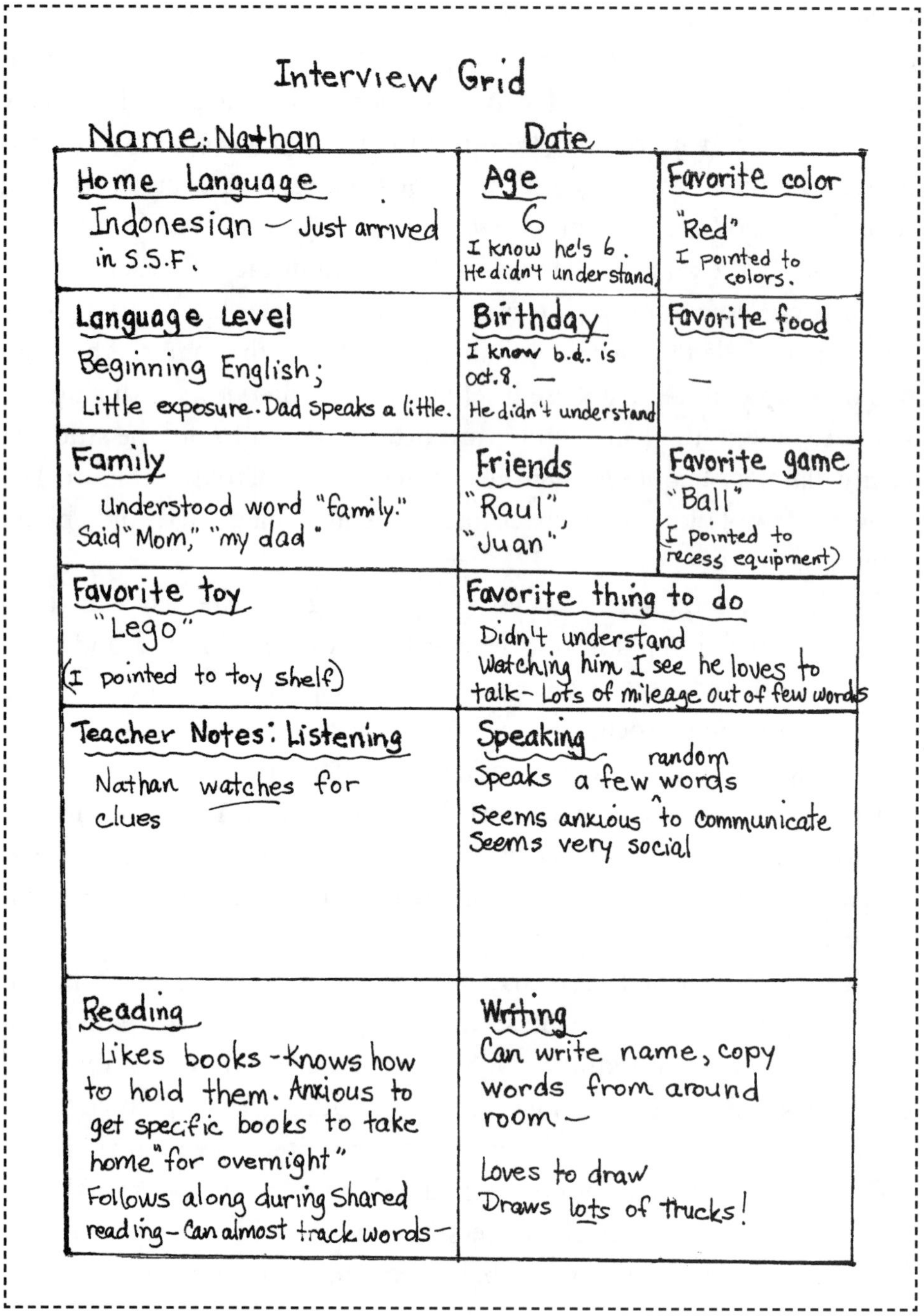

Interview Grid

Name: Nathan   Date

Home Language Indonesian — Just arrived in S.S.F.	Age 6 I know he's 6. He didn't understand.	Favorite color "Red" I pointed to colors.
Language Level Beginning English; Little exposure. Dad speaks a little.	Birthday I know b.d. is oct.8. — He didn't understand	Favorite food —
Family Understood word "family." Said "Mom," "my dad"	Friends "Raul", "Juan"	Favorite game "Ball" (I pointed to recess equipment)
Favorite toy "Lego" (I pointed to toy shelf)	Favorite thing to do Didn't understand Watching him I see he loves to talk— Lots of mileage out of few words	
Teacher Notes: Listening Nathan watches for clues	Speaking Speaks a few random words Seems anxious to communicate Seems very social	
Reading Likes books – knows how to hold them. Anxious to get specific books to take home "for overnight" Follows along during shared reading – can almost track words —	Writing Can write name, copy words from around room — Loves to draw Draws lots of trucks!	

Drawing Games

If the child being interviewed is nervous, or does not speak any English, I sometimes initiate a cooperative drawing game. I will draw something at the bottom of a sheet of paper and then push the paper toward the child. Without oral language, I am saying, "My turn, your turn." We can make a totem pole drawing, taking turns sketching one creature or thing on top of the partner's drawing. I may draw a turtle. I point to the top of the turtle. The child draws a dog on top. I draw an elephant on top of that, and so on. This is a quick, fun, silly, playful way to get to know your students and to create a relaxed learning atmosphere.

When I play this art game with Nathan, a student from Indonesia, he giggles, moves his hands a lot, and tries out some English with me as he draws. Once Nathan begins to try to communicate verbally in our class—right away—he doesn't stop. He does an amazing amount of verbal communicating with few words at the beginning. Almost immediately his verbal ability snowballs and he really takes off!

Anthony Browne's Drawing Game

Another art game is the Shape Game, which Anthony Browne describes in his book of the same name (2003). To play the shape game, two colors of pens (or one pen and one pencil) are used. The first player draws a shape. The second player uses a different color pen or pencil to change the shape into something else. Then player number two draws a shape and the first participant changes that by adding to the drawing. This game sparks lots of creativity and can open up lines of communication fast. I like to teach it to my class and provide pens in children's desk boxes so that this activity can take place often and spontaneously.

Sometimes these drawings lead to individual or class stories. It is fast and easy to put up several drawings to reflect on by using magnets on a large whiteboard. In this way we can layer things we are working on, and the board becomes a reflection of what is going on in class each day.

An activity for older students is the commercial game called Oodles of Doodles. There is a drawing book of the same name.

Yes, Indeed I Care!: Developing Caring Relationships with Students

Pierre: A Cautionary Tale in Five Chapters and a Prologue is a classic chapter book by Maurice Sendak (1991). It is about a boy whose stated philosophy is "I don't care!" He repeats this phrase throughout the story. At the end of the book, when Pierre is rescued from inside a lion, he decides, "Yes, indeed I care!"

In the classroom, amazing things can happen when children know *we* care. This is the ingredient that transforms struggling, indifferent students into energized learners.

When Beatríz sees how excited I am when she tells me, "Good morning," she makes a point of saying it every day. Soon she goes a step further and tries out other bits of language as well. Beatríz has been silent most of the year, except for occasionally chatting in Spanish. I have tried to encourage her to speak in her home language, but she hasn't wanted to talk very much. And even when she speaks in Spanish, it is difficult for us to understand her.

When Beatríz begins speaking more, in both English and Spanish, the other children and I are thrilled with her progress, and we all let her know. Beatríz takes risks because she knows in our classroom we will celebrate her efforts, just as the children do for me when I learn or try something new in Spanish.

Irvin, a new child who does not yet speak any English, begins to try out some words and phrases. I believe Beatríz has spurred him on to take some risks and use some language himself.

Of course, if having spoken embarrasses a child, all this attention could backfire. It pays to be sensitive to each student. Beatríz loves the attention, and it propels her to try new things.

Innovative Ways of Collecting Information Directly from the Children

I always love to point out to children how much better and freer they are at drawing than most adults are. Drawing—and reading drawings—is one of the best ways to communicate as we are learning to speak together, listen to each other, and see what we're saying, see what we mean. Aliki writes of this experience in her wonderful back-to-back picture book, *Marianthe's Story: Painted Words, Spoken Memories* (1998). The sixty-four-page book contains two carefully written stories about Marianthe's experiences in her new country.

In the beginning of the book, on the side titled *Painted Words,* Marianthe is newly arrived from an unnamed country, where her family experienced the terrible hardships of famine and war. When children in

Marianthe's new classroom laugh at her because of her inability to speak their language, her sensitive and caring teacher gives her art supplies and time to paint. He also lets her classmates know that their behavior is unacceptable. Through art Marianthe shares many details of her former life with her new classmates. She also astounds them with her painting talent, which props up her floundering self-confidence as she struggles to learn English.

When the reader flips the book over, Marianthe tells her sequel: *Spoken Memories*. In this story she can tell her own tale because now she is a speaker of English. Not only does this book give hope to children that they too will progress in language and related social and academic skills, but it also shows clever clues for ways to communicate without spoken language.

Sharing Touches Us Way Down Inside

I frequently ask my English learners for information about their lives and invite them to draw and paint. In return I see some good drawings and gain a lot of knowledge, some great sharing, and some insights about cultural diversity. As Beatríz became more comfortable in our class, she drew us a very involved picture of her school in Mexico. A surprise came in her second drawing: the detailed graveyard scene of her close friend's funeral. Beatríz dictated the simple yet moving words to me in Spanish, and I printed them on her poignant little picture: En Mexico murió un amigo mía. (In Mexico a little friend of mine died.) (See Figure 1–4.)

Figure 1–4
*Beatríz's drawing
of an important
event in her life.*

This is a drawing that aptly reflects Beatríz's life in Mexico. I believe it is crucial for me to know about the cultural heritage of my students and to be acceptant of and interested in things kids wish to share.

The Importance of Writing Down Children's Words— in Any Language

Taking dictation, collecting language experience stories, as I did with Beatríz, is a wonderful way to help children communicate and acquire language. I believe this is worth doing even when I do not know the language the child is speaking. I just write down the phonetic sounds of the words a child says to me. This way I can read words back to the child and get her idea of whether I am correctly repeating what she means. This will give me a record of what the child said, and perhaps this student will be able to put it into English at a later date. Although I'm certainly not transcribing Chinese, Urdo, or other languages correctly, I'm putting down the children's stories in a way that will allow us to access them again later.

This exercise honors the child's language; stresses that it is a real, authentic way of speaking; and creates a cultural bridge between us. I also let children know that I do not know how to write their language correctly, so I just put the sounds I hear. In this way, I am modeling what I want the children to do when they attempt to write English.

If I keep my phonetic words handy, on a special place on the whiteboard, I can easily look at the board and use those words with the children. Salim, my Indonesian student, is thrilled each time I tell him, "Terimah kasih" (Thank you), in his language or ask him, "Apa kabar?" (What's new?). I refer often to the list of words and phrases Salim is teaching me, and we add to it together.

Drawings Are Windows into Children's Lives

Irvin, newly arrived from Mexico, did a telling drawing on his first day with our class: a miserable-looking child, alone in the midst of strangers. Since he did not want to talk about it, in English or in Spanish, I left it without any dictated caption. Roberto and Fernanda shared drawings of the animals they missed on the ranches where they lived near Guadalajara. James drew his large extended family, all left behind in Nicaragua. And Hee Sun, from Korea, frequently drew different festivals and children in Korean dress. She also brought in photos and wrote about these experiences with her family for family homework. (For more on family homework and books, please see Chapter 12.)

When the children share their drawings with me, I attempt to take their dictation and add their dictated stories to their art. In some cases children are just not ready to speak, even in their own language. I believe it is important to honor this preference for silence.

Thought Balloons

From Beatríz I learned a wonderful new technique: cartoon thought balloons. When these are drawn next to sketches of the children, it is easy to indicate pictorially what a child is thinking. Beatríz began doing this early in the school year as a way to show me what was important to her.

I extended Beatríz's idea (letting everyone know it was *hers*) by making photocopies of empty thought balloons for children to use (see Figure 1–5). I taught a self-portrait art lesson for the class. We put these portraits on display next to thought balloons with drawings or words showing children's thinking.

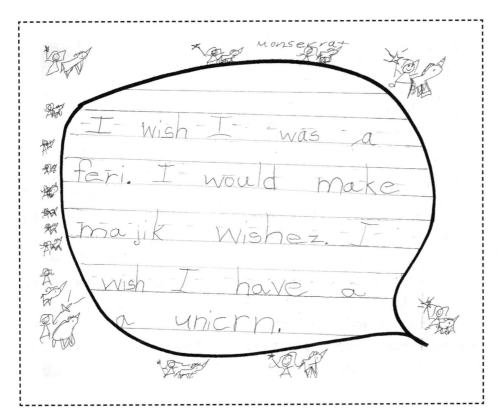

Figure 1–5
Monserrat writes her wishes in a thought balloon.

The children found this fun and intriguing, so we began keeping each child's portrait and current thought balloon up on our magnetic whiteboard. (See the Appendix, page 202, for a thought balloon template.)

Survival English, Sign Language, and Labels

I believe that it is crucial to teach new students survival English and some sign language right away. Children also can be assigned buddies to help them get around: physically, socially, and academically. The buddy strategy is discussed in more detail in Chapter 4. Having a buddy helps children feel comfortable and taken care of. I want them to know they are important people in our class community.

Right away I teach words and sign language for crucial phrases. These are mounted where children can see and refer to them. The following are some words and phrases that are taught right away. (Please see the references, page 229, for suggested sign language books.)

Good morning
Yes
No
Bathroom
Water
I feel sick
I need help
I have a question

I also use sign language charts to help teach immediate survival English. The sign language gestures will help children remember the words through kinesthetic memory as well as give them a way to express what they mean if they have forgotten the words in English.

In addition, I work with the children to put up signs (labels) all over our classroom to identify vocabulary items they will see: wall, computer, door, desk, and so on. This is an ongoing activity throughout the school year. I put up labels in several languages to honor all the children in the classroom as well as to propel us all to become interested in other languages.

Creating an Anxiety-Free Classroom

At the beginning of first grade, the children and I begin many activities and start working toward becoming a close classroom community. One of my main goals is to create a classroom climate that is low on anxiety and high on zest for learning. As Stephen Krashen tells us in his work *Explorations in Language Acquisition and Use* (2003), anxiety creates a block, the affective filter, which closes students to comprehensible input and gets in the way of learning. One of the most important things I can do is to keep anxiety at bay. I work with my children to keep our worries minimal and our joys great as we spend our year together.

CHAPTER 2

Structuring the Classroom Environment to Propel English Learners Toward Success

I hear and I forget. I see and I remember. I do and I understand.

—Chinese proverb

Imagine two different classroom scenarios: In one classroom the teacher is talking as she stands in front of a table with art supplies: torn-paper scraps, construction paper, and glue. Children look on, some expectantly, some of them with blank faces. The teacher continues talking, talking, talking, and a few students ask questions. The teacher answers and children go to their seats to work on art projects. Many students have no idea about the objectives of the lesson or about what is expected of them.

As they are working, a few children may ask, "Is this right, Teacher?" The overall atmosphere in the classroom is one of confusion and indecision rather than joy in experimentation and creation.

At the end of this lesson, children clean up, put their pictures away, and then go on with studying in another area of the curriculum.

In the second classroom scenario, the teacher also stands in front of the children, next to a table of art supplies. There are some art prints, a picture book, and a whiteboard and marking pens as well as construction paper, paper scraps, and glue. As the teacher talks, he briefly gives his vision of the meaning and objectives behind the lesson—why they are doing it, what they hope to accomplish. He may use a few *brief* sentences in Spanish or another relevant language so that all the students will have some idea of what is going on. As the instructor describes the objectives—ways to create with paper scraps and how to use glue—he *demonstrates* them in a minilesson. For example, when he talks about how to glue, he shows how to lift up the topmost construction paper scrap, put glue under it, and press down the paper. He shows how to wipe the top of the glue bottle with a tissue and then turn the cap to close it. And he demonstrates how to tear paper. He uses loops of tape or magnets to stick the simple glued torn-paper examples up on the whiteboard.

This teacher gestures a lot, tries to avoid complicated sentence construction, and also uses a second language to briefly clue students in to what is going on. (If he cannot do this in another language, he could call on a student for translation help or employ the help of a parent volunteer.)

This second teacher models different kinds of things that can be done with the paper scraps: sandwiched layers of different colors and sizes of paper, three-dimensional bits and pieces, and overlapped shapes. He reinforces these ideas by showing some art prints and picture books illustrated with paper techniques. The students have many opportunities to talk and respond. If children have questions, the teacher gives them wait time to get their words out and their meaning across. In so doing, he reinforces for his students that it is OK to struggle for self-expression and that the class and teacher will be patient and help the child make himself understood. By listening to their peers and especially their buddy partners who can translate for them, English learners are able to at least get the gist of this lesson.

In just a few minutes these children have seen a variety of work created with paper scraps. They have watched a demonstration about gluing and have heard a brief translation of the teacher's English words. They have practiced tearing scraps. When this group goes to work on their own creative projects, more of them will have an idea about what is expected and what the lesson is all about. They will be free to experiment with materials, to use their imaginations, and to create their own artwork.

After the creative expression part of this art lesson is over and the class has cleaned up, students meet on the rug with *their* projects. The completed work is laid out on the floor or quickly stuck up on a whiteboard or bulletin board with Fun Tac (see Resources, page 226, at the back of this book), blue painter's tape, pins, or magnets. Children and the teacher discuss the completed projects. They talk about the work in relation to the original goals for their lesson. Individual students may choose one or two pictures that they feel fulfill the lesson goals and objectives or that demonstrate good use of glue and paper scraps or interesting shapes or color combinations.

As an alternative, the group can make riddles about the work and find things in question in the art display; for example, "I see a tide pool with a hermit crab and some seashells. The tide is in and there is a lot of water." Vocabulary is reinforced as children describe things they notice or play guessing games. They enjoy talking about what they have made, what they were thinking, what gave them ideas. Some of the children's words may be written down on a large shared writing tablet. These reflections may be placed on the bulletin board with children's finished work. Any instant or digital photographs taken during the lesson may be added to the display as well as the teacher's reflections about his goals and objectives for the lesson: things he noticed happening as the children worked.

This is a rich lesson. Children have used and expanded their vocabularies, practiced gluing and tearing paper, and created their own compositions using torn-paper scraps. Language wraps around this lesson, from start to finish. Children have gained in art expertise as well as learned new words and reinforced current language capabilities. There is also a good feeling of class community.

Students who may not have gotten the gist of things at the start of the period have a much better idea about what was going on by the time that they have experienced this variety of related activities, seen their teacher's minilesson, and participated in the wrap-up, where they have seen the work created and heard their classmates talk about it.

The Importance of an Overview

All children, but most especially English learners, need an overview—a snapshot view of what is going on—at the beginning of any lesson being taught. When students understand the context of a lesson, a lot of small pieces will make sense and fall into place. They will more easily understand vocabulary words and English explanations when they see them as part of the whole.

27

*Structuring the
Classroom
Environment to
Propel English
Learners Toward
Success*

Aside from modeling and showing children what we are doing, one of the most important strategies to help English learners is to provide consistent and clear classroom routines. This will alleviate a lot of anxiety, as children will be able to follow procedures even if they aren't totally sure about the oral directions. When a child sees events unfolding the same way day after day, the words that accompany these routines become clear. "Team 1 may line up" makes sense when the child hears the words and sees identical results happen over and over. Much vocabulary is learned this way, especially those tough words such as *on, in, under, on top of,* and so on. Repetition helps children learn how to handle the classroom and how to manage materials, and it helps them gain understanding and language capability.

Here is a brief list of directions, words, and phrases that children might hear and see acted out day after day. My students also enjoy miming these activities.

- Put your backpacks and jackets in the cubbies.

- Put your homework/overnight books/folders on your desk/table.

- Get your morning paper from the table tray.

- Stand for the flag salute.

- Sit with your partner on the rug.

- Team 1 may line up for recess.

- Read with your partner.

- Team 2 may get lunches or lunch tickets and line up.

- Tear out page 10 in your math book. (It is important to consistently write page numbers in the same place on a board or whiteboard so that children know where to look for help.)

- Put your math book in the basket under the desk. (Our bins don't hold all our materials, so we have a plastic crate under each team's table.)

- Ask your partner _____.

- Tell your partner _____.

And so on.

Total Physical Response

James Asher's program Total Physical Response, also known as TPR, is a method that uses body movements to help make language input comprehensible. Teachers give commands or directions, and students perform the actions. Asher's book *Learning Another Language Through Actions* (2000) has many lessons that apply TPR in the classroom.

For some creative, child-centered variations of this program (Simon Says—Our Style!), see *Everything You Need to Know to Teach First Grade* (Dragan 2003).

Classroom Spaces and Places

Another way to help children with routines is to introduce them to different areas of the classroom and then explain and show what can be done in each part of the room. Reviewing and giving children time to restate their understandings of room management helps solidify concepts such as these:

■ Where will you put your completed papers? *in the team tray on the table* (With our new classroom furniture, four to six children sit at a table and form a team.)

■ Where can you go to read with a partner (or group or by yourself)? *book nook, front library area, carpeted areas, tables*

■ What can you do with these math tubs? When can you use them?

■ How do you use the listening center? Who is in charge of the tape recorder? *the team captain for the week*

■ Where do you put this PE equipment? *in the blue bag in the green bin* How do you make sure nothing is lost? *count the balls*

Labels on different materials and different areas of the classroom also help children handle themselves knowledgeably in the room.

Ways to Get Children's Attention

Students also need predictable brief signals for getting their attention. There are many different ways of letting children know they need to look and listen. With second language learners, the more predictable the signals are, the easier it is for them to respond to them. Here are a few possible ways to get children to stop and look and listen to their teacher:

- Say, "Close your lips and look at me."

- Flick the classroom lights or turn on the overhead projector.

- Say, "Look and listen." Put your finger in the air.

- Begin a class song or poem.

- Clap a rhythm and encourage children to join in.

This year I have been trying out a wonderful new attention-getting method I learned from Paula Rogovin's book *Why Can't You Behave?* (2004). Paula relates that she learned this technique from a parent who had been teaching students some African dance steps. The parent said, "Ago," pronounced "AH-go" (Swahili for "I want your attention") and taught the children to answer "Ame," pronounced "AH-may," which means "We are listening." As Paula suggested, I sang "Ago" in a "quiet, songlike way" and taught my students to answer by singing the response "Ame" with a low volume.

I find this to be a wonderful, very respectful way to ask children for their attention, and I like the fact that we are all learning something special about another language and culture far across the world.

It is important to have good, calming attention-getting routines in place in any classroom, but it is especially crucial for language learners that routines are clear and consistent. Sometimes children appear to be ignoring class procedures. It may be that they just do not understand what is expected of them and clarification is necessary.

Rules and Classroom Management

When children make classroom rules together and illustrate them, they are much more likely to buy in to them and to follow them. Role-playing the class rules is a good strategy to help English learners and other children as well. You can photograph this role-playing and put the photos on a chart next to the rules and guidelines. Some photos may be placed under the international symbol for *no*, a red circle with a line through it. Children enjoy acting out and making this kind of visual reference for the classroom.

Create a Classroom Full of Meaningful Print

Student- and teacher-made charts are an aid to literacy as well as an aid to understanding and behavior. We read these references together frequently. Children read with me as I track the words with a pointer. Quite soon our words are memorized, internalized, and are a good reference for children looking for specific words to write and spell. Children learn to read these before they know it, and some of the literacy skills transfer over into other literacy activities.

Reading these charts gives children confidence. One day as we walk around together and read the room, I mention that it is *so* powerful to see a word—really look at it—say it, and hear it all at the same moment. As I turn back to the chart I hear a little voice say, "I feel those words going into my brain right now!" This thought spreads like wildfire, and everyone admits to feeling those words getting up into his or her brain, where they can be used and read again and again!

Children also enjoy reading the room as a center or independent activity. They can look for specific words; words that begin or end with certain sounds; categories of words to collect, such as animal names or words that show action; and so on. Kids love this kind of scavenger hunt! (See Figure 2–1.)

Another helpful tool for English learners, as well as all learners, is a large posted daily schedule. This can be displayed in a pocket chart.

Figure 2–1
Alejandro, Juan, and David read the room.

A paper clock next to each activity listed not only helps children see their day but also helps them to learn to tell time.

It's Great to Grow! We Celebrate Learning

I know from my own experiences in language learning what a toll it can take on learners' confidence when they can't speak the language of a culture and can't interact or connect with others. Language learning is ongoing and takes time. I make sure my kids see me enjoy a bit of struggle as I grow in reading and speaking Spanish and small bits of other languages. I stress my satisfaction and joy in improving and gaining language competence, and I strive to make these examples brief and fun. I want each of my first graders to have positive experiences as they work on acquiring language. As part of this acknowledgment of growth and success, we frequently meet in a circle on the rug to celebrate things we can do or have learned. Children hold a starfish or other small artifact as they speak and keep it moving if they wish to pass.

We also make a "Celebrations" bulletin board together. I fold a large piece of fadeless paper so that each student has a personal square. Achievements and feats are recorded here. Children decide what they want to celebrate and we write and illustrate notes about their successes. These notes and illustrations are added to the "Celebration" board with magnets or tape. (See Figure 2–2.)

In addition, we keep a series of "Great Idea" charts going. If someone has an inspiration, we write it down to celebrate and acknowledge it and to motivate others. (See Figure 2–3.) Children also enjoy making their own celebration banners. (See Appendix, page 203, for directions.)

One of the literature books we love that highlights this celebration of personal growth is *Leo the Late Bloomer* by Robert Kraus (1994). At the beginning of the book, Leo's friends are all accomplished in many ways. He is not. Leo's father watches him for "signs of blooming" until his mother tells his dad that a "watched bloomer doesn't bloom." Then, one day, "in his own good time, Leo blooms." This is a very satisfying story. We all want to bloom, and the sooner the better. It's helpful for children to watch a storybook character struggle and have to wait for success.

Other supportive books on this theme are *Wemberly Worried,* by Kevin Henkes (2000), in which Wemberly Mouse worries about everything until she gets a handle on things; and *Amazing Grace,* by Mary

Figure 2–2
Student writing from our "Celebrations" board.

Hoffman (1991), in which Grace learns that she can achieve anything she wants to if she sets her mind to it and works at it. *Whoever You Are,* by Mem Fox (2001), reassures kids that there are children just like them all over the world. They may look different; they may speak a different language; their lives may be quite different too, but inside, they are just like them.

There are many inspiring folktales about being and becoming. A favorite in my classroom is *The Story of Jumping Mouse* by John Steptoe (1989). A young mouse, feeling woefully inadequate, undertakes a dangerous trip. Along the way he meets Magic Frog who tells him, "You will reach the far-off land if you keep hope alive within you." These words give the small mouse courage on his long and perilous journey. He faces many obstacles and sacrifices much to help others. But his compassion and faith in himself are sources of great power that help him fulfill his quest. And when we see this small creature succeed, we are empowered to dream and strive ourselves!

Figure 2–3
A "Great Idea" chart.

Matching Stories with Realia

We can help children understand and internalize stories we read by bringing in real items to illuminate the written text. A pirate headband with an eye patch and bandana and a toy ship help contextualize *Tough Boris,* a picture book by Mem Fox (1998). One or two small puppets are fun to use with *Borregita and the Coyote,* an Ayutla trickster tale retold by Verna Aardema (1998). These small items draw children into stories and make read-alouds both comprehensible and exciting. Children are propelled to retell and reenact stories when we provide small props for them to use.

Using Videos

Clever use of real items extends to helping children understand movies and videos as well. I was privileged recently to watch Stephen Cary, author of *Going Graphic: Comics at Work in the Multilingual Classroom* (2004), teach an ESL lesson to my first graders. Stephen showed a short video clip from *The Black Stallion* (1979). He then brought out a small black plastic horse and created a cobra for the children using a piece of paper, a pen, tape, and his own belt. As one boy lay on the rug, enacting the sleeping child, Stephen and the kids used the horse and snake to replay the movie scene and talk about it—with great drama. Children's language exploded out of them as they sought to describe what they had seen—and what they had experienced when they used the props. This was a powerful activity to see and hear. Reluctant speakers clambered to be heard and express themselves. Stephen coaxed language and built on it. And when he tried to leave, my children waylaid him. They ran for their notebooks and pencils and began writing down his email address and his every word. (See Figure 2–4.)

Figure 2–4
First graders hang
on author Stephen
Cary's every word.

This use of real items doesn't just make kids more comfortable with stories. It helps them understand them from the inside out and respond to these tales with passion and intensity.

A great deal of our work in the classroom has to do with giving children opportunities like these. We want our students to experience success. When we make provisions to tailor learning experiences to their language level and other needs, we help them achieve it.

CHAPTER 3

Demystifying Second Language Acquisition

The limits of your language are the limits of your world.

—Ludwig Wittgenstein, from *365 Daily Thoughts
and Inspirations About Teachers*

Acquiring a second language can be a giant challenge for both children and adults. This is an issue that can greatly affect self-esteem and profoundly affect our future: who we are, how we approach life, and what we become. I think my first job as a classroom teacher is to let my kids know that no matter what our language capabilities are, I'm OK, and so are they! Nothing stifles language acquisition quicker than worrying about it. My intent is to boost children's confidence in their abilities to communicate and to validate their ways of speaking. I want them to know that I have faith in their capacity to learn. I am the bridge between my kids' home languages and the academic and social language of Standard English they need to acquire to succeed.

Because I want all my children to be language learners, I model this myself by learning some words in the languages of all my students. It doesn't matter whether I am great at this endeavor; I think it is important—and fun—to make the effort, and it takes very little time. With this thought in mind, I make sure that my students hear me speak a few words of Indonesian to Salim, a little Korean to Ho Sun, some Portuguese to Luan. (The children teach me these words or phrases and I write them down phonetically to help me remember the pronunciation.) The rest of my class can learn these words too. And we all have a good time learning some sign language.

I do use some Spanish in class as well, to clarify things and help my Hispanic children get an overview of what we're doing. English speakers can pick up some Spanish at this time. This year this is helping out two little boys who let me know they felt uncomfortable because they didn't know any Spanish. When I read an English–Spanish bilingual book with good pictures (the pictures help us *all* know what's going on!), I sometimes say, "Listen to me read. When I practice, I think I get better at this." My kids marvel when they *do* hear improvement, and they nod their heads sagely. "The teacher is getting better at Spanish," I hear them say.

I want to help my students feel that we are all in this quest for knowledge together, puzzling out best ways to learn and grow. If children can see that language acquisition is a wonderful opportunity for us all, not just a skill for a few special learners, they will find it easier to accept the challenge and will feel less anxiety about language mastery.

I once heard Leonard Olguin, an expert on language and bilingualism, speak at a CABE (California Association for Bilingual Education) conference. Olguin had great perspective on the value of language, and he spoke about how fortunate we are if we are multilingual. "People talk proudly about all the languages they speak," he said. "No one ever brags that they can only speak one language."

The Tower of Babel

I love to share with my children an art print of *The Tower of Babel* painted by Pieter Bruegel the Elder in 1563. (See Resources, page 222, for some addresses and websites for obtaining art prints and transparencies.) This work of art shows the biblical story of the building of the tower and the confusion that resulted when people began speaking many different languages and could no longer communicate with each other. (This ancient story is a good metaphor for us all!) Talking about the painting leads us into a discussion of strategies for exchanging information when people speak different languages. We also talk about how much fun it is to know some words in other languages. This can be surprising for other people who don't know how clever we are!

See and Say

A wonderful picture book to use in our language acquisition endeavors is *See and Say,* written and illustrated by Antonio Frasconi (1972). This is a great resource for teaching children some information about language. The author, a graphic artist who illustrated the book with woodcuts, originally wrote it to teach his young son, Pablo, about differences in languages. He soon realized his work could introduce young minds to an understanding of vast cultures.

Frasconi spoke about his work in a lecture at the Library of Congress in 1989. "I was looking not for a book to teach a child a foreign language but for one that would show that there are different ways to say the same thing, that there is more than one nation in our world, that there are many other countries where people speak different languages," he said.

These are important ideas. I once met a ten-year-old who heard a child speaking another language for the first time. She asked why the girl was speaking "baby talk." Children really need a good overview about the world and its languages to give them some perspective.

Planet Earth, Where People Live

Another children's book that expands the world for children and gives them information about the Earth and its inhabitants is *People,* written and illustrated by Peter Spier (1988). This book gives facts about languages and cultures, interests, customs, and physical characteristics of people all over the world. It can lead to wonderful nonjudgmental discussions about ways people are the same and different.

And nothing is more visually exciting than three books by Barnabas and Anabel Kindersley: *Children Just Like Me* (1995), *Children Just Like Me: Celebrations* (1997b), and *Celebrations: Festivals, Carnivals, and Feast Days from Around the World* (1997a). The Kindersleys traveled the world, interviewing and photographing children. These books record the children's own hopes and dreams, their beliefs, and details about their lives. Photos give us a look at how children in other places live and what matters to them. In my classroom, children love to pick a place on our large world map and then find a child from that country to read about. Usually the first countries picked are countries of origin for children in the class.

The Kindersleys' books, and others like them (see the References) get a lot of talking and thinking going in my classroom. They teach a lot of English through content. And they give support and credence to other languages and cultures as well as help children build self-esteem. They are also good takeoff points for stimulating talking and writing about contrasts in the ways children live in America and in other parts of the world.

A book that shows startling contrasts between my students' lives and the lives of other children is *Kids at Work: Lewis Hine and the Crusade Against Child Labor* (Freedman 1998). This is a great book to pull out when my children occasionally grumble about something they have to do. The book is full of large black-and-white photos, most dating to the early part of the 1900s in the United States, showing children at work in terrible circumstances: shucking oysters in the cold, lifting heavy bolts of fabric in a factory, and so on. I point out, trying to be subtle, that many children in the world still live like this today. Many never get the chance to go to school. I try to introduce this book without saying much and let children take the lead in discussions. We all feel pretty lucky after a glimpse into the world of this book.

Interaction Is Crucial to Language Acquisition

Discussions in which children are speaking about and listening to things that matter to them are very important ways to help them acquire language. According to Krashen, Krashen, and Terrell, who developed the theory called the Natural Approach (1983), language is acquired naturally when we understand it, when it is comprehensible to us. Krashen discusses this further in *Explorations in Language Acquisition and Use* (2003a). He makes a distinction between *learning* language (studying language rules and grammar at school, for example) and *acquiring* language. It is language acquisition that gives us both fluency and accuracy. Acquisition doesn't rely on grammar rules and repetition drills or a lot of work with textbooks. When we hear language, and it makes sense to us, and then we *use* it, we get it.

An anxiety-free environment is also important for language acquisition. This is Krashen's Affective Filter Hypothesis. According to Krashen, if the language learner is anxious, stressed, has low self-esteem, or does not consider himself to be a potential member of the group speaking the language, comprehensible input does not reach the part of the brain Chomsky calls the language acquisition device. It is blocked, so the learner does not understand or make progress.

This information points out how important it is to provide exciting and meaningful language experiences for our students, in a nurturing, comfortable classroom atmosphere. When we focus on great content, language comes naturally, fulfilling our need to communicate and express what's going on. It is a by-product of some significant learning. When we use these principles to guide us, everything we do can help children learn to speak, understand what they hear, and write and read in English.

Ways to Help Children Acquire Language

Here are some exciting ways I work on language acquisition in my classroom. Children acquire language when they

- Listen to a story read aloud or read a big book with me

- Read books *they select* alone or with companion(s) of choice

- Practice reading alone, reading books at their own reading level

- Choose books to take home overnight

- Act out math problems and clamber to explain their thinking

- Ask for a class meeting to help them solve a problem

- Negotiate conflicts in a class meeting

- Describe the feats of our pet hermit crab or goldfish

- Write about classroom pets—and anything else that *matters* to them

- Explain a personal or group art project

- Write a story with me (shared and interactive writing) or work on their own writing during writers workshop

- Chant, sing, rap, and read poems and songs we love

- Illustrate poetry charts, books, and stories

- Interview each other about special toys, skills, hopes and dreams, and things they want to share

- Retell a story, a personal experience, a playground event

- Talk to assembly performers after a show

- Write letters to thank the local firefighters or other guests for visiting us

- Write letters and notes to send through our class post office

- Send notes schoolwide through our Wee Deliver postal project

- Create special art and make connections between what we are learning in many different curriculum areas

- Write family stories about something they want to share (This can be a great family project.)

- Work with partners and small groups on curricular-related games and projects

- Patiently *listen* to each other and *support* each other's endeavors; pull for each other as members of the same school family and citizens of planet Earth (see Figure 3–1)

Figure 3–1
Bridget helps Cassandra by listening to her story.

When we try to become accomplished in another language, we take risks. The job of the classroom teacher is to minimize these risks for students by scaffolding their language and creating an atmosphere conducive to trying things out, expressing things the best ways we can, as well as having a good time doing it.

Interaction with the Teacher

An important element of a good program for English learners is interaction with the teacher, the key English model in the classroom. In some rooms with many non-English speakers and a child-centered approach, children may be spending the majority of their time speaking their native languages or learner varieties of English. It is important that they receive regular teacher-directed instructional activities or formal instruction as well (Fillmore 1991). If children are to be successful in their challenge to acquire English, they need frequent meaningful interactions with accomplished English speakers.

I find one of the most compelling ways I can work with my first graders to influence their language is through sharing books and big books with beautiful language—language children will love hearing, will anticipate, and will enjoy repeating. Participation books—stories with language that reoccurs in patterns—are stimulating for kids. The children look forward to exciting parts of the story and the chance to echo and enact the patterned words. The following are some of our favorite participation books.

- *Each Peach Pear Plum* by Janet and Allan Ahlberg (1999)

- *Chicka Chicka Boom Boom* by Bill Martin Jr. and John Archambault (2000)

- *Brown Bear, Brown Bear, What Do You See?* by Bill Martin Jr. (1992)

- *Oso pardo, oso pardo, ¿que ves ahí?* (Spanish version of *Brown Bear*) by Bill Martin Jr.

- *Polar Bear, Polar Bear, What Do You Hear?* by Bill Martin Jr. (1991)

- *Farmer Duck* by Helen Oxenbury (2003)

- *The Napping House* by Audrey Wood (1991)

- *Seals on the Bus* by Lenny Hort (2003)

- *The Wheels on the Bus* by Paul O. Zelinsky (1990)

- *"Fire! Fire!" Said Mrs. McGuire* by Bill Martin Jr. (1996)

- *Possom Come A-Knockin'* by Nancy Van Laan (1992)

- *The Big Fat Worm* by Nancy Van Laan (1995)

Please see the References, page 231, for other selections. Many of these books are available in other languages as well as in English.

Success Begets Success

Gaining skill in one activity can convince children—and the rest of us too—that they have achieved success in other areas as well. One monumental day Beatríz brought in the Spanish version of *Brown Bear, Brown Bear, What Do You See?* (*Oso pardo, oso pardo, ¿que ves ahí?*). She put the book down in front of her, opened it smugly, and *read* it to all of us! The children and I were thoroughly impressed, and Beatríz basked in our surprise and approval. She took the book to recess and read it to other kids and repeated this activity at lunchtime. In the afternoon I helped her make an audiocassette of her reading, and we made the book and the tape available at the listening center.

At the end of the day, as Beatríz was standing in line to go home, she measured herself against Andrea and was thrilled and surprised to find that they were, for the first time, the same height. (Beatríz *was,* and continues to be, several inches shorter. However, such was the power of her belief that she even convinced Andrea of her sudden growth spurt.) Beatríz gained in stature that day, no doubt about it!

There's Nothing Like Practice

When children hear a favorite book many times, they memorize it and internalize it and frequently even speak the words of the story. And because they know the tale so well, they find it easy to make substitutions and create a whole new story line. During the weeks before Halloween this year, my class invented a clever takeoff of *The Wheels on the Bus:* an entire cast of spooky creatures on the bus—many beasties making their own noises as they headed for a scary party on Halloween night.

We turned this writing into a homemade big book, illustrated it, and enjoyed reading it in unison. I made typed binder-sized copies so that each of my kids had his or her own edition to read, illustrate, and show off.

The Great Power of Reading and What It Can Do for Us

I have struggled for years, since the bilingual program in my school district ended in the 1980s, to keep my Spanish current now that I am doing most of my teaching in English. Each year I build up my skills, and then they drop off over the summer, and I work on them all over again throughout the next school year. A couple of years ago I decided to do a lot of reading in Spanish to see if that would help me keep my language skills alive. I had tried this idea previously but rather halfheartedly.

This particular summer of great resolve, I read almost totally in Spanish, with just an occasional English book in between. I read picture books, chapter books, and poetry. I read Spanish editions of Roald Dahl's *Matilda,* Madeline L'Engle's *Wrinkle in Time,* Katherine Paterson's *Bridge to Teribithia,* and the first four of J. K. Rowling's Harry Potter books. I read many of my favorite books, which I'd previously read in English. I enjoyed them all over again, in surprising new ways.

I read slowly at first, looking up many Spanish words, but as time went on I began to read much as I read in English: I kept going if I didn't know a word and got the information from the context. I was helped by the fact that I had previously read all of these books in English and knew what was going on. I realized I noticed many things when I read in Spanish that I missed when I read in English, perhaps because I'd been reading too fast in my native tongue.

I began to *savor* the books I read in Spanish. Each time I picked one up, it took a bit of time to get into again, but that wait time soon shortened and became less bothersome. When I had trouble getting into a text again, I frequently reread several pages. I enjoyed feeling that my skills were increasing. And when school started I was flabbergasted: I could say absolutely everything I wanted to say when I spoke with parents and children. My fluency in Spanish was at an all-time high! And I had enjoyed myself while I worked to make this happen.

The Power of Reading

Stephen Krashen writes a lot about this phenomenon in his book *The Power of Reading* (2003b). I had read the first edition of this book before but had forgotten about it (consciously, anyway) when I devised my own summer reading plan. So when I reread the new edition of Krashen's book, I had my own experiences to refer to as well as Krashen's suggestions, which made everything doubly powerful. It absolutely worked to read in Spanish to increase my fluency, comprehension, and language skills. And it gave me a wonderful feeling anew of what it is like to learn to read and to savor both the experience and the text.

Controlling the Learning Rate Through Personal Reading

Speech goes by so fast that it is difficult to latch on to partially understood phrases or sentences. When I read, I could reread, refigure, and puzzle things out, just as I urge my own students to do. I also found that all this reading in Spanish much improved my writing and spelling in Spanish. This is another corollary to the Krashen premise called the Input Hypothesis (2003a), which I found to be true on the basis of my own personal experiences. As well as my ability to speak and understand spoken and written Spanish, my spelling and vocabulary really took a big leap.

I had always thought I was practicing Spanish when I spoke it, but I never felt that I made much headway when I worked on my language capabilities this way. As Krashen says, "Talking is not practicing." When I read, it makes a big difference. I now find that when my students have time each day to practice their reading in English, by reading previously read guided reading books at their own level (see Chapter 7), they make tremendous gains in *their* reading and in their written and oral language abilities as well.

The Student *Appears* to Understand . . . Is This the Case?

Language acquisition is an ongoing process. Once a child begins speaking English fairly fluently, this is a crucial time. The impression this learner leaves with teachers is that she understands the curriculum and academic language of involved coursework. This is often not the case. As a struggling Spanish speaker, I too know the strategies of nodding my head, striving to look like I get it, and appearing to understand, even when I'm not sure I do. It can take several years for students to achieve fluency in academic language. Learners need ongoing help and support—realia, maps, drawings, artifacts, charts, gestures, specific vocabulary development, and assessments—to make sure that they are *continuing* to make progress in language growth and so that they do not experience comprehension difficulties due to lack of specific subject matter vocabulary and context.

Language Is a Treasure: The Importance of First Language Maintenance

I spend a lot of time speaking with my children and their parents about how lucky they are if they keep up their home language skills. Maintenance of the family's common language is the most important underlying tool that helps family members stay connected. When lines of communication stay open through and across generations, this facilitates closeness between family members and keeps family ties alive. The kids who maintain this ability to converse with grandparents, parents, cousins, and friends in their heritage language have a treasure beyond words. They will be able to celebrate the richness of their home culture together. And their family stories, songs, recipes, jokes, and proverbs, as well as family pride, will enrich everyone's life.

More opportunities in life will come to those who speak more than one language. Our society will benefit. Students will benefit by acquiring more skills and knowledge, more confidence and self-esteem. Literacy and content knowledge in a child's first language will transfer to the second language and will assist children in learning that language. By helping children respect and acknowledge their heritage, we help them negotiate many different worlds.

CHAPTER 4

Getting Started Teaching ELLs—A Look at the First Twenty Days of School

(And then Twenty More and Twenty More and . . .)

Marianthe knew this day would come. [The first day of school in a new land.]

"I won't know anyone . . . I won't understand what they say. They won't understand me," she said. "Everything is so different."

"Only on the outside," said Mama. "Inside, people are the same."

—Aliki, *Marianthe's Story: Painted Words, Spoken Memories*

Starting school in a new grade can cause anxious moments for many children. The trip into a new classroom can be much more difficult for a child who doesn't speak the language and more difficult yet for children coming from another country. Things may be the most difficult of all for the limited English speakers who enter class after the year begins. All eyes are on them as they join an already-established community of learners.

There are many things we can do right away to help children feel welcome and comfortable and to help them believe they are a valued part of our classroom community. It doesn't take a lot of specialized materials and equipment to make this happen. Top on my list of strategies is to be aware of the child's body language and facial expressions; to smile; and to try to be as nurturing, helpful, and sensitive as possible. I also get some help from my students.

47

A Friend in Need

The first thing your new English learner needs is a buddy. Since most of my students are English learners, *everybody* gets a buddy. I try to seat students so that a buddy who speaks their language is seated on one side of them. Children who have less proficiency in English get a second buddy on the other side—if possible, a child who speaks both English and the English learner's home language. Depending on the needs of children and their patience level, I pair children with more language capability with children who have an average and an above average command of language. I match students with middle-level language development with those children in need of more help with language. I try to pair children who like each other. These partner decisions also take into account the personalities of individual students.

At times no one else speaks a new student's native tongue. I make sure this child gets a really competent, nurturing buddy who can patiently *show* her how to do things. Later I will try to get help from someone—a parent volunteer or tutor—who speaks both the child's home language and English. If I know about a child's language needs before school starts, I try to arrange for a parent volunteer or cross-age tutor from another classroom before the opening bell rings.

It is important to model for the class ways that buddies can help each other. Children need to speak clearly and look at their partners as they speak. They can *show* their partners what they should be doing, point to the page number, demonstrate what to do with materials, and so on.

It is crucial that children are patient and show respect for their partners. It can be tricky expecting young children to translate information correctly and patiently, but they really can be quite helpful to newcomers and to children who do not understand much English. Many of these children have already spent a lot of time translating for their parents or siblings and have a lot of experience in this area.

Buddies can help their partners learn classroom routines and show them what they need to be working on. Early in the school year, what could be called copying from someone else's paper is perfectly acceptable: it is a way for new students to participate and begin to learn.

Last year I had an English learner who copied feverishly at the beginning of the term. I think this allowed her to feel that she was a participating, authentic member of our class. Like everyone else, she was *busy*! Later in the year, I tried to limit her copying so that she could use and rely on some of her own knowledge.

How to Make the Best Use of Buddies

Here is a list of ways buddies can help their English learner partners:

- *Show* their partners the work to be done

- Answer questions and give reassurance

- Read a story or part of a story

- Point out or demonstrate the classroom routine to be followed, such as stand up, go to the meeting place on the rug, or turn to page 3 for reading in unison

- Point to words being read when the class reads a poem or piece of literature together

- Help the English learner practice the alphabet song, alphabet letters, numbers, and simple vocabulary

- Show how to practice counting in English

- Play simple word games

- Show their partners how to get lunch and get settled in the cafeteria

- Play with partners (at least for a few minutes at break time) and teach them how to participate in recess activities

- Join buddies at the listening center: help with tapes and finding the printed words that match those heard on the tape

- Help partners learn to communicate by sharing a few simple words

- Learn some words in their partners' language

- Work together at centers

- Work together on art projects; play art games (see Chapter 1, page 17, for sample games)

- Talk with partners and share recreational reading books together (see Figure 4–1)

As teachers, we need to be on top of the buddy situation by checking frequently to see whether partner pairs are working out. Some pairings may need to be changed if the helper seems drained by the experience or if children seem tense and annoyed with each other. And occasionally we may find children who prefer to work alone and would rather not

have a buddy. It is important to honor this need and to allow these students to work with a buddy part-time if they change their mind.

I think it is essential to change partners every six or eight weeks to keep children from becoming too dependent on each other. Some children also need a break from their buddy partners.

Parent Volunteers and Cross-Age Tutors

It can be helpful to have parent volunteers or cross-age tutors for children with little or no home language support in the classroom. It is reassuring for them to have at least one person with whom they can communicate! Naturally a parent volunteer or older student from another class (cross-age tutor) cannot be present all the time. But even having one around for a few minutes a few times a week can be helpful. It is best if there is a regular schedule so that the student in need of help can rely on it.

One of the jobs a parent volunteer can do before school begins is to make a cassette for a new student that gives information about the school and the class in the child's home language. This cassette should include school rules and information about what is expected in the classroom as well as specifics about bathrooms and fire drills. A nice touch is to include some music or poetry or a story in the child's home language.

This can be a helpful present for your new English learner on the first day of school.

If you *are* able to borrow an older student for a few brief minutes on day one, it would be helpful if he could translate directions, answer questions, and be sure the child understands where bathrooms are and when to use them, knows about emergency drills, and so on. Of course, if this isn't possible, your children can show their new classmate most of these things.

Your parent volunteer or tutor may be able to explain math assignments, translate math story problems, give tips on printing or writing, and read easy reading materials in unison with a student. A wonderful job for parent volunteers, and older students as well, is reading one on one to the student in her home language. If you do not have any reading materials in this language, perhaps your volunteer could bring books, newspapers, or magazines from home.

Children *love* this one-on-one reading time, and it is an easy way to make good use of a parent volunteer or a cross-age tutor.

Sensitizing Your Class to Newcomers: Reading Aloud Can Teach Children Many Things

Read-alouds are a wonderful way to help your class realize what it is like to be a new student who has not yet learned English. One of my favorite books, mentioned in Chapter 1, is *Marianthe's Story: Painted Words, Spoken Memories* by Aliki (1998). Another favorite is *The Color of Home* by Mary Hoffman (2002). In both of these picture books, the child protagonists use art to communicate with their new classmates, showing them where they used to live and what their lives were like in their former countries. Both children in these two stories use art to help become part of their classroom communities and create new lives for themselves.

The Name Jar, by Yangsook Choi (2001), is the story of a Korean girl who involves her classmates in helping her choose the name she wishes to be called. And *My Name Is Yoon,* by Helen Recorvits (2003), tells of a child who thinks her name looks happier in Korean than it does in English. The name problem reflects Yoon's unhappiness because she is living in America rather than Korea.

Pa Lia's First Day, by Michelle Edwards (2001), conveys a lot of vocabulary about feelings and relates some difficult first-day-of-school experiences. In *How Many Days to America: A Thanksgiving Story,* Eve Bunting (1990) tells the tale of a family that flees a small Caribbean island and lands on American shores. Family members then celebrate a very personal Thanksgiving.

All these books tell good stories, give children awareness of cultural diversity, and help create an atmosphere of acceptance and empathy in the classroom. The books are good vehicles for discussion. Coupled with a classroom map, they are an easy way to teach meaningful geography. They are also valuable for teacher reference about cultural conflicts and values and geographic and linguistic backgrounds of students.

Other helpful books tell about the experience of leaving a beloved home for a new one. Among them are *Good-Bye, 382 Shin Dang Dong* by Frances and Ginger Park (2002), and *The Morning Chair,* Barbara Joosse's 1995 story about a little boy's worries as he leaves Holland to go live in America. In *Angel Child, Dragon Child,* Nguyan Hoa (Surat 1989) has not only started school in a new land where she doesn't know the language but also has had to leave her mother behind in Vietnam. Her new classmates find her different and have problems adjusting to her until they understand some of what she is going through. Ultimately they help her with her biggest problem, and her mother is able to join her in America. (See the bibliography for some other wonderful read-alouds.)

I once visited a children's art and writing exhibition in a museum in Madrid, Spain. The exhibit, titled *Un día tuvimos que huir* (One Day We Had to Flee), shared three children's heartbreaking experiences in photos, paintings, drawings, and words and showed their dangerous journeys to refugee camps in Kenya. I purchased the exhibition book, *Un día tuvimos que huir* by Sybella Wilkes (1994). It reminds me, as does *Angel Child, Dragon Child,* that some of the children who enter my classroom have been through incredible heartbreak and danger and are in great need of kind and compassionate teaching and care.

Cultural Diversity: Videos and CD-ROMs

Many wonderful children's books are available on video, DVD, and CD-ROM. Some of the best are *Reading Rainbow* books: specially selected literature that has been made into videos and CD-ROMs. Aside from retelling the story, these materials give other background information about the topic addressed. (See the bibliography for a sampling of titles.)

Children can gain a great deal from videos, DVDs, and CD-ROMs. The images give them visuals to rely on as they work to puzzle out and acquire language. Stephen Cary's book, *Second Language Learners* (1997), contains good ideas about using videos, films, DVDs, and CD-ROMs in the classroom. Stephen has written a new book on this subject, titled *Going Hollywood,* which will be published by Heinemann in 2006.

Big Books and Transparencies

Whenever possible I use big books for large-group shared reading so that children can see the words and pictures as I read. This is a wonderful aid to help students acquire language and literacy. I also use transparencies on the overhead projector for sharing poetry and shorter pieces of literature.

Here in the Meadow We Help Each Other . . .

I like to retell the story *Hickory,* by Palmer Brown (1978), to my children at the beginning of the school year because it sets up the kind of atmosphere I hope to achieve in my classroom. In this chapter book, Hickory the mouse decides to move to the meadow. On his first day in his new home, a grasshopper saves him from being eaten by a cat. When Hickory tries to thank Hop, the grasshopper, she brushes away his gratitude. She tells him, "Here in the meadow we do what we can to help one another."

As I explained in my book *Everything You Need to Know to Teach First Grade* (2003), I find this chapter book to be quite powerful in helping me create a classroom full of sensitive, caring, and helpful children. Because the book has several chapters, I often retell the story at the beginning of the year and read the full story later on. If I don't have the book handy, I retell the story when I feel it is needed.

On the last day of school last June, I experienced personal results that may have come from having shared this story. My hands were sore that day from doing a last-minute classroom task. When Cristian asked me to open his ketchup packet at lunch, I said, "Could you please ask Juan? My hands are hurting from using the bookbinding machine."

On hearing this, Andrea stood up and looked at me indignantly. "*Why* didn't you ask us to help you?" she demanded.

And Brenda, also upset, added, "You *know* we're always *here* for you!"

I was torn between bursting into tears of gratitude and feeling embarrassed at having been chewed out by two six-year-olds.

Inclusion Through Music

Music is another great way to bond your group and make everyone feel included. CDs and cassettes fill in and make it easy for children who don't speak much English to participate at their own level, as I did in Mexico. Some easy songs have simple sounds and rhythm, such as the Israeli tune "Zum Gali Gali":

> Zum gali gali gali,
> Zum gali gali.
> Zum gali gali gali,
> Zum gali gali.

The tune for this song can be found in the book and cassette set *Wee Sing Around the World* by Pamela Conn Beall et al. (2002). It is a very easy song to sing. I often teach just the first verse of a song, especially at the beginning of the school year.

The Wee Sing series has several different sets of music, finger plays, and songs. Each set comes with a booklet with musical notation and words as well as a cassette. See Chapter 6 for further information about incorporating songs, games, and poetry into your curriculum.

Another good music reference is the CD *Songs for Singing Children*, sung by John Langstaff (2004). Some of the words have nonsense syllables, such as "Keemo Kymo" and "Sing song kitty catch a kymee-oh." Many other songs contain just a few words or sounds, and repeat them frequently, such as "If You're Happy and You Know It" and "Oh, A-Hunting We Will Go." Mother Goose rhymes are also short and easy to sing.

I teach the songs in echo fashion: I sing a line and then the children echo me. Other references I use are *Jazz Chants* by Carolyn Graham (1979), and piggyback songs—songs with new words put to old tunes. A good collection of this type of song is *Piggyback Songs: New Songs Sung to the Tunes of Childhood Favorites* by Jean Warren (1983).

Participation Games

"Who took the cookies from the cookie jar?" is a game-chant children love. The group asks questions, and one child, chosen ahead of time, answers:

> *Group:* Who took the cookies from the cookie jar?
>
> *Selected Child: [naming a classmate]* _____ took the cookies from the cookie jar!
>
> *Named Child:* Who, me?
>
> *Group:* Yes, you!
>
> *Child:* Couldn't be!
>
> *Group:* Then who?
>
> *Child names a different classmate and the game repeats.*

This old game has been turned into a picture book, *Who Took the Cookies from the Cookie Jar?* by Lass and Sturges (2000). Ashley Wolff illustrated it with animal characters from the American Southwest. In my classroom I used photos from our class picture to change this into a very personal four-fold booklet. Children illustrated it, sang it, played it, and read it frequently. (See the Appendix, page 204, for this template.

Songs and games like these give children a chance to actively participate and to play as they try out words and phrases. (See more on this curriculum in Chapter 6.)

Instrumental Music

Musical instruments also have an important place in helping children develop meaningful language. Rebecca Coolidge, a colleague of mine, is very committed to the arts and to providing them in her kindergarten and first-grade classroom. As she says, music supports mathematics, reading, writing, and all subject areas. It involves us kinesthetically, engages our emotions, and empowers us to listen and create.

Rebecca recently wrote a grant and purchased a large xylophone and plastic boom-whackers (cylindrical plastic tone pipes of different lengths). Aside from giving the children musical enrichment experiences—Rebecca's intended objective—she says that using the xylophone has already helped her students extend their vocabulary and concepts. They are now using words such as *higher, lower, tone, melody,* and *beat.*

When I visited Rebecca's classroom, several children were playing the xylophone and discussing whether they preferred the sound of the soft mallet or the hard mallet as they tried out different notes. Then one little group of four played together, listening to each other to sensitively compose as a group. One child announced proudly, "*This* one is called 'The Jungle'!"

Rebecca has planned several projects to incorporate the xylophone with other curriculum. Her students will perform *The Three Bears* using readers theater scripts that they helped write. Children will compose their own musical interludes to enhance the readers theater performance. Students will also have many opportunities to create background music to play as they retell their favorite stories. Music could also be a counterpart to movement and language games.

There are so many ways to use these instruments that Rebecca can't wait to pursue them. "Music education is powerful," she told me. "It engages all parts of the brain."

Giving Children Many Chances to Share

Children may wish to share a song or chant (or play a tune if an instrument is available) in their home language. I like to provide time for this if a child is willing or eager to sing for us, recite a chant, make music, or share a recording from home. Some children also like to tell stories. One of the most memorable moments in my classroom took place when we had a visit from my neighbors' granddaughter. Emma is of part–Tlingit Indian heritage and lives with her family on Hoonah, a small village on the northeast shore of Chichagof Island, forty air miles west of Juneau, Alaska. She was a first grader at the time and asked to come to school with me one day.

Emma loved meeting the children in my class and getting to visit a local school. But her favorite thing of all was getting to meet Crab Louie, our large hermit crab. Wanting to show off our classroom pet, the children and I put Crab Louie in the center of the room and sat cross-legged in a large circle around him. Some children sketched; others watched or gestured for him to come close. (Strange as it may seem to refer to a crab as "him," this was the children's decision.)

Not much happened at first—Crab Louie curled up in the shell and was still and unmoving, until Emma began spontaneously singing a Tlingit lullaby. Incredibly, the crab came out of his shell and headed right for her. I have always been sorry not to have this experience on video or at least on audiocassette.

We learned many things from Emma that day, but we all gained the most when she shared her beautiful song in the Na-Dene language of the Tlingit people.

Exciting Ways to Get Children Talking

Children love language for its own sake. They treasure words as they treasure keepsakes.

—Padric Coluum

One of the most powerful ways to help children acquire language is to plan such exciting, active lessons that students become totally engaged and just can't wait to talk to each other about what they are doing. When we involve children in meaningful activities, they forget their reticence to speak. They use all kinds of authentic language. And they use language for real purposes: to communicate things that matter to them.

This thought reminds me of the time I went to a Chinese restaurant with a group of college friends. We were served food with chopsticks, but no forks. And I was really hungry. I had always assumed I'd learn to use chopsticks someday, but I hadn't tackled them seriously. Without any thought at all, on this particular evening, out of both intense need and interest (and the knowledge that my seven friends weren't going to leave me much to eat if I didn't get a move on), I found myself able to use chopsticks immediately. My technique may not have been great, but I did get some dinner. I realize now that I had put off learning this skill because I was worried about doing it right. When I learned to use chopsticks from genuine need, I stopped worrying about doing things perfectly. My goal was just to be able to eat. And presto! I had learned something quickly that had always been on my list of things to accomplish. I then refined my chopstick technique on future trips to Chinese restaurants.

Excitement Stimulates Lots of Talk

When English learners are propelled to use language for their own *real* reasons, their defenses are down, and their affective filters are low. ELLs aren't worrying about whether their language is correct; they are expressing themselves as quickly and as well as they can because they are excitedly focused on the activity they are doing and sharing. With this in mind, I planned a kite-flying event to celebrate our hundredth day of first grade. One of my goals was to generate a lot of language—and to use students' own language to reach them and teach them!

Hundreds Day Kites

The children and I made quick and easy kites to celebrate the hundredth day of school. The materials were quite simple: all that was needed for each kite was one piece of copy paper, one drinking straw, a few pieces of transparent tape, two one-yard lengths of string, and two pieces of crepe-paper strips for the tail. (See Appendix, pages 205 to 207, for the kite-making directions and pattern.)

When the kites were put together, a task that took only about fifteen minutes, children were free to decorate them with crayons or marking pens. I brought ministamper-type markers for children to use so that they could stamp patterns in groups of ten and create decorations of one hundred stamps (or ten different patterns of ten stamps) on their Hundreds Day kites. There was a lot of interest and enthusiasm about these kites as we went outside to the windy space between buildings. And then the atmosphere was one of pure joy . . .

Children ran, pulling kite strings behind them, and kites and kite tails swirled through the air. (See Figure 5–1.) More than a few kites ended up tangled, but we were all in awe of the majesty of our kites taking to the sky and actually reaching the height of the school roof and beyond.

Children spent a wonderful fifteen minutes running madly, calling to each other, admiring the kites, and being amazed by what the wind could do with just a little piece of paper and a few bits of other things.

Figure 5–1
*Maria ecstatically
flies her kite.*

When we went back into the classroom, my students couldn't stop talking about the kite-flying marathon. Their words formed some beautiful poetry as they listened to each other's language and worked to clarify each other's ideas.

While children were still enraptured by the activity, I wrote down everything they said. They built on and scaffolded each other's language as I wrote, and two results were class poems that captured some of the intensity of the experience. The first poem was a somewhat sequential telling about the kite flying, but with the second poem, children hit their rhythm.

Flying Kites

It was fun flying kites.
You can run and run,
    Faster and faster
And the kites can go up,
    up, up.
The kite flies high and
    Goes away from you.

Kites look
Wonderful
Pretty
Fast
Very high

Moving like dragons
Moving like ocean waves
Moving like airplanes in the sky

Moving like birds and butterflies
Moving like snowflakes
Moving like eagles
They swoop.

—Room 7 Super Star Kids (my students' name for themselves)

I knew the word *swoop* had come from a recent song I had taught my kids: "Baby Eagles" by John Archambault and David Plummer (1997). I was delighted to hear the word being used by several children.

"Your language is *beautiful*!" I said as I wrote down children's words and read them back to them.

They said, in total surprise, "It *is?*"

Our discussion continued for quite a while as students talked about their kites, discussed how high they flew, and tried to describe the swirl of kite tails, the colors moving through the air, the image of kites suddenly taking to the sky, and even how many sets of tens we sent up into the atmosphere. For me, the project was a beautiful marriage of math, language, and poetry.

I wrote the children's dictated poems on poetry charts and they illustrated them. I also made copies so that each child could keep them and illustrate them for their individual poetry binder collection. (Read more about these collections in Chapter 6.)

Using Children's Language to Promote More Language

My next step was to use the copy machine to enlarge some of the photographs I had taken of our kite-flying experience. When the children saw these photos, they were full of yet more expressive language. They couldn't help but talk about the pictures and how they felt about the whole activity. Some of them chose to write about their kites during writers workshop. I brought in books about kites, and these literature and nonfiction books generated even more language. I decided then that the way to really get children talking and trying to express themselves was to provide the most exciting activities I could, weave them throughout the curriculum, and then harvest children's own language from these experiences to use in helping them acquire even more language. (See the bibliography for a listing of some good kite books and stories.)

Special Celebrations

We need to *do* things together so we have things to talk about, remember, and celebrate—experiences that will connect with our learning. Here are some of our favorite classroom activities that weave in and out of our curriculum and, incidentally, stimulate lots of oral and written language:

- Creating jack-o'-lanterns and telling Halloween stories

- Harvesting and cooking pumpkin seeds

- Making Chinese brush paintings of dragons and Chinese zodiac animals (see Figure 5–2)

- Planting daffodils and sketching them in our school garden

- Constructing origami houses

- Building a city and port; creating a city of the future

- Visiting a local tortilla factory and writing about the assembly line, the taste of fresh tortillas, the smells and sights during the tour

- Going eye-to-eye with an alligator at the end of an assembly program—and surviving to talk about it

- Using telephones to stimulate conversation and practice calling 911 for emergencies

- Creating body-sized puppets and acting out favorite books and stories

I like my monkey. He's waiting for his mom to get home to play with him.
—Juan Basulto

Figure 5–2 *Juan's Chinese brush painting.*

■ Wearing pajamas, robes, or sweats over clothes, drinking hot chocolate, and listening to a retelling of Chris Van Allsburg's wonderful story *The Polar Express*

Playing to Learn: Acting "As If"

One way to get children speaking and writing is through play. Playtime facilitates exciting language learning, which is one reason children pick up playground language so quickly. Nothing is as engrossing as play, deep play. There is magic in it, power, and control. When you play, *you're* in charge of the world—you and your companions—not your parents, teachers, or politicians. You invent alone or together—"No, you be this, and I'll be that"—creating, refining, adjusting, *talking it out* as you go along.

I miss being able to play in this way, although sometimes I can come close to the depth of the experience when I am writing or creating art. When I visited my brother's family years ago, I envied my nephews their time around the Legos and *Star Wars* table with all the children in their neighborhood. My nephew Dan told me recently that the summer before he left for college, he and his brother Will got up many times in the middle of the night to go back to *Star Wars* and Legos and act out the world.

Some people are able to hold onto this sense of playfulness and invention and take it with them throughout their lives. We all need to keep this part of us alive. Without play, nothing creative will ever be accomplished.

Play Is Constant with Children

Everywhere we see children, they are playing. It's their job. They make the most of it and have fun doing it. Play is a way to try on life: When you play you can be someone else, turn broom straws into gold, travel the known universe and beyond. You can take risks and make incredible things happen—past, present, and future—because you're in control of it all. Imagination is supported, nurtured, and encouraged. As Einstein once said, "Imagination is more important than knowledge."

Play is a child's most natural way to explore the world and make sense of it. It's an elemental, creative force that propels children to grow, gain skills and confidence, and learn about life. Play is a license to be silly, fool around, and *make* the impossible happen.

Teachers can facilitate language and literacy by giving children opportunities to link some literacy experiences to play. Reading, writing, and oral language can all enhance playtime activities. For more on this concept, see the book *Literacy Through Play* by Gretchen Owocki and Sue Bredekamp (1999).

My Best Present: Artistic License

When I participated in a residential California Art Project (Bay-CAP) inservice a few years ago, we were all given a very special gift at the end of the two-week program: an artistic license. Art project staff members had made color copies of a document resembling a driver's license. Each participant was photographed (headshots only), wearing an unusual hat chosen from a large selection of headgear. The photos were glued to the licenses, which were presented to us with great fun and fanfare. I have kept an enlargement of my artistic license in my classroom, within view, ever since. It reminds me to "sing, dance, create, play, act, draw, and emote." When the license expires, I'll renew it. (I'll paste a new expiration date on this cleverly created pseudodocument!)

I believe we all need to have both artistic license and creative license throughout our lives so that we'll remember to play, have fun, create, imagine, dream, invent, and try new things. I make one of these documents for each of my students (see Figure 5–3 for sample license; see Appendix, page 208, for license template).

Play in Children's Literature

A lot of children's books are about play. One of my all-time favorite picture books is *Roxaboxen* by Alice McLerran (1992). Children in the story go to a place they call Roxaboxen to build their own houses (outlines of stones and beach glass), drive (a small circle or hoop to hold and steer is all that's needed), ride horseback (a stick is enough), and *be*.

The book reflects the magic of being able to hold onto an imaginary thought and run with it. There is flexibility, creativity, zest, and total engagement. The picture book is part of a memoir told by the author's mother, who *lived* the story fifty years before. As an adult, she went back to the place she and her friends had named Roxaboxen, and it was still there. And, of course, it had been alive in her memory all that time.

Figure 5–3
*Gabriel's artistic
license.*

Play Is Crucial

With the ever-increasing and out-of-control demands on children to learn, to test well, and to produce, children need a chance to play as never before. They need some time each day when *they* are in charge of what they do, and what they learn, both at home *and* at school.

I try to keep a variety of creative toys and manipulatives in my class-room (many purchased at garage sales). Complete sets are not necessary; incomplete sets are cheaper. Following is a list of some of the kinds of things I believe children need. I try to provide open-ended and creative materials.

■ Legos

■ Building blocks, large and small; bricks, Tinkertoys, Lincoln Logs, and other building toys (see Figure 5–4) (To add interest and another dimension to big blocks, I attach typed poems to some of the blocks and cover the text with wide transparent tape. Children love discovering poems they know. Sometimes they change their play themes to incorporate the poetry.)

■ Blocks and Marbles

Figure 5–4
David, Victor, and Alejandro negotiate castle design.

- Puzzles, geometric shapes, labyrinths

- Word games: Upwords, Scrabble, Perquackey

- Flannel board, cut-out felt figures, numbers, and felt scraps (Great for storytelling!)

- Stuffed animals (lots of bears), dolls, small movable figures

- Toy dollhouse, castle, circus, schoolhouse, and so on (settings for play)

- Art and craft supplies—as large a variety as I can come up with (Kids like to help organize these.)

- Puppet theater and puppets

- All kinds of manipulatives: number tiles, geometric figures, magnets, linker cubes, buttons, kraft sticks, and so on

Linking Play to Curriculum

Some days after math and other afternoon activities, children jump at the chance to engage with the play paraphernalia in the classroom. I have spent time with them exploring these materials. They know what is available, how to use things, and how to put them away. Small chalkboards and chalk, pencils and paper—and, of course, books—are also available to use with play materials.

I also try to provide play links to curriculum and make opportunities to play and have hands-on time in a variety of subject areas. We have math manipulatives and games, science tools, tubs of rocks and magnets, and other pieces of equipment. Some of our best resources for play are children's books, both fiction and nonfiction.

Nonfiction Books

Nonfiction books are easy to pair with manipulatives: a tub of rocks and books about rocks, tiny trucks and books about vehicles, a box of magnets and books about magnets, and so on. I have a basket of plastic bugs and some bug books, some postage stamps and books about stamps. It is fun to put things together this way, and the children enjoy it. They help me add to our collections. Children pore over nonfiction books and love the opportunity to play and fiddle with real items like those shown in books.

Children's Literature: Make Play-the-Book Centers

Children's literature books are a great impetus for imaginative play. I keep many books in plastic tubs, banker's boxes, and large envelopes or freezer bags. I match the books with possible items children might need to act them out. For example, children love to reenact Nancy Shaw's story *Sheep Out to Eat* (1995). The sheep are hungry and go to a restaurant. They have difficulty ordering because they can't read the menu. (This is a great plug for wanting to be able to read for *real* reasons!) When the waiter brings the food, the sheep don't like it. In their ignorance about the menu, they have ordered crazy food! Eventually, after a lot of sheep misbehave, the waiter throws them out of the restaurant. The sheep discover that they love the tasty green grass outside the diner, and they eat their fill. They decide they'll come to eat here again.

Children like this book so much that they find it fun to have some time to read it, act it out, and play with it (see Figure 5–5). I keep three or four copies of the book in a manila envelope or large plastic bag. I put a few props in, too, in case children want to create materials or reenact the story. I try to stay away from organizing things, though—the children are in charge.

Figure 5–5
Children love acting out Sheep Out to Eat.

Here are a few props and materials I put in the envelope or bag with the *Sheep Out to Eat* books:

- Twelve-by-eighteen-inch white paper, folded in half or thirds, in case children want to create their own menus

- Sample menus to look at for ideas (Some restaurants, especially family-oriented eateries, are glad to donate these.)

- Magazines, glue, scissors, and marking pens, crayons, and pencils

- A towel and an apron for the waiter or waitress

- A pencil and ordering pad for the waiter or waitress

- A cook's hat and a spatula, in case a cook wants to get involved

- A small chalkboard and chalk (or whiteboard and pens) for the "Special Foods of the Day" chart

- Rubber chickens and other rubber or plastic food

And so on. I also add related picture books, such as *Frank and Ernest* by Alexandra Day (1988), which is full of diner lingo, and *Pigs Will Be Pigs: Fun with Math and Money* by Amy Axelrod (1997). (I add some play money to use with the *Pigs* book for adding up food bills.)

Children will be propelled into writing if they need food words or advertisements on their menus or names of dishes on a restaurant specials board. When they *really* need to write to enhance their play situation, the act of writing takes on new importance and credibility. I am available to help them, and they also get help and ideas from books and magazines and each other. (See Figure 5–6.)

When children have books available, they will use them as part of their imaginative play. They will read them, refer to them, and enjoy the literature and the whole experience. This works best with stories the children have already listened to and love.

It is very powerful to involve students in brainstorming book titles to put in the play center as well as collecting toys and manipulatives to go with the reading materials. Kids can take charge of centers and plan book and toy sets.

Figure 5–6 *Monica made a terrific menu for her restaurant.*

Storytelling

I like to provide storytelling experiences in the classroom, giving children a chance to visualize and to suspend disbelief. When books as well as toy and play items are provided, children enjoy storytelling as well. In a situation without pressure, storytelling becomes a valued play experience.

Generalized Materials for Acting Out a Literature Book

Most picture books can be brought to life with just cutout drawings of characters adhered to kraft sticks. These simple puppets are used to enact the whole story. A large paper bag (place the bottom on the desk, cut a hole in the front, and lower the puppets into the bag) can be a backdrop for the story. Just stick on story details, inside and outside of the play theater, with cut paper and glue. (See Figure 11–2, page 181.)

Other Book and Play Ideas

Another way to act out *any* picture book story is to use paper towel rolls, cut in two- to four-inch lengths, three-by-three-inch cardboard squares (optional), paper, scissors, and pens or crayons.

Children can make main characters and details of settings with paper and pens or crayons. Then they can cut out these items and attach them to pieces of paper rolls. They can glue the rolls to squares of cardboard for stability, so that the whole scene can stand alone, or students can move pieces around to reenact a story.

To add to the fun, design a story mat using about one square yard of butcher or tablet paper. Glue or tape on setting details, move the figures onto the scene, and let the story begin!

Little Red Riding Hood

A recent story map my kids enjoyed creating went with the story *Little Red Riding Hood* (Hyman 1983). The base was a four-by-four-foot piece of green fadeless paper. The children glued on paths and flowers and other aspects of the landscape. They created trees from cut paper and attached them to cut paper tubes to make a three-dimensional forest. Little Red's home and Grandma's cottage were created the same way, as were story characters: They cut out paper pictures and attached them to stand-up paper tubes. These characters became puppets the children moved around to retell the story.

A theatrical variation of this idea is to use a large empty box to store paper roll puppets and story elements such as trees, houses, and mountains. Children can create story scenes with crayons, pens, or cut or torn paper on twelve-by-eighteen-inch construction paper. Attach a story scene to the front of the box with paper clips or clothespins, and change scenes as needed for dramatic enactments.

Readers Theater

To add a reading-practice element to the center with the box of props and scenes, provide book copies and/or readers theater scripts, and keep them in the box with the puppets. Then children can read the story as they move puppets and change story scenes at appropriate times. (See Figure 5–7. For more ideas about using puppets, see Chapter 11.)

The following is a sampling of some children's books I package with additional play materials. I think the best books for this center have at least one great character and scenes children remember and want to play with.

Figure 5–7

Scene enactment of Where the Wild Things Are.

- *Pierre* by Maurice Sendak (1991). I include our large stuffed lion as part of this center as well as a toy stethoscope and a briefcase for the doctor.

- *William's Doll* by Charlotte Zolotow (1985). I keep multiple copies of the book and a small baby doll.

- *Chewy Louie* by Howie Schneider (2000). I include a stuffed dog with copies of the book. Children can create lots of "chewed-up" props by making drawings of items, cutting them out, and cutting "bites" out of them.

- *Mean Soup* by Betsy Everitt (1995). This book is packaged with a large bowl, a small pot, and a wooden spoon.

- *The Tub People* by Pam Conrad (1995). I put multiple copies of the book in a cardboard soft-drink tray with paper towel rolls, tape, paper, and marking pens. Kids make their own Tub People and glue them onto the rolls. With paper rolls for backing, these cutout figures will easily stand and are easy to manipulate.

- *Frog and Toad Are Friends* by Arnold Lobel (2002). I keep multiple copies of the book with small plastic figures of Frog and Toad. (These figures were sold with the book for a limited time.) I include a button, a flower, tablets and pencils for lists, plastic cookies, and other small props. Children also like creating their own Frog and Toad characters and attaching them to kraft sticks to make simple puppets.

- *Building a House* by Byron Barton (1990). Pair this book with a plastic hammer, saw, wrench, and other tools, and some blocks of assorted sizes.

- *Doctor DeSoto* by William Steig (1990). Create a dentist's office. Add pulleys and string if you have them. Make paper and scissors available for making the mice, the fox, the ladder, and dental tools.

- *Rumplestiltskin*, retold by Paul O. Zelinsky (1986). Build a castle with blocks and details attached to stand-up paper tubes. This castle may also be used with other folktales and fairy tales as well.

- *Art Dog* by Thacher Hurd (1998). Make a three-dimensional art museum from construction paper. (See Appendix, page 209 and 210, for directions on how to make this scene box from a piece of twelve-by-eighteen-inch construction paper. See also Figure 5–8.) Decorate

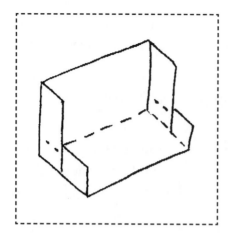

Figure 5–8
A construction paper scene box is a good substitute for a shoe box.

the walls of the museum with tiny art. Remember to add Art Dog, the protagonist of this picture book. Some other museum books are *Willy's Pictures* by Anthony Browne (2001), *Katie's Picture Show* by James Mayhew (2004), *The Magical Garden of Claude Monet* by Laurence Anholt (2003), and *Linnea in Monet's Garden* by Cristina Bjork (1987). This scene box could be used for any book.

Children really enjoy these "play-the-book" centers. The activities are a mix of theater, art, and literacy. They allow children to really use their imaginations while giving them good practice in a variety of skills—language skills in particular. Five or six book centers can be used at the same time, with children grouping themselves to play their favorite stories. Student-made props may be kept in a box or bag at a center and used again and again. (See the References for other children's books relating to play.)

Using Picture Books for Language Learning

Read-alouds are a wonderful way to stimulate language learning. I taught the children a song about a farmyard, and they talked a lot about a farm field trip most of them had taken in kindergarten. I then shared Jane Wattenberg's picture book *Henny Penny* (2000) with my group of English learners. I explained to the children that I had heard Jane talk about her book and her art. She does not use drawings to create her illustrations; she uses a combination of photography, computer technology, and collage techniques. She takes some photos herself and also uses photographs from magazines.

The language in this book is complicated but lots of fun to say. Children first experienced more traditional Henny Penny folktales, and then I read Wattenberg's variation. After students had a good idea about the book and had heard it once or twice, I invited them to repeat some parts of the story after me, using the echo technique. When I use this method, I say the words, gesturing to myself, and then children repeat the words as I hold my hands out toward them. They loved repeating the words of Wattenberg's retelling: saying sentences such as "Shake, rattle and roll! The sky is falling!" and "Don't loiter, Lurkey. Let's LAUNCH!"

This book also contains great synonyms, which help children comprehend the text and increase their vocabulary. For example, Henny Penny "RAN and RAN. That she-hen, she HUSTLED, she HURRIED, and she BUMPED right into that he-chicken, Cocky-Locky, a rooster of fine repute."

I shared with the children two other versions of the same story: *Chicken Little,* by Stephen Kellogg (1987) and *Henny Penny* in *Nursery Classics* by Paul Galdone (2001). They enjoyed making comparisons.

Creative Expression Extends Language Learning

I believe a lot gets done when children converse as they work. As students gathered at tables to illustrate a favorite scene or character from one of the *Henny Penny* picture books, there was a lot of talk and discussion. Donald Graves says, "Busy hands make good thinking" (2004). "There's nothing like good conversation while our hands are busy doing something else," he continues. "We're not staring at each other; the talk flows easily while we work. A study of very young children working on crafts showed that their language and ideas were richest when they were doing something with their hands."

When I brought out actual acorns (a detail from the story) and passed them around, children were totally fascinated. They begged to keep them. I went on a subsequent acorn hunt so that I would have an acorn for each child.

An interesting related lesson, which I have not yet proposed to my class, would be to invite the children to afix an acorn to a piece of paper with glue or Fun Tac and add marking-pen or crayon drawings to illustrate a special part of *Henny Penny.* Children could write their own stories or dictate them to me. I could then type the finished tales and tape each under a watercolor painting or final illustration. This technique might also be an interesting way to create a mural of this traditional tale.

Songs and Picture Books That Inspire Talk

Last week my ELL students enjoyed listening to and acting out the folk song "Fire! Fire!" This song from *The Tiger Sings on CD* by the Mc-Crackens (1999), tells the story of old Mrs. O'Leary and the great Chicago fire of 1871. Children got into a circle and mimed the actions to the story-song as they sang. Their favorite part was showing how the cow kicked the bucket over, blinked her eyes, and yelled "Fire, fire!" We made large poetry charts of the song lyrics and children illustrated them. I also put the lyrics on an overhead transparency so that we could read them together and track them while we sang. Children enjoyed listening to Gail Gibbons' picture book *Fire! Fire!* (1987) as a complement to the song. Another related picture book we all liked was *"Fire! Fire!" Said Mrs. McGuire* by Bill Martin Jr. (1999).

Quick and invigorating experiences with words and music, made comprehensible by picture books, go a long way toward developing language. I believe that when children are perked up by music, they are more receptive to language—to understanding it and to using it.

Charlotte Diamond

Charlotte Diamond is a musical genius. I use her CDs daily as a way to sing our way to literacy. These experiences are lots of fun, and the children beg to sing and act out Diamond's songs. One of my students' favorite songs is "I Wanna Be a Dog." They choose it on a regular basis. When children can make up their own variations of songs and poetry, I know that their language has taken a big leap.

Midway through our first-grade year, this song took on a life of its own for our English language group, as they began spontaneously saying and singing what else they "wanna be." I wrote down the children's words on chart paper (during shared writing), scribing for them. About halfway through our list, the word pattern changed, and then it changed again. A definite beat or rhythm took over. The children loved rereading their list. On another day they illustrated it and acted it out.

A final activity was a performance: The kids added animal details to headbands. They wore their costumes and acted out the written animal list they had created. They chatted with each other about which animal they had chosen and what their animal could do. The non-English speakers were definitely included and supported as they repeated the "I

Wanna Be" list with the class, joining in when they could and copying others in acting out the animals and the animal antics.

Children ended up loving their creation so much that I typed them copies for their poetry binders and they illustrated them their way. The actual rap created by my class went as follows.

I Wanna Be . . .

> A fast-running cheetah
> A racing lion
> A roaring tiger
> A little blue pony
> A kitten that climbs trees
> A barking poodle
> A little white rabbit
> A giraffe in the zoo
> A rabbit that's real and he goes to the city
> A unicorn that flies
> A fast-swimming fish
> A black and white zebra
> And *then* I wanna be ME!

Children also enjoy singing the song as it was written and pretending to be dogs. A fast and easy costume, if needed, is a headband with ears attached. I like to integrate this song with other curriculum. I give children the opportunity to talk to their partners and then to the group about their own dogs or dogs they know. We make lists of kinds of dogs and I read aloud several picture books about dogs. One of our favorites makes us howl with laughter: *Chewy Louie* by Howie Schneider (2000). Chewy Louie, the puppy protagonist, nibbles, chews, and bites everything, as the illustrations demonstrate. Louie's behavior is more extreme on each page. Just as he is about to find himself homeless, he grows up enough to control some of his behavior. Other dog books children love are *Harry, the Dirty Dog* (Zion 1997) and *The Stray Dog: From a True Story* (Sassa 2001).

Another favorite Charlotte Diamond song is "I Wanna Be a Pizza." This song has a lot of repetition: each line repeats, and the tune is easy to sing. The song is fun to act out, as there are many steps to show what happens to the pizza. Children love to create this favorite food with scraps of felt and scissors. We don't glue this project. The pizza pieces (felt scraps) can be taken apart, stored in an envelope, and reassembled another day. If enough felt pieces (or paper scraps) are available, this makes a great partner activity!

Want to Generate Language? Plan a "Quiet" Activity!

One of the best ways to get children talking is to put on a video—preferably a video they know and love, and one that relates to curricular themes being covered in class. First graders' preferred way of watching a video is to *talk* their way through it. If left to their own devices, they will move their chairs into clusters, walk around between groups, chat, and predict to each other what is going on and what will happen next. It makes no difference whether they have seen this video or not; this is their way of enjoying it to the max!

And if they find out that you, their teacher, have not seen this video and they have, you will be fair game. This will make their day. Their greatest joy will be to talk you through it so that you will know what is going on. Children love being the experts!

I brought in a video of *The Lion King* for the children to watch during their Valentine's Day party. I did this to create a celebratory atmosphere. Also, I wanted to listen to children's language as they watched. What I didn't realize was that they would be using as much or more language than there was on the video!

Maybe the fact that the room was slightly darkened, rendering reluctant speakers somewhat anonymous (and the fact that many children *really* knew this video and even had it at home), accounted for the barrage of language it inspired. The film didn't have a valentine theme, but it was certainly about love and loyalty, and we had been enjoying a lot of picture books on these themes.

I was plunged into first-grade culture as I leaned back to eavesdrop, think about children's language, and ostensibly watch the movie. The classroom scene looked more like a cocktail party than a theater, as the children walked around and chatted with each other, mostly talking about what was happening in the film and what would happen next.

The hit of the party for my students was being able to tell me what would be happening next: "He's gonna die now." "His father is gonna die." "No, not yet." "He'll die when he climbs the rock. Then he'll fall and die." "Now it's gonna happen." "It's so sad." "The animals will run on top of him." I soon realized that this was no quiet period for watching a movie: this was an opportunity for language practice and acquisition!

I had brought the video to create a special treat for my children, but I think I enjoyed the experience more than they did, watching them as they related to the video and realizing all the language it generated.

Through this experience I learned that seeing a good video or DVD on a theme being studied can really *stretch* language. Many of my first graders had totally memorized different scenes, and they dramatized them in their way throughout the film. They all acted out scenes when the opportunities arose. A few of the children I overheard talking animatedly rarely got going like that in class. It was a great afternoon of discovery for me.

CHAPTER 6

Facilitating Oral Language Acquisition Through Poetry and Music

Poetry and Hums aren't things which you get, they're things which get you. And all you can do is to go where they can find you.

—A. A. Milne, *Winnie the Pooh*

Words come to life when we say and sing them. When we teach children poetry and songs and then provide time for them to recite them, and sing, chant, and read them, we are strengthening their language in exciting ways. Poetry gives us words and images that can live on in our minds and hearts. It gives us voice and ways to express ourselves. Learning through poetry is a magical experience for us all and a wonderful tool for children who are struggling with language acquisition.

When I lived in Mexico, for a total of four or five months over two summers, I visited an elementary school and took a look at children's reading textbooks. Although there were some stories and essays, the books were filled with illustrated poetry that got progressively more difficult each year. I was able to purchase some texts and I continued studying them on my own. The illustrations helped me figure out the meaning of the poems. I soon realized that learning simple poetry and song lyrics gave me a real edge in learning Spanish and gave my language acquisition capabilities a big push! When I recited and sang, I enjoyed myself. I made new connections with my first graders. Perhaps most surprising of all, I discovered that I could effortlessly remember all kinds of things

I hadn't specifically studied. And I internalized a lot of information about the way the language worked.

Memorizing poems and song lyrics is a great way to learn the structure of a language and internalize rhythm, rhyme, and vocabulary. Working this way, I grew in self-confidence as I gained facility in Spanish. Since this worked so well for me, I decided to emphasize these strategies in my classroom.

I have always taught a lot of poetry and music: I love it, it's always been important to me, and we all *need* it. But after my own foreign language struggles, I became even more aware of the benefits and great joy in learning—and teaching—this way. I found, as an added benefit, that these collaborative experiences with poetry and music help build classroom community. When our voices join together in reciting a common piece of literature or music, each individual is supported, and weaknesses and mistakes don't matter. We become a bonded group, and the experience transcends the struggle with syntax, pronunciation, and vocabulary words.

When a Child Does Not Speak

I once had a Spanish-speaking student named Ricky who barely spoke all year. Even though I realize that we all need to go through a silent period before we begin speaking another language, I was concerned about his reticence. The breakthrough for Ricky came late in the school year when our class had an on-site field trip. It was a visit from a local nature van, complete with an assortment of small animals and a docent to tell us all about them.

The children and I sat on logs placed in a circle on our school grounds near the foot of San Bruno Mountain. We listened and watched as the docent handled animals and told us stories about them. We learned about native birds and other creatures, held some of them, and felt a heady reverence for life. As we watched the docent show off a small brown mouse, Ricky looked at me, smiled, and spontaneously spoke, in the words of poet Rose Fyleman: "I think mice are rather nice" (1990).

I almost fell off the log, but I recovered in time to show Ricky how excited I was about his gift of language. This experience seemed to be a true epiphany for Ricky. He continued speaking English, began taking many risks to express himself, and never clammed up again.

Teaching Poetry

I teach poetry to children in many ways throughout our days together. One way is the echo technique. First I read or recite the poem. Children respond and sometimes want to talk about it. Then I say the words a line or two at a time. The group echoes what I say. We practice, adding on a few lines each time, and soon we can repeat the whole poem together.

I sometimes say, in the words of my literature mentor and former children's literature professor Kay Goines, "Give me a soft, gentle rhythm." The children and I tap our knees in unison and recite the poem, clapping and tapping as a counterpoint to the words.

Personalizing Poetry

I also use another strategy that is a cause for joyful celebration: After the group has heard a poem and has reflected on it and talked about it—with the children's ideas driving this discussion—I substitute a child's name for the name in the poem. Children want to repeat the poem over and over using different classmates' names. They could go on at some length enjoying this activity, but I always try to stop before they are tired of it. In this manner we chant, "Kelcie [instead of Isabel] Met an Enormous Bear," "Roberto [not Fernando] Has a Basketball," and so on. See Joanna Cole's book, *A New Treasury of Children's Poetry* (1984), for the poems "Adventures of Isabel" and "Fernando."

Children clamber for turns to have their name included in the poems. Effortlessly they recite and relish the words, putting in lots of expression and hamming things up. Usually I am the person who wants to stop and go on to another activity. We do this for many days with the same poems, all chosen by students. This suits me just fine. I like it when my kids beg for poetry.

Poetry Charts and Craft Activities

After I teach a poem or song I put the words on a twenty-four-by-thirty-six-inch piece of manila tagboard or a piece of colored poster board. Children draw or paint; we cut out the artwork and glue it around the poem. Sometimes I put poems on overhead transparencies as well. (See more about this in Chapter 7.) Often we make murals to illustrate poems and stories, with torn-paper images that embellish the words. Puppets are another great item to use when we recite poetry.

Retelling: Making Poetry and Story Booklets

Another related language activity is to make small booklets that go with these murals: We retell the poem or story and put our words both on the mural and in the books made from one piece of photocopy paper. (See Appendix, page 219, for directions for making these booklets.) I write the children's words on paper, make copies, and fold them into eight-page booklets. Children illustrate these and read them over and over, gaining fluency and confidence and internalizing language rhythms and structures.

Zomo the Rabbit

My first graders loved the book *Zomo the Rabbit* by Gerald McDermott (1996). They asked me to read the story daily for several weeks. Finally, we practiced retelling the story. Then we made a Zomo mural and illustrated it with both cutout oil-pastel illustrations and computer printouts of our story synopsis. The words from our retelling also made their way into the small type of booklet described previously. I noticed that when some of my English learners were illustrating their booklets, they would look at the mural, match the cutout words attached there with words in their little books, and then would know what part of the story to draw. The mural scaffolded children's independent reading and drawing. (See Figure 6–1.)

Children enjoyed a similar experience with Ashley Bryan's picture book *Beautiful Blackbird* (2003). When they learned I would be seeing Bryan at a Reading the World conference in San Francisco, the kids begged to make a mural for him. (See Figure 6–2.) The *Beautiful Blackbird* mural was hung at the conference reception, and my class received a beautiful thank-you postcard from Bryan.

My children were so involved with the book and the mural that they talked of Bryan constantly. They wrote him notes, and one child even created an illustrated poem for him. (See Figures 6–3 and 6–4.)

1 Zomo is very clever.
He wants wisdom.
He asks Sky God.
Sky God says Zomo has to do
three impossible things.

3 Zomo the Rabbit played his drum
so loud it went way to the ocean.
Big Fish came out and danced faster
and faster, and his scales fell off.
He was naked.

2 Sky God says, "You must bring me
the scales of Big Fish, the milk of
Wild Cow,
and the tooth of Leopard."

4 Zomo got his hat and put the scales
in his hat and went to the forest.

Figure 6–1 *A sampling of pages from an 8-page* Zomo the Rabbit *retelling booklet.*

Figure 6–2
I loved sharing my students' Beautiful Blackbird *mural with author Ashley Bryan.*

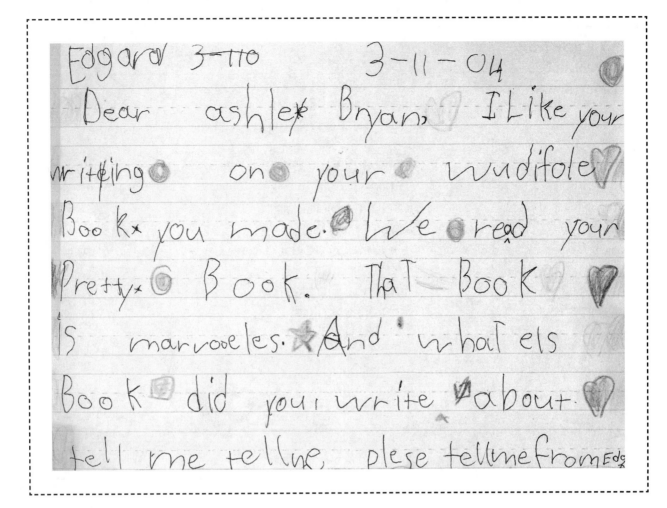

Figure 6–3 *Edgard's letter to Ashley Bryan.*

Photo Poetry and Book Excerpts

Best of all, at times we include our own cutout photographs on the charts and murals as well as in the small booklets. This helps personalize the written words. If we can see ourselves in the poetry or songs, we activate our imaginations in a special way and view it all from another dimension.

There is a lot of power in the melding of our images and the text: We can *be* what we can imagine. In this way we become *part* of the literature we are reading. Our photos place us in the poem or story excerpt alongside real and fictional characters, in real and imaginary worlds and settings. We have passed through a magical doorway to become part of it all!

Figure 6–4
*Ricky's illustrated,
spontaneous poem
for Ashley Bryan.*

Hey, Ashley Bryan,
I just made a song for you:

Beautiful Blackbird
In the sky,
Beautiful Blackbird
Singing up high
Beautiful blackbird
Watching us fly
Beautiful Blackbird
Shining up high.
—Ricky

Poetry Puzzles

We admire our artwork as we recite the poems or sing the songs. We also make puzzles and games with these poems, for example, by putting cut-up sentence strip versions back together in pocket charts. We refer to these often for shared reading, to make connections with other pieces of literature, and to enjoy the words and the visual images they evoke (Dragan 2001, 2003).

Poems, Music, and the Visual Arts

I believe in extending experiences with poetry and song lyrics by providing children with many varied opportunities to illustrate the images the words evoke for them. When they think about a poem or song they have learned or created, and then draw or paint how *they* saw it, how they feel about it, what they *heard,* children are taking real ownership of the words and their meaning.

Occasionally an individual child will illustrate a poetry chart. Sometimes I send charts home and parent volunteers illustrate them. Children also get a chance to illustrate poems individually as well as collaboratively in a smaller size format. Each student has a poetry binder filled with poems we have learned. They practice and illustrate poems during poetry center time and sometimes during other parts of the day. (See *Literacy from Day One* [Dragan 2001] and *Everything You Need to Know to Teach First Grade* [Dragan 2003] for more information about centers.)

Adding Movement and Drama

When we add movement and mime to our bag of creative literature experiences, children have an opportunity to move around and to interpret story and poetry in yet other dimensions, expressing themselves without words. Sometimes we act out poems and songs as we recite and sing them together.

When the group sings, "Put your finger in the air," this amounts to a TPR lesson (see Chapter 2, page 28 for more on James Asher's program of Total Physical Response). Doing the motions and touching correct body parts as we sing "Head and Shoulders, Knees and Toes" is a fun and easy way to play with and learn vocabulary words. (For more on related drama activities, see Chapter 11.)

Using Poetry Booklets and Charts to Assess Language

I learn a great deal about children's language capabilities when I see their drawings in their booklets and on poetry charts and as I listen to their reflections. One of the most revealing incidents for me was seeing the Caterpillar tractor Ricardo had drawn to illustrate a poem about butterflies. It seemed like a somewhat sophisticated mistake: this child really knew his construction equipment! But I realized that we were way off on comprehension and that I should have modeled, drawn, and read more books and shown more photos when we were learning the poem.

In this way, enjoying and evaluating children's artistic and verbal responses to poetry lets me know how my children are doing in terms of language. These pieces of student work also let me know how *I'm* doing in getting concepts across to my first graders.

Formats for Showcasing Poetry and Art

A new idea I implemented last year, thanks to a template from Nancy Andrzejczak's Project RAISE workshop on building literacy through the arts, was the use of a seven-by-seven-inch black-line frame for artwork and poems. To use this template, I draw the frame on photocopy paper and keep the image on my computer so that I can type poetry underneath the square. Sometimes the poems are original writing by students; often they are poems and songs we have learned. My students illustrate these poems within the black-line border. Different types of frames can be used too; children can also invent their own borders.

I sometimes type up students' poems or stories and cut them out and glue them on their original work. If this will not fit, I staple the typed version to the other side of the paper. This way I can see both original and edited work and the final product. (See Figure 6–5.)

Sometimes the art is done on separate seven-by-seven-inch white construction paper or cardstock and is then glued onto pages with the frames and the text. This is especially important for watercolor illustrations.

Poetry Board Display

I make a permanent bulletin board display with collections of these illustrated poetry templates from each child. The board has permanent pins for hanging stacks of children's work. I punch two holes at the top of children's papers. In this way, I can quickly place new illustrated poems on top of each child's group of collected work. This ongoing bulletin board is visually interesting, always new, and keeps our art and

Figure 6–5
Kelcie's original writing and typed story.

writing in view all year. It is a special way for children to show off their wonderful art illustrations as well as their own writing.

Children love to lift up papers and look through the work that has been written or illustrated by classmates. (See Figure 6–6.) And the professional look these black-line or decorative frames give to children's artwork is amazing.

The idea for the template came from Project RAISE, Lake Elsinore Unified School District, Lake Elsinore, California. (See Appendix, page 211, for a poetry frame template.) The Project RAISE workshop is filled

with ideas for helping children learn to write through access to the visual arts. (See References, page 235, for source information about this wonderful program—Andrzejczak 2003.)

English Learners Are Poetic!

I have found that English learners are very poetic when they are exposed to poetry, literature, music, and song. There is something about poetry, and its freedom of expression, that empowers children to give up struggling and say things their own ways . . . and beautiful are the words they use. When Fernanda told me, "In Mexico, a little bird died," the reverent way she said her new English words gave them import, power, and the feel of poetry. Antonio told me about the "moon-eater snake-cloud" he "saw in the night"; and Maria, just beginning to string words together in English, was stimulated enough by seeing her newly emerging permanent tooth in the mirror to say, over and over, "This little tooth want time to grow!"

Adrian used symbols, letters, pictures, and some words and dictation to describe his cable car ride in San Francisco: "We went on a cable car and we almost crashed because a car got in front of us. We went to pier to eat. I ate chocolate cookie Magic." He ended with the words "And the moon was turned orange and it was night. We came late to home."

All these thoughts and writings seem to me to be small poems. I type each of them on the computer, one poem per seven-inch frame template, and the children illustrate their work. At the end of the year I bind these collections for each child or staple them with covers and send them home.

I believe part of my job is to be as conscious as possible, alert to the incredibly beautiful things children learn, do, and say as they begin to express themselves. In this way I can help make their words permanent for them and publish or display the poems and stories so that we can all enjoy them.

Poetry Collection Covers

These stacks of poetry written and illustrated by each child are terrific collections of individual students' work. Children make beautiful mandala covers for their poetry collections. Mandalas are geometric or pictorial designs usually enclosed in a circle, representing the entire universe. Children love the format and seem calm and centered as they use it.

I give students copies of my template of a circle with nine empty boxes to use for their mandalas. I enlarge class pictures and give children copies of their photos. If they prefer, they can use photos from home; I photocopy these for them and return the originals. Children use their photographs and oil pastels, marking pens, or colored pencils to create very personal mandalas. They may use words as well as images. These mandalas are cut out and glued to colored construction paper or colored cardstock of the children's choice. Some children choose to further decorate around the mandala on this background paper.

I have shared with my class seven symbols to use for creating patterns and interesting designs to liven up their artwork. These symbols are dot, half-circle, circle, loops, spiral, diagonal line, and triangle. The students often use these symbols as parts of their cover designs. Covers can be laminated (especially if they are illustrated with oil pastels) or left as is. They are extremely personal and very beautiful. (See Appendix, page 212, for a copy of this circle template.)

We also work on language to use on the mandalas. We brainstorm descriptions, such as "likes to make things." I explain that another word for this trait is *creative* since we like to create. When Daisy says she "likes math," I explain that *mathematical* is another word to describe this characteristic. I was pleased to see that Daisy used the word in her mandala. (See Figure 6–7.)

Figure 6–7 *Daisy's mandala book cover.*

Enjoying Words and Images

Our poetry collections live on the classroom wall. They show off many illustration techniques and a variety of poetic voices, as well as different types of language exploration lessons. For example, when my group was learning to read and come up with different *-ing* words, I read David McPhail's picture book *Those Can-Do Pigs* (1999), which has a lot of *-ing* words. The children thought of many *-ing* words for me to jot down on our large shared writing tablet. Then they went off to write, to see if they could come up with their own poetry or stories that contained some *-ing* words.

Edgard, who has a lot of fluency in both English and Spanish, wrote a piece, "I'm at the Zoo": "I see tigers running. I see lions drinking water. I see tarantulas sleeping. I see birds flying. And I see otters swimming under water." His artwork showed everything that he had written about. Ricky wrote "Growing Butterfly," with some thoughts about our butterfly unit (see Figure 6–8). And Alejandro wrote a very evocative story-poem about a butterfly he saw while he was outside playing (see Figure 6–9). All of these were beautifully illustrated.

Other language patterns may be used as well. They are simple for language learners and act as an aid to comprehensible writing. I give my class many other opportunities for writing. I don't want to restrict my children's writing to patterns and formulas. I just try to use formats occasionally to help them succeed. Here are some patterns my children have used successfully:

- I can _____. (Repeat six or seven times in the pages of a small eight-page book. See Appendix, page 219, for directions on folding the booklet.)

- I can _____, but I can't _____.

- I used to _____, but now _____.

- Do you like _____? Do you like _____?

- I like _____, but I don't like _____.

Sometimes poetry and song and play go together, as in the game "Who took the cookies from the cookie jar?" (see Chapter 4, page 55).

Figure 6–8
Ricky's butterfly poem.

Growing Butterfly
I grew from an egg. I chewed my way out.
And I went from one week old, two weeks old, four weeks old.
I was a chrysalis. I went my way out.
Eight weeks. I'm a butterfly at last!
—Ricky

First Choice: Poetry!

At the end of school this year my children and I were filmed for part of a district television program. District Coordinator of Community Relations, Bruce Grantham, organized the shooting of an overview of our school, Martin Elementary in South San Francisco. The footage showed the children greeting our principal, Mario Penman, in front of the building, as well as several views inside our classroom. Most of the classroom views focused on children's art and work that was still on display all over our room.

Finding a Butterfly

A butterfly is flying
And I'm playing soccer
And I see it in the flowers.
—Alejandro

Figure 6–9
*Alejandro's
butterfly poem.*

After this part of the filming, Bruce told me he would like the cameraman to get pictures of "the kids *doing* something." Before I could even ask for ideas from my class, the children said, "Oh! Let's read our poetry books! Ooooh, can we do it with partners?" Within thirty seconds the children had moved into little groups and partnerships and were happily reading, reciting, and discussing poetry together.

The cameraman seemed amazed at both the children's level of enthusiasm and involvement and their quick transition. Bruce, a former teacher, commented to me, "Don't you *love* this time of year? Think about the beginning of school when you just *yearn* for moments like this!"

Poetry Anthology

The poetry books the children were reading so enthusiastically were an anthology of poems *they* had selected and illustrated as an end-of-the-year project. Each child had chosen a favorite poem that we learned during the year. I typed the text of the poetry on the computer, one poem per page. Sometimes I invite children to mime their chosen poems while I take photographs, but this year I used enlargements of students' school pictures. I made enlarged photocopies of their photos (head, neck, and shoulders) and cut them out. Each student pasted his or her photo on the page with the selected poem and illustrated the rest of the page with fine-line black marking pens and ballpoint pens.

I feel strongly that this is one of the most important projects we do all year long. The children had to come up with the poetry that mattered to *them*. They drew details to incorporate themselves inside the poems. I made a book for each child as an end-of-the-year gift. And children read, recited, and dramatized these poems because *they loved* the poetry, loved saying it, loved playing with it. They were also intrigued by seeing their own and their classmates' drawings and photographs.

Poetry Games

It took me a long time to realize that I needed to include a table of contents in the poetry booklets and then number booklet pages accordingly. When children sit together on the rug with their books, I can ask, "Which poem should we read first?" and then "What page is that one on?"

We can make up poetry riddles:

Which poem is about animals? ("Always Be Kind to Animals")
Which poem is about a ship? ("The Allee-Allee-O")
Which poem is on page 18?

And so on. After the children guess the answer to each riddle, we read the poem.

The Great Poetry Program

One year I asked a colleague, a resource teacher, to film the big event where children see the completed poetry books for the first time and read them together and individually. It was a very exciting period. Children did not want to stop choosing and reading the poems. After enjoying poems as a group, I gave them time to read with whomever they wished, or alone, anywhere in the classroom. Most children read with partners or in small groups. A few read to classroom animals. Some read under tables or in nooks and crannies. One child read the table of contents to himself. I counted the day as a big success.

The next day two children did not come to our class meeting area with the rest of the group. I glanced up to see them lying on tables. One student held a shark puppet, and the other child's head was partly inside the puppet's mouth. The two children were vigorously reciting John Ciardi's poem "About the Teeth of Sharks." My mouth flew open. This was an incredible idea!

I asked my colleague to come and film yet again. I met with my children and suggested we take twenty to thirty minutes to plan a quick poetry program. They were excited about the idea and got started. They had approximately a half hour to meet with a group, select a poem, and plan a way to present this poem to the class through any medium they wanted: drama, dance, recitation, art, tableaux, mime, and so on. I made all art materials available, as well as our classroom puppets, stuffed animals, and realia. The children worked diligently, and when my colleague arrived half an hour later to videotape, they were ready for the show to begin.

The Great Poetry Program, as it came to be called, was one of my favorites of all classroom events. My children outdid themselves working collaboratively to present poems. The first group enacted "I Asked My Mother for Fifty Cents to See the Elephant Jump the Fence." They used an elephant puppet and an accordion-pleated paper fence.

In the next act, "Five Green and Speckled Frogs," children sang a counting-down song as they took the parts of frogs and jumped off paper logs. They were followed by "A Thousand Hairy Savages Sitting Down to Lunch," enacted with the use of plastic and rubber food and utensils. Each act was even better than the one that had come before. My personal favorite was this traditional poem:

As I was standing in the street, as quiet as could be,
A great big ugly man came up and tied his horse to me.

As children recited this poem, one little girl stood alone in the "street." Along came Jeremy with a jump rope. Attached to the end of it was a classmate, acting the part of the horse. Jeremy, the "great big ugly man," tied the "horse" to Darling, patted the animal on the head, gave it an apple (from someone's lunch), and fell over the rope. This brought down both Jeremy and the house.

Although this video is very rough and amateur, it is such a treasure to me. Without it I would have felt that in my memory I had exaggerated the quality, fervor, and passion of these little performances. Each and every act, and there were about twelve of them, was performed by children who knew the poem well and presented it with passion, knowledge, and great creative sense of play.

English Learners Begin with Many Gifts

Part of the success of The Great Poetry Program lay in the fact that children come to school with a lot of already well-established skills and characteristics, including great creativity in using language, perceptions about language, terrific imaginations, and pleasure in finding fun in all the things they do. They can read facial expressions and gestures very well. They can make good guesses about language. They know a lot of vocabulary and a lot about language structure through knowledge of the languages they speak at home. They love to play. And of course, they love to talk!

Using Shared Reading and Picture Books to Help Children Acquire Language and Learn to Read

You should see me in my future, 'cause I'm learning to read and I'm learning SO much!

—Ricky, age 6

The more passionate I am about children's literature and sharing it with my students, the more success I have in creating readers—children who love books, take them home each night, and talk about them as if they're old friends. This approach works for my English learners as well as the rest of my first-grade class. Of course, I include many other types of instruction in literature, writing, and phonics in my reading program, but the heart of it all is the time I spend reading aloud to the children.

Although the majority of my students speak a language other than English, they can experience the text through pictures as I read a picture book aloud. When I am reading a big book, as I do most days, children can see and say the words with me as I read and track the text with a pointer.

Sometimes I get an almost electric tingling up my spine as I am reading a book aloud. And when I sense this same sort of silent electric hum coming from the children as well, then I *know* the book is reaching all of us! This happened recently when I read the kids David Shannon's picture book *A Bad Case of Stripes* (2004). Children had so much to say as they worked to uncover meaning in this imaginative tale. Even my reluctant English speakers were excited enough about the story to make comments.

English learners gained some understanding of the text from the illustrations in the picture book. Comments from their buddies and other classmates also helped them puzzle out what was going on.

Shannon's book is the story of Camilla, who wakes up covered with stripes. The stripes turn into other patterns throughout the story. Ultimately we find out what causes these odd happenings and how Camilla solves her problem. Crucial to the plot is the fact that she is craving lima beans but doesn't think she should eat them because her friends don't like them. Here are some brief samplings of the children's thoughts about what was causing Camilla's spots, stripes, and other difficulties:

"I know! It's bacteria!"
"Ohhh! Camilla didn't wash her hands."
"She should wash her hands all the time."
"If somebody says something, she changes into it."
"Or she changes into the color of it."
"If somebody said, 'Make Camilla turn normal,' she'd turn
    normal. But nobody said it."
"The lima beans are magic."
"Maybe she ate too many lima beans when she was little."

There was much discussion over whether doctors should give Camilla worms, jelly beans, magic beans, medicine, or lima beans to turn her back into herself. There was a lot of use of the word *normal*.

"Maybe there's regular, normal lima beans and magic lima beans.
    Is that what you're thinking about, buddy?" (One child said
    this to another, to help his friend sort out his thoughts.)
"This story is like *Imogene's Antlers*!"
"It's like *I Wish That I Had Duck Feet*."
"Camilla wanted lima beans *soooo* bad!"
"She's not eating what her body wanted."
"If she ate lima beans and changed back into normal she should
    eat lima beans every day. I solved the case!"
"You know how you say, 'I got a frog in my throat'?" (This child
    grabbed his throat so I'd get it.) "She mighta said, 'I got a
    chameleon!' Get it? You know, Camilla, Chameleon?"

101

*Using Shared
Reading and Picture
Books to Help
Children Acquire
Language and Learn
to Read*

"And now she has a bow with a rainbow color."

"And now she eats lima beans always."

I was astonished at the children's spontaneous comments and discussion as they made meaning together and built on each other's thoughts and ideas. They were *thinking* as they talked and listened to the story. These children were doing just the kind of thinking done by smart readers of any age: mulling over visual connections, making inferences and predictions, determining what was important in the unfolding story, and evaluating the events and the story solution.

This momentous discussion was spontaneous: I was trying to read the story, but the children were trying to figure it out. I finally came to my senses and moved out of their way. I continued reading the story, pausing for kids' comments before and after reading each page. English learners who wanted to speak echoed or built on comments made by classmates. In this way their language was scaffolded by the other students.

As different children spoke, I jotted down their thoughts. Even as I read my own words now, I am reminded that sometimes my first graders know what they need even sooner than I do.

This was an amazing event for me to observe. All my students were dying to talk about this book, get their hands on it, pore over the illustrations, and read it. Looking back, I see that this would have been the perfect book (if I had had multiple copies available), and the perfect moment, for literature circle study groups. Children would have loved to meet in small groups to discuss this story, find relevant passages, and argue and prove their points. But probably nothing would have been as powerful as *this* student-organized, unprompted, and spur-of-the-moment whole-class discussion!

Starting Our Day: Picking Overnight Books

Let's go back to the beginning of the morning and I'll tell you how we use our reading time. After coats and lunches have been put away and I have taken attendance, I look to see who has returned overnight books. These are the choice treasures selected by the children to take home to read and have read to them. Students put books and homework at their seating places, and I can easily see if a book or paper is missing. I make little marks on a grid to remind myself who is missing an item. B means missing book; H means no homework. I remind children who have not returned a book and usually they bring it back the next day. This checking and time for reminders, if any are needed, takes just a few seconds (see Dragan 2001).

And now the fun begins: Children return books to special bookcases in the front of the room, team by team, and choose another book to take home for overnight. There is a lot of competition to get popular books, and students are quick about making selections. Each table team has an assigned day of the week to choose first. There is great joy in getting to take a special book home. Esmeralda hugged her reading choice one morning, on the eleventh day of school, and said, "I've been waiting *forever* for this book!" This year, Salim, my limited-English-speaking Indonesian student, had been waiting several days to choose a large picture book about trucks. When he finally got his hands on the book, he enfolded himself around it and hopped around the room, yelling gleefully, "My turn! My turn!"

I have already read these books aloud, so children are familiar with them. This particularly helps English learners. They have heard me read the story, have seen the pictures, and have spent time with a partner who speaks their language, looking at the book and retelling the story. There are paired copies of some books, one in English and one in another language. Children may take one or both home. I try to make sure that there are some books written in all of the home languages represented in our class. I keep just a few more books available for overnight than there are students. This makes it easier for children to focus on the reading material they *really* want to spend time with. Each child prints the title and reads it to me, getting help from classmates if needed. I write the title on my weekly grid. Now they are all free to read!

Free-Choice Reading Time—Hooray!

Independent reading time is one of the most crucial and valuable parts of our day, but it doesn't have to take long. Sometimes the period is as short as seven to ten minutes while other times it lasts twenty or thirty minutes. And rainy-day recesses can be wonderful additional reading periods. This special time for books helps turn children into avid, lifelong readers.

Any book or magazine in the classroom is available to students, and they may read wherever and with whomever they wish. Many children want to read in our book nook, a cozy classroom area with more than one hundred books placed with covers out on rain gutters on the wall. (See Figures 7–1 and 7–2.) Stuffed animals lurk there, waiting for children to read to them. The nook has a race-car rug to sit on, some special pillows (one in the form of a giant frog), as well as additional tubs and tubs of books. Only four or five children fit comfortably in this special space, so we take turns by table teams. One table gets to go to the book nook each morning. Other children read on the classroom carpet in the library area, and some hole up to read under tables, at

Figure 7–1
Children love to read in the book nook.

Figure 7–2
The book nook is a great place to read, write, and think.

desks, or in little clusters in other places in the classroom. A few children choose this time to read alone while others read in pairs, little groups, or to classroom stuffed animals.

There's nothing like sharing a good book with friends. "Look," says Brenda, with great excitement. "A mouse lemur!" She is reading an issue of *Ranger Rick* magazine with Irvin and Edgard. All three children are thrilled to learn about the mouse lemur. I'm pretty thrilled too. I didn't know there was any such kind of lemur. I mention this to the children so they will see my enthusiasm and will realize that I am a learner too. I'm also delighted that Brenda is able to figure out the information that's written about this animal. Edgard, who is fluent in both English and Spanish, explains all about lemurs to Irvin, who is just beginning to learn English. The magazine article has wonderful photographs, and these visuals help all three children access the text.

Several children are sitting on the floor, surrounded by open books and reading about reptiles together. Maria and Obdulia are choral-reading *Sheep in a Jeep* by Nancy Shaw. Other children are comparing English and Arabic editions of *Come On, Daisy* by Jane Simmons (2000). And Jesús, Ariel, and Cesar are folding paper airplanes and hovering over a large book full of different kinds of planes to make (and fly after school or occasionally during a brief afternoon break). Believe me, I thought long and hard about making this paper airplane book

105
*Using Shared
Reading and Picture
Books to Help
Children Acquire
Language and Learn
to Read*

(and copy paper) available to children during free-choice independent reading time. Finally, I decided that learning to read directions was a pretty terrific skill. If I were a better instruction reader myself, I would have a lot more luck programming my VCR, and I know plenty of other adults who aren't so great at reading and following directions either. So this book choice remains a standby until squabbling breaks out for a couple of days. Then we give the book a rest.

Although children are free to choose books in several different languages, often students just pick books they like, regardless of language. I love to watch children make reading and browsing choices based on their own intense interests in specific topics and books.

Throughout the year Andrea has chosen several picture books and nonfiction books about animals. One spring day I comment to her that she is so lucky to know some things she is interested in already, such as wild animals. Andrea sidles up to me at recess and confides that she really wants to be a zookeeper when she grows up. She has many questions about this job, so I help her write an email to the education department at the San Francisco Zoo.

One of Andrea's main questions is whether she needs to be a veterinarian to work at the zoo. She also wants to know how to tell when animals are sick and whether part of her job would be to "wake up the baby animals in the morning." We are all thrilled when Andrea gets a helpful email back from Cindy Cameron of the education office at the zoo. The message has reassuring information for Andrea, and she continues picking books on this topic.

The next week in the school library, Andrea asks me to help her choose a book about working at the zoo. Such nonfiction titles are shelved too high for first graders to reach. I hand down to Andrea a book with many large photos of wild animals. She peruses it and literally sticks her head into it. I hear her saying something to the book over and over. I lean in and whisper in her ear, asking what she is saying. "Too scary! Too scary!" she replies. I hand her a different book and a little while later, she tells me, "You are so incredible to find me just the book I need to be a zookeeper!"

During free-choice reading time in my classroom, many of the students excitedly peruse large reference books they can't really read, but they learn a lot from the captions, photographs, and pictures. The children's intense interest in specific topics carries them past the difficulties of the text. They just take in whatever information they can and use the "group brain" to figure things out. At the beginning of the year, when we are just beginning to develop special relationships with books and reading, I do a lot of pretending and acting "as if." I just act as if the children are real readers, passionate about books and learning. And pretty soon I find that this really is the case.

Most of my students are English learners and may not have access to books or other reading materials at home. They *desperately* need this time to connect with books (and to watch me model my own excitement as I read too). When children experience the passion of stories, non-fiction, and the written word, it makes sense to them to learn to read. This glorious time of freedom to read and talk about books settles children into our day. It makes it easier to get their cooperation with other tasks when they have begun by spending this special time with books and with friends.

Enhancing the Basal Series

Next, we put independent books away and join up at the class meeting area for the flag salute, some music, and, of course, a read-aloud or big book. I am obligated to teach a basal reading series, and I do so during this time period. We sit together on the rug for this part of our day. The basal includes organized lessons encompassing phonemic awareness, phonics, a story to read, comprehension activities, and practice in other literacy skills that relate to the text we read. Because phonics makes so much more sense to children in the context of the story, we do a scavenger hunt in our basal readers for the words that go with the phonics part of the lesson. This helps reinforce these skills. While I believe in more authentic activities with literature, the basal teachers manual and student books give structure to this part of our reading period. I adapt this basal series to the needs of my group of children, and I make sure that I have time for shared reading, guided reading, and other important elements I feel must be part of my reading program.

Previewing Text

I make a point of gathering my English learners together to preteach parts of a lesson: introduce vocabulary, show photos, look at realia, and talk about children's related experiences. Then, later in the day or the following day, when I teach this lesson, these children have a head start on vocabulary, as well as comprehension. They have an overview of what we are doing. This strategy develops confidence and self-esteem as well as understanding of text. Children get a few more pieces of the reading puzzle.

Shared Reading

At the beginning of the year when the basal stories are too difficult, I frequently modify them by enlarging story pages on the copy machine and we read the story together as a homemade big book. This activity helps children transition to using the actual basal reading books. And it provides a way for our English learners to participate with us, even by just looking at the pictures to get the gist of the story. Sometimes I make transparencies of stories and we read them together from the overhead projector. These transparencies are a great resource for children to use during centers, especially since they love to use the overhead projector.

This week the basal teachers manual has a story for children to listen to and visualize as the teacher reads the text. There are no pictures. Because the majority of my students are second language learners, it is imperative that I omit or modify this lesson. No one will get anything out of an auditory activity without any props, realia, illustrations, or clues about the text. I decide to turn the story into a drawing tale and I draw pictures of characters and events as I read. These are not great drawings, but they give some meaning to the text, and my class is fascinated, watching pictures appear on the whiteboard.

At the end of the story the children form a circle, sit down, and we choose characters to enact the tale, creative dramatics-style. I feed characters the lines, but they can say them however they wish and are free to make up their own dialogue. Children act out the story, without props—we just imagine them. Simple headbands with character names or small drawings attached could also be used, but this very simple enactment seems to work well. The class is enthusiastic about the drama, and our follow-up discussion indicates that children have understood the story.

Sometimes the simplest activities can make a big difference in helping children get it. At the end of this lesson, Betsy, a child with an emerging command of English, comes up to me with her arms folded, hands across her heart. She is all eyes. "That was a lovely story," she says.

Children Need to Have It All

I believe that children have got to have it *all*—many different types of reading instruction: phonics, shared and guided reading and writing, literature books, big books and basal readers, fiction and nonfiction, large- and small-group instruction. Who knows what specific types of lessons will help all the pieces fall into place for a child? I believe that children learn lots of phonics and vocabulary through many activities woven throughout our day. As I described in my book *Literacy from Day One* (2001), we play word games with our overnight book titles. We do many phonics and language activities in the context of our reading lessons with both basal readers and leveled books, as well as when we read and recite poetry and songs. Reading and writing their own stories also reinforces phonics skills for children and many other skills as well.

Small-Group Instruction: Guided Reading

By recess time, we have enjoyed our independent reading activities and participated in our basal reading program. After recess, children go to small guided reading groups with me. Guided reading is when I teach a small number of children, usually four to six, to read books at their *instructional* reading level. These reading levels are determined by taking a running record for each child. For more information about taking running records and teaching guided reading groups, see *Guided Reading: Good First Teaching for All Children* by Irene C. Fountas and Gay Su Pinnell (1996), Regie Routman's *Reading Essentials: The Specifics You Need to Teach Reading Well* (2002), and *On Solid Ground: Strategies for Teaching Reading K–3* by Sharon Taberski (2000).

The guided reading lesson begins with a quick introduction of the book and a brief chat about our own prior experiences related to the book's topic. Any unfamiliar vocabulary is mentioned orally. Sometimes we take a picture walk through part of the text and look for specific words. We review pertinent strategies we could use if we are stuck on words: look at the pictures, think about what would make sense look at the letters in the word and try blending, and so on. I like to mention to the kids that figuring out words is a little like trying on clothes. If something doesn't work or fit, we try something else. This helps cut frustration and the feeling of being right or wrong.

After the introduction, I pass the books out and the children begin reading aloud, quietly, at their own pace. If they wish, they can use phonics phones (see page 190) to hear themselves without disturbing others. As children read, they make every effort to use strategies to figure out the text. I listen to each child read and make small anecdotal notes about reading achievements and stumbling blocks.

We wrap up the lesson by focusing on what strategies the students used successfully and by talking about the meaning of the story. It is important that comprehension is addressed early in first grade. Children need to get *meaning* from text. They need to practice *thinking* while they read and after the reading experience as well. We also spend some time on word work—practicing reading and spelling specific words and sounds from the story on a whiteboard or with plastic letters.

109

*Using Shared
Reading and Picture
Books to Help
Children Acquire
Language and Learn
to Read*

Practicing What Counts

Guided reading is not round-robin reading, where children take turns reading parts of a story. It is not whole-group instruction with a lengthy skills-based introduction and twenty to thirty children reading the same story. In guided reading groups, children are spending their time engaged in the learning activity that will help them the most in their efforts to become literate: *reading*.

When beginning English learners read in small groups with me, it is more of a shared reading lesson than guided reading. Depending on the group, I may key the kids in to the story theme using Spanish. We discuss our own experiences. We take a picture walk and talk about the story. Then we practice reading the story in unison, choral-reading-style. All the children are successful. There is no pressure. They just chime in whenever they can.

And what, pray tell, is the *rest* of the class doing during this time? In the past, I always provided centers during the guided reading period, when I meet with about two or three groups a day for about ten to fifteen minutes each. I finally realized that even though I spent hours getting centers ready, sometimes I saw minimal learning going on. I still provide center time for children, but we do it later in the day. Now during guided reading, children who are not reading with me meet in their leveled groups to hone their reading skills. During this practice time on their own, children break into little groups of four to six students around tubs of leveled books. These materials, many with multiple copies, are books that children have previously read in guided reading, and now they reread and enjoy them socially as well as intellectually.

We make some little retelling booklets in our guided reading groups. Children tell the story, and I print it out for them on the computer so that they can practice reading and illustrating it. This is another activity that can be done independently while I am busy with other children. These practice books become artifacts or mementos of our reading sessions.

As I teach one guided reading group, I sneak little peeks at the rest of the class; I enjoy watching the interactions as students help and energize each other and build fluency and comprehension as they read and reread, talk about the stories, illustrate, and take charge of their own learning. At another time in our day children will read silently, by themselves.

Helping English Learners Practice Reading

While I am busy with guided reading groups, one little independent group reads together at the listening center. They have organized stacks of four or five leveled books in front of them, coordinated with a cassette they helped make. They create these tapes with me, with all of us reading in unison, after we read the books in the guided reading group. These children speak little English yet, but they are able to read book after book, following along as they listen to the taped stories. The stories are comprehensible because of simple pictures and our prior activities and discussions.

Students are successful at all the reading activities because they have already had small-group lessons with these materials. The books selected for this independent practice are at their specific learning level, and children are relaxed and in charge. As they connect with text and life and even each other, there is an atmosphere of play. I think that is what the children are doing: playing. They are using spontaneous expression and gaining fluency as they work to say the words, read with understanding, and make the books come to life. And they are having a great time doing it.

This interlude is great practice and a validation for the children that they *can* read and understand text, whether a teacher or parent is with them or not.

Many Supports for Reading

There are many background scaffolds or supports for these reading practice sessions. Children have experienced written text in many ways: through a variety of opportunities to listen to real literature read aloud, big book shared readings, and reading trade books and basal texts together, often from an overhead projector. They have all been part of guided reading lessons in small groups with leveled texts. They read and create poetry charts, act out books they love, and have many writing experiences through minilessons, classroom interviews, and writing their own poems, memoirs, and stories. There is an emphasis on oral language and on connecting language with visuals to help language learners understand what is being said.

More than anything else, my students are gaining a language to depend on. They listen to stories they love read aloud over and over again. Many of the books are participation books, with repeating phrases and sentences. Children begin to speak the language of these stories, play with the words, and try them out in their own lives. Reading aloud to children gives them vocabulary, concepts, and language structures they need and helps them *own* all of it.

Hearing and reading glorious works of children's literature fills the children up with heaping helpings of language and story. As the great children's author Bill Martin Jr. once said, "Students will only learn to read when they have language inside of themselves" (2004). And the kids also seem to understand the importance of the work we are doing with literature and with each other. One of my children, Sabine, told me, "Reading is for getting smart." And another child, Monica, said to me this year, "It's like it's magic when you can read."

Enriching Language Learning Through Language Arts and Visual Arts Connections

Drawing is not just for children who can't yet write fluently, and creating pictures is not just part of rehearsal for writing. Images at any age are part of the serious business of making meaning—partners with words for communicating inner designs.

—Ruth Hubbard, *Authors of Pictures, Draughtsmen of Words*

When children find out it's time for art, they are excited and raring to go. They need this opportunity for self-expression, experimentation, and play and for connecting their art experiences both to their lives and to other curriculum areas. When children are given good instruction, art materials, and time, they create intense personal responses to their world. They internalize lessons that cannot be learned through other experiences. And they have a great chance to joyfully express the things that matter to them. The benefits of art are even more important for English learners, who may be limited in their outlets for communication and self-expression.

The arts are another language for English learners to use while they are acquiring English. Salim, my Indonesian student, was brand-new to English when school started. He had a very limited vocabulary and great difficulty talking with me as well as with his classmates. But after just a few weeks of school, he has involved conversations with his partner and other children that evolve from his very intricate drawings and rich fantasy life. Salim's art is helping him connect with our class. Through his drawings, Salim says to us, "This is who I am, what I care about, what I value." We know a lot about Salim because he has shared his drawings and his keen interests with us.

Art Connections

I believe in teaching through art across curriculum areas, as well as giving lessons on artists and art history and how to use art materials and media. I want to weave related language and vocabulary into the context of the lessons as well. This is important for all students, not just English learners. But I never want to stifle my students' own endeavors to express themselves in ways that make them feel most truly alive.

As Robert Regis Dvorak says in his book *Drawing Without Fear* (1985, p. 5), "When you draw, you make something that has never been made before. It cannot be made by anyone else on this earth or in this universe. It can only be made by you." I believe that this empowering thought also describes the things we say and write. If children create, speak, and write honestly and try to express their own deepest truths, these are also one-of-a-kind personal expressions, even if they are not yet polished or well crafted.

I want my students to experience the incredible individuality and uniqueness we all bring to the arts and have the chance to be part of it. The arts will give each of them a voice.

The visual arts are a natural way to facilitate language learning. Children become involved in personal creative experiences and are eager to express themselves and share their work with others. They acquire vocabulary and language naturally as they work two-dimensionally, three-dimensionally, and then orally, sharing their creative work and perceptions.

In the Beginning

In planning my art curriculum, I frequently refer to the State of California *Standards for the Visual and Performing Arts* (2005). I also use the sequential art media program created by my art mentor, Dick Sperisen. Dick is Art Coordinator Emeritus at the San Mateo County Office of Education in Redwood City, California. Working with a committee of teachers, he put together a sequence of art techniques that teaches children a repertoire of ways to proceed in art. Once they know how to manipulate materials and know some simple basics, children can use this knowledge to create art in many media, across all curriculum areas. As Dick explains, "There is no need to make elaborate plans for art lessons. Use the art media sequence of activities, and let art grow right out of the curriculum. Give youngsters many opportunities to use art to *respond* to what they are learning in other subject areas."

The more simple we keep things, the more time we have to make art an integrated part of our core curriculum. For more information on Sperisen's media-based art education program, see *Everything You Need to Know to Teach First Grade* (Dragan 2003).

Art Prints Bring a Museum into the Classroom

It is early in the school year, and my first graders have been excitedly looking at some art study prints and talking about things they've noticed. They are enjoying the time to give their own impressions and opinions. There seems to be some competition about who can notice and talk about the most details. Even reluctant speakers find things to say.

The large photos show a variety of different media: art throughout time and across many cultures. I mention to the children that what is so special about these examples is that *people* create art and have done so for thousands of years. Ricky is particularly inspired by this thought. He stands up, flings an arm up in the air, and says in a voice full of emotion: "I was *born* to do art!"

The children and I are caught up in this moment, and for just a heartbeat time seems to stop. Then other voices join in: "I was born to learn!" "I was born to make stuff!" "I was born to read!" "I was born to color!" "I was born to play soccer!" "I was born to go to school!" "I was born to be taught by the teacher!" The children are fired up and eloquent. I type a sentence frame using some of Ricky's words, "I was born to _____," and make copies. Children now have the opportunity to personalize this sentence by drawing their ideas and by spelling words their way. If they prefer, they can dictate their words for me to write, or they can write down their own thoughts. We subsequently make these into four-fold booklets that the children illustrate and read over and over again. (See Appendix, page 213, for a booklet template.)

Modeling and the Chance to Be Part of It All

115

*Enriching Language
Learning Through
Language Arts and
Visual Arts
Connections*

The "I was born" sentence frame is not an assignment or required work. Students may be working on other art and writing during this time. But I find that when a class member comes up with a great idea, most of my children want to be part of it. I model this by doing my own illustrations and writing so that I can be involved too. Of course, I don't share my endeavors until the end of our work period when we meet to look at our masterpieces. I want to support children's efforts, but I don't want to interfere with their *own* thoughts and creations.

This small piece of integrated art and writing is especially meaningful to us all since it grew out of Ricky's emotional response to art and our own spontaneous class discussion.

Art Levels the Playing Field

Children are curious, earnest, and intense. They want to know about life and to become competent in their abilities to understand things and do things. And they *love* to create. Time for artistic expression is crucial for any group of students, but it is even more important for English learners. Art levels the playing field for these children. It's another language for learning, and it gives us all a way to communicate nonverbally.

Art production stimulates children to use words as well as images because they become so excited about what they have created that they can't wait to share with others. They enjoy chatting while they are working. And they often forget their reticence to speak and become caught up in the excitement of the moment. Some of the best classroom discussions occur at the end of art lessons when we meet to share and talk about our work.

Time to do art also gives English learners a respite from the difficult work of focusing on acquiring their new language. It gives them a break and a time to recharge. In this way *all children* can be an active part of our class community. This can't help but increase students' confidence and self-esteem.

Art Is Another Way of Seeing and Knowing

On a different day children look at an art print and talk about line and color and how these are used to create city and neighborhood scenes. They notice the most miniscule things, some of which I never would have seen. Students enjoy related picture books. Three I especially like to use with this activity are *Madlenka* by Peter Sís (2000), *My New York: New Anniversary Edition* by Kathy Jakobsen (2003), and *The City by the Bay: A Magical Journey Around San Francisco* by Tricia Brown and the Junior League of San Francisco (1981). After hearing and viewing a picture book, children go to their tables to create their own marking-pen and oil-pastel neighborhood drawings.

My students get involved in their art at different degrees of intensity, but no one else works at the feverish pace of Beatríz. Perhaps this is because she speaks almost no English, and her level of speech development in Spanish makes it difficult to understand her. But Beatríz is gifted in communicating in other ways. Through pens, oil pastels, crayons, paint, and torn paper, she works fervently to make herself understood, to make her mark. We all marvel at what she creates. Art is another language for Beatríz and she speaks to us eloquently through this medium.

The visual arts are a simple, straightforward way to facilitate language learning as well as thinking. I like to use one or two art prints or transparencies at the beginning of each art lesson. They help children zero in on what I'm teaching: different art styles, elements of art, or thematic ideas for their own creations. This activity helps them see and get revved up to create. It teaches vocabulary in a context that makes sense.

Art prints and transparencies fit right in with children's natural love of talking about themselves. As students look at these images, they talk about things they notice and relate things to their own lives. Making connections like this is very powerful: it helps us all make sense of personal experiences as well as facilitates learning in many curriculum areas. Big books, as well as picture books, are other wonderful tools for sharing visual arts and language. Some adult books with large art illustrations are also good resources. These visuals give us information about what we're doing and help us all to begin on the same page, no matter what oral language we speak.

Van Gogh Visits . . . or Does He?

A few years ago, when I was teaching a unit on Impressionist art to my first graders, Tom Gaffney (then South San Francisco superintendent of schools) came to visit. He was taken with the children's paintings and surprised by the depth of their learning about Monet, Gaugin, and some other artists. Tom loaned us his own book about French Impressionists and came back a few weeks later to revisit our art gallery. The children had a lot to say about their favorite paintings and painters. And since they had many of their own paintings on display, they had a lot to say about these as well. One child was overcome with excitement about getting to talk with Tom personally when she returned his art book for the class. "You are the most *wonderful* painter!" she said. After Tom left I found out that Roxane had mistaken him for Van Gogh.

I just couldn't make myself disillusion her. A first grader doesn't have a clear grasp of time and place anyway, and some things just won't be clear because of the developmental stages of the children. It didn't matter that Roxane had not really met Van Gogh: she had gotten to know his art! And the whole painting and art gallery experience and the classroom visit of someone obviously important could not have been more powerful for her.

Imitating a Famous Artist

Around the time my children were getting to know Van Gogh, Gaugin, Manet, and other artists, we spent some time learning about Matisse. I focused on teaching about his paper cuts. Children particularly loved the art transparencies of his *Circus* cut-paper collage series as viewed in the book *Jazz* (Matisse 1947).

After looking at art prints, viewing transparencies of Matisse's cut outs, and then talking about and practicing cutting flowing shapes, students created their own individual paper cuts in the style of Matisse. They also made some incredible class murals. I placed three different-colored six-by-eight-foot pieces of fadeless paper on the carpet and made scissors and all colors of construction paper available. I also set out our wonderful scrap box full of paper remnants from other lessons. This is always a great place to find small bits of paper as well as unusual cut shapes that haven't been used.

My children decided on their own themes: playground games and kites. Children cut incredible paper shapes, turning the construction paper as they cut, and took turns placing the large cutout shapes on the colored background sheets. In table teams and during a whole group meeting, we played with the paper placements and moved things around. Sometimes we even switched cutouts from one background

117
*Enriching Language
Learning Through
Language Arts and
Visual Arts
Connections*

piece to another. Language flourished, and children learned about shape, color, design, and composition as they internalized the work of one of history's greatest artists.

Later, a few children took turns gluing things in place by carefully lifting (and *not* moving) the corner of a shape, putting small drops of glue underneath, and pressing the shape down. They slightly lifted and glued other areas of the shape as well. In this way our original creations were not disturbed while they were being made permanent.

An Art Exhibit Led by Docents

The murals were so stunning that there was a universal need to share them. I talked with my group about museum docents and how they studied the work of artists and led people through museum displays, sharing their knowledge. The children thought docent jobs sounded like a great idea, and we decided as a group to invite other classes, as well as parents, to visit. We picked out a few Matisse prints to put on display with our work. Some children chose to meet in groups to practice talking about our murals while others researched information about Matisse. A small group of students chose to work on social language. They practiced greeting visitors and thanking them for coming. Everyone had a part in our exhibit, and it was a great success with children and adults, and especially with our class. And all my students profited by practicing and using social and academic language in context.

Yes, Indeed, They Know About Matisse!

One of my most smug and satisfactory teaching moments came soon after our art show, when we took a field trip to a local art gallery and nearby science museum. In our trip between exhibition areas, we passed through a public building. By coincidence, there was a large framed Matisse print on display. Children gathered round, excited to see a work of art they knew . . . but then were dismayed by what they noticed. "It's upside down!" several of them cried out. The rest of the class gathered to look, and we all agreed. Passers-by and people who worked in the building smiled indulgently, and I heard one receptionist say to another, with a smirk and a laugh, "As if *they* would know!"

But the children *did* know. I was insulted for them. But they were insulted for Matisse, a beloved fellow artist.

Art from China

Even more exciting to my students than the work of such masters as Van Gogh and Matisse was the artwork of children from China. With the help of Dick Sperisen, I was able to borrow some pieces of original art from a large exhibit of Chinese children's art. William "Billy" Lee, a retired architect from Portola Valley, California, spearheaded this exhibit. Through the Children's Art on the Environment Project (CAEP), a collaborative effort sponsored by the 1990 Institute in the United States and the Center for Environmental Protection and Communication of the State of Environmental Protection Administration in China, Billy worked with the government of China to plan a countrywide study of the environment and the creation of follow-up artwork. As a result of Billy's idea and the backing of the Chinese government, children of China created more than a million pieces of art on the theme of the environment. Through Billy's efforts, a massive judging took place in Beijing. During the second phase of the project, a two-year traveling art exhibit began touring several cities in the United States.

Some wonderful art that was not selected for the touring art show was made available to local schools on loan through Billy Lee and the efforts of Dick Sperisen. I was twice able to use this art in my classroom over a monthlong period as part of our thematic unit on the environment.

These original art pieces by Chinese children intrigued my students far more than commercial prints of famous, priceless pieces of art ever could have. I focused on one or two drawings at a time to share and discuss with my class. I used the art label on the back of the artwork and our classroom map and globe to show my class the exact home of each child artist. My students had a lot to say about why the young artists created things the way they did. They made many comments about the environment and talked about the way each piece of art was executed. They were excited to be viewing the art and making comments, and vocabulary and speaking abilities took a great leap. This thematic unit became part of my ESL block. (See Figure 8–1.)

There is no better way to give students critical thinking experiences than through the arts. As children create, they are posing their own problems and challenges and must think and work through these to their own solutions: how to attach paper sculptures to a background, how to create clothing for a foil figure or scarecrow, how to design and

119

*Enriching Language
Learning Through
Language Arts and
Visual Arts
Connections*

Figure 8–1
Students talk about children's art from China.

balance a mobile, and so on. Through art we learn to be flexible, divergent thinkers and to puzzle out different ways to invent and create. There is never a correct answer. We extend our abilities to think laterally rather than remain satisfied with just one obvious solution, or just doing the same things over and over. We learn to take chances and grow from trying out our ideas.

My Letter of Thanks

I wrote a letter to Dick Sperisen that he shared with Billy Lee. I wanted Billy to know just how empowering it had been for me to use art from another culture, especially because it was created by other children. The result has been several meetings with Billy and an invitation to join his art advisory board.

Dear Dick,

Being able to show children the art from China has been a wonderful experience for the last four weeks! We have been fortunate to have the use of both portfolios of children's art.

I have used the artwork to teach geography and many other curriculum areas. My first graders all know where China is on the map and globe, know the best route to get there, and are in-

121
*Enriching Language
Learning Through
Language Arts and
Visual Arts
Connections*

terested to note all the products we use that are made in China. I have also used the art as part of my English–Second Language program for the past month. Talking about the artwork is providing a very rich experience.

Each day the children hope to see a new piece of art. They like to tell what they notice in the artwork, talk about their ideas regarding the art, and make up stories about it. Sometimes they work in little groups to craft stories to present to the whole class. Other days they ask to see two specific pieces of art together and talk about them both.

The children are absolutely fascinated with the artwork. They can tell the media used and have a pretty good grasp of what each artist's intent was in executing the art. The children also want to create works of art themselves that reflect *their* ideas about caring for the planet we live on.

Dick, I can't tell you what an enriching and rewarding experience this has been for me and for my first graders. Please give my personal thanks to Mr. Lee, and also many thanks to you for making these experiences possible.

I am including a sampling of some of the things I have heard my children say as they have looked at the artwork. All but four of the children are second language learners. I have transcribed the children's comments exactly as they were expressed, in the order comments were made. I haven't corrected or changed their language.

Sincerely,
Pat Barrett Dragan
First-Grade Teacher
Martin Elementary School

Children's Responses to the Art from China

Here are descriptions of two pieces of the artwork and a brief sampling of my children's reflections. It is important to note that these discussions took place at the end of the school year, after children had completed a full ten months of English instruction.

Description of the Art   The first marking-pen drawing, done by a first-grade child, shows three goats crying in a barren field. It is aptly called *Goats Crying in the Field*. The children in this group are emergent speakers of English. They are more advanced in their language than the children in the next reflections.

Children's Reflections

- "It's a really good picture, and it's very important to keep the land and sky clean."

- "I got a clue. I think the Chinese words say the ground needs water and the sky needs to be blue. The sun is crying too."

- "The goats are sad. It's hot, and their food is dying. It wouldn't taste good all dried up."

- "The goats are trying to find food and water and they can't find it. That's why they're crying."

- "The goats need another valley with green trees and food to live happy ever after."

Description of the Art   Another picture shows a design of a star with wood pieces inside it. There is a design pattern of red and gold around the star. There is a view of planet Earth seen from a distance. It is full of cracked soil and tree stumps. One stump has green leaves sprouting. These children are working hard, but enthusiastically, to express what they see in this picture.

Children's Reflections

- "I know what's going on there. There's chopsticks. People cut down all the trees. They can't grow anymore."

- "It's a wreck right there. Things won't grow. Only one tree has a little things growing. All the trees are cutting down."

- "Maybe they could make little holes and plant seeds and grow more trees."

- "They cut the trees to make wood for houses and thousands of chopsticks."

- "They can't make even a tree house now, 'cause there's no more wood."

- "That valley doesn't work good anymore."

- "If they cutted down more trees they won't have oxygen. 'Cause trees make oxygen."

- "There's cracks in the ground 'cause they cut the trees and there's no water."

In both reflections children didn't let their difficulties with vocabulary or sentence structure deter them from expressing themselves. They had a lot to say and they just went ahead and said it.

A Sampling of Art Lessons

There are many different types of art lessons with different goals and objectives. Some lessons are for the sole purpose of teaching how to use specific materials or media. Others focus on ideas beyond the art and connect with other subject areas. Children need a variety of these learning experiences. The following is a list of some types of lessons that demonstrate different reasons for teaching art.

- How-to lessons on use of specific materials, such as glue and scissors

- How-to lessons to teach specific skills: how to tear paper, make rubbings, do crayon resist, and so on

- Lessons focused on learning to use specific media, such as block printing, watercolor paints, and plaster of Paris

- Lessons that connect with cultural themes: *papel picado* (cut-paper Mexican banners), Mexican bark paintings, Italian *impasto* paintings, Russian fairy tale boxes, Kwanzaa weavings, Chinese New Year dragons, Black History Month portraits, and so on

- Lessons connected to holidays and seasons: leaf prints, scarecrows, pumpkins, elves and Santa, snowmen, spring flowers, Mother's Day gifts, Fourth of July projects, and so on

- Lessons linking to other curriculum, such as music, dance, drama, math, social studies, science, language arts, children's literature, and physical education

- History lessons about specific artists, art periods, or art movements

Art and Story

The arts are evocative and strike many chords within us. Art tells us stories and helps us produce, record, and tell our own tales. It can make our experiences bigger than life. The arts can take us across cultures, across the world, and even through time, to see in new ways what other people have created, what they believe, and how they live and have lived.

One of my favorite poems, "In the Museum," by Charlotte Zolotow, evokes what it means to create art.

In the Museum

The horse from 200 B.C.
is made of stone,
but the way he holds his head
shows
someone long ago
loved a horse like him,
though now,
both horse
and sculptor
    are dead.

—Charlotte Zolotow

I love sharing this poem with students and coaxing out their thoughts about art and what it means to them. On one occasion I paired the poem with the wonderful Mongolian folktale *Sujo and the White Horse*, retold by Yuzo Otsuka (1981). This picture book tells the story of the tragic parting of a boy and his horse and how this event led to the creation of the horse-head fiddle used by Mongolian shepherds.

Children loved the picture book, and they worked in teams to create a mural together. One group painted the Mongolian steppes on long fadeless background paper. Other groups used crayons, marking pens, and scissors to create and cut out yurts, horses, soldiers, the Emperor, and Sujo—the child protagonist. When the painted background paper was dry, children worked together to place their detailed cutout artwork on the background and reconstruct the story. They were intense about their project and there was much discussion and decision making involved. Children retold the story and then created their own small four-fold booklets. We put the mural up on a whiteboard (quickly attaching it to the board with magnets) and sat together, admiring the art and recapping the experience.

As with our other art experiences, the children had worked on this mural with their whole hearts. They pooled all their skills and pieces of knowledge and gained in awareness of art techniques, elements of art, and knowledge of folktale and culture. They achieved great self-expression and realized an idea of what it means to be a unique and extraordinary human being. This mural was never just an art project to my students—it was a magnificent experience in bringing a timeless story to life through the arts. And my first graders knew just how to do it!

CHAPTER 9

Thematic Teaching

Making Connections

*When we try to pick out anything all by itself, we find it hitched to
everything else in the universe.*

—John Muir, *My First Summer in the Sierra*

My first graders sat on the rug on a rainy January day, excitedly eyeing
three packages from Australia. I had purchased some children's books
during a children's literature trip to Australia the previous summer.
January was the perfect time to rip off these wrappings because we were
going to begin a thematic unit on the rain forest. With our world map,
the secret parcels, some personal photos and stories, and a good plan,
I was all set to begin.

I loved telling the kids about my adventures in the Michael Noonan
Rainforest in Maleny, Queensland, with Australian book publisher Jill
Morris and several other friends. The beautiful, sunny Australia day had
turned cool and dappled within the thick grove of the tropical rain forest, and high above us the canopy was dense with broad leaves. As we
hiked through this ancient area on Jill's property, Book Farm, we slipped
and slid on wet roots, and we were sometimes caught, even trapped, by
the sticky wraparound branches of the wait-a-while plant. These tricky
plants were best avoided. They were difficult and time-consuming to
escape from without damaging clothes (and skin!). Jill pointed out sev-

eral species of small animals, birds, and foliage, and a couple of us stopped to sketch and make notes.

While pushing my way through gigantic vines and trees, I suddenly thought of Jeannie Baker's picture book *Where the Forest Meets the Sea* (1988). I visualized Baker's collage illustrations, made from a vast array of natural materials. Like her story protagonist, I could almost *see* the faint outlines of an aboriginal child leaning up against an enormous twisted tree trunk. In my mind's eye I saw the primeval forest, barely perceptible dinosaurs, and other now-extinct creatures. Just being there in the rain forest in Maleny, I felt as if I had fallen smack-dab into the pages of Jeannie Baker's book. And knowing this piece of literature heightened and deepened the experience for me.

I believe that my friends, also children's literature enthusiasts, felt the same way. Some of us climbed up into a huge three-hundred-year-old hollow strangler fig tree, and when we emerged again at the bottom, feeling as if we had been far, far away, we saw a poisonous trap-door spider, a green tree frog, and two kinds of snakes. Several of us also managed to career down a steep narrow path slick with mud, narrowly avoiding a drop into the Obi Obi Creek.

Now back in the classroom once more, I shared some personal photographs, talked about my brief adventures, and read Jeannie Baker's book, transporting my kids, along with me, into the world of story.

I chose this rain forest theme in part because it is used in the basal reading program adopted by my district. I was also excited to share with my first graders my own learning and experiences in this Australian habitat. (The basal is a required *component* of my reading program. See Chapter 7 for a more complete account of the ways I teach reading.)

K-W-L Chart

After experiencing a picture book, a nonfiction book, some photos of the area, and a look at the world map, my children had an idea about some of the birds, animals, and plants that live in the tropical rain forest. They did a lot of talking with each other as we worked together on a K-W-L chart (the initials stand for *know, want to know,* and *learned*). I scribed for the kids as they listed things they knew about the rain forest and things they wanted to learn.

Figure 9–1

*K-W-L chart about
the rain forest.*

Later on, at the end of our thematic unit, we filled in the last column by adding things they *had* learned. These discussions scaffolded language for children and gave them a way to express themselves and listen to each other. The completed chart helped them see both the direction of their inquiry and all they had accomplished. And it was a wonderful assessment tool for me. (See Figure 9–1.)

Children may also benefit from the chance to create their own individual K-W-L charts and illustrate them with drawings of things they have learned. (See Appendix, page 214, for a K-W-L chart template.)

Investigators in the Classroom

My students were eager to figure out information from photographs of Australia and to locate these areas on the classroom map. And they were wild to open the packages of picture books and see what *they* could find out about this unusual area of the world "down under." Most of the books had a large number of illustrations, so after our warm-up activities, children knew some things to look for and had success in finding some comprehensible information no matter what their reading and language levels.

Most of the time when I begin a thematic study I don't have access to so many new books. But a trip to the public library and the school library is always a good way for me to supplement my own book collection. Photos are another helpful instructional aide. *National Geographic* magazines and old calendars are excellent sources. At the beginning of a thematic unit I like to bombard my kids with books and images and give them time to make some discoveries of their own, as well as time to talk about them.

Getting the Big Picture

There is a great deal of power unleashed when we entice our students to learn. And when learning is organized thematically, the results multiply: we can approach content through all areas of the curriculum. Teaching with themes gives kids the big picture. Concepts will stick because they are interrelated with interesting content, and vocabulary is repeated and reinforced. All the information is connected in meaningful ways.

Choosing Themes

When I choose a theme, I pick a core topic from mainstream curriculum. This way, all students, whether they are English learners or fluent English speakers, have access to the core materials.

When there is material I am required to teach, such as the animal and rain forest unit in the basal reader, I look carefully to see what else I can add to enhance it and help make content comprehensible to my English learners and other students as well. I look for links I can make to other curriculum areas: reading, math, social studies, science, and art, as well as learning centers. However, I don't think of this endeavor as making a *collection* of everything I can find. I pick and choose carefully, selecting materials that make the point clearly and directly and that mesh with my own goals for the thematic study. I select the best literature books available—materials that speak to the heart, the real meat, of the subject matter. As much as possible, I make choices with links to children's lives and experiences.

It isn't necessary to have something from every curriculum area to add to a theme. I pull in what works. I don't want to overwhelm my students, and we need time for many learning experiences during our school day.

I believe themes should be topics of high interest to my students, with content area concepts that will be appropriate for their grade level and experiences. I make sure we have materials from a variety of genres: nonfiction, fiction, fantasy, and poetry, among others. I also make sure I have activities to interconnect and develop each area of language learning: listening, speaking, reading, and writing. Literature books and related art lessons can help extend, cement, and clarify learning, as do meaningful class discussions.

How to Organize a Thematic Plan

There are many ways to organize thematically. I like to make a simple web or sunburst, with the name of my theme written in a circle in the middle of a page, and use it to brainstorm. I draw rays coming from the circle and write ideas for other curriculum activities within these spaces. This is the skeleton I use to build on related lessons. In a glance at this web, I can see how lessons connect and find possible areas that need to be addressed. For example, if there is no music or poetry listed, I look for some good poem and song additions to my basic plan. (See Appendix, pages 215 and 216, for two reproducible web templates.)

Children enjoy knowing about and using a web organizer. When I am getting ready to launch a new theme or area of study, I like to make a large tablet-sized planning web *with* my students, including *their* ideas in the mix—I write down all their thoughts about the topic. This helps kids see how to make connections to their own knowledge and experiences. They also like to create their own webs individually and in small groups. These can be made with both words and illustrations. I give each group time to present and explain its work, and then we put these webs up with magnets on our front whiteboard.

This activity introduces a lot of vocabulary and allows time for children to use language in *real* ways as well as time to play with and warm up to concepts that will be developed in the unit. We keep these student-made webs on the classroom wall and add to them, and they become good resources for children to use in their thinking, speaking, and writing. They form a vocabulary word bank for kids to reference. This activity may be done with the whole group or with a smaller group of English learners, as a way to preview and review material to be taught. (See Figure 9–2.)

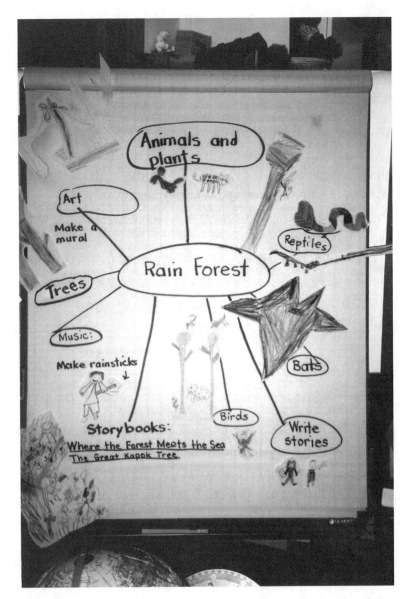

Figure 9–2
Sample web for organizing rain forest theme.

Small-Group Work

As with the web activity just described, I always model for the whole class the work small groups will be doing and show a completed project sample. I emphasize with the children that when they work together, they will

- Talk with each other and share ideas
- Listen to each other with respect

■ Share books, art supplies, and other materials

■ Do their best thinking and help each other succeed

Sometimes I plan the small collaborative groups while other times children pick their own teams. I like to keep assigned language buddies in the same groups (see Chapter 4 for more information on buddies) so that English learners can get help from children who speak English as well as the English learners' home language. I never want to put ELLs in a situation in which they would have no possible way to understand what we are learning!

Another important component for success and accountability in small-group work is that students are expected to *share* their work with the whole group. This gives kids a *reason* for getting something done!

Planning Sheet

In his book *Second Language Learners,* Stephen Cary (1997) uses a planning sheet to present an overview of his chosen theme. This template includes a place for goals for the unit of study, as well as space for recording activities, and resources, and materials that will be needed.

I find both the web I use and Cary's planning sheet to be helpful. The web gives me a view of curriculum areas I am linking in my teaching. The planning sheet organizes me sequentially and reminds me of materials and resources I will need to have available to present my lessons day by day. (See Figure 9–3.)

I have to admit that in my hectic life in the elementary classroom, because I'm planning for and teaching all subject areas, my typical planning notes are scribbled into a blank template or even on the back of an envelope. But knowing the format keeps me centered and organized. I frequently remind myself to save these notes in a thematic unit folder so that I won't need to reinvent them another year.

It's a good idea to keep all books, resource materials, and notes used for thematic units in labeled boxes, such as banker's file boxes or copy paper boxes with lids. Once you have everything figured out and planned, it would be a shame not to be able to use the ideas and resources again.

Theme: Rain Forest

Key Concepts and Skills

1. Instill respect for Earth, its habitats, and all living things
2. Study animals of the rain forest in Australia and South America
3. Investigate, peruse books, and look for information
4. Discuss ideas; provide time for critical and creative thinking
5. Learn songs and poems and read them
5. Create poetry charts, personal stories, and illustrations
6. Make a class mural
7. Make and illustrate a small eight-fold booklet about the rain forest

Activity	Context Clues and Materials
Teacher: Tell personal stories, share photos of an Australian rain forest and rain forest animals.	*Personal photographs *Calendar and magazine photos *World map
Invite discussion. Teacher may wish to take quick dictation of children's beginning-of-unit ideas in a small notebook.	
Read picture book.	*Where the Forest Meets the Sea
Show rain forest areas on map.	*World map
K-W-L chart: Teacher scribes; students list what they know about rain forests and what they want to know. Later they will list what they learned. Children illustrate our K-W-L chart and read it together.	*Easel with large tablet paper and marking pens *Drawing paper, crayons, and pens for children's illustrations

Figure 9–3 *Rain forest planning sheet*   (continues)

Activity	Context Clues and Materials
Students open packages of children's books from Australia; investigate, share, and reflect.	*Picture books and nonfiction books about the rain forest, from a library as well as from classroom and teacher collections
Teacher shares picture book and cassette: *Crocodile Smile: 10 Songs of the Earth as the Animals See It* by Sarah Weeks.	*Picture book, cassette, and tape player
Sing together and pick songs and poems for poetry charts.	*Twenty-four-by-thirty-six-inch manila tagboard, or large tablet paper and pens
Students illustrate poem of choice; read and sing the charts together. Charts can be illustrated in groups, or everyone can create illustrations for a single chart. These are cut and attached. Make multiple charts, depending on level of student interest.	*Marking pens for illustrations
Teacher shares books about rain forest animals. Discussion time.	*Australian Frogs: Amazing Amphibians* by Jill Morris *Australian Bats* by Jill Morris *Green Air* by Jill Morris *The Great Kapok Tree: A Tale of the Amazon Rain Forest* by Lynne Cherry *El gran capoquero: Un cuento de la selva Amazonica* (Spanish version of *The Great Kapok Tree*) by Lynne Cherry (Other books listed in References.)

Figure 9-3 *Rain forest planning sheet (continued)*

Activity	Context Clues and Materials
Students watch a video about rain forest animals. Lots of reflection and discussion.	*National Geographic's *Really Wild Animals: Totally: Tropical Rain Forest* (South America) or *National Geographic's *Really Wild Animals: Wonders Down Under* (Australia)
Students are invited to create their own stories and illustrations about an animal of their choice.	*Seven-by-seven-inch white paper *Crayons and watercolors or marking pens *Nine-by-twelve-inch white paper for writing and mounting the artwork (see Chapter 6 for sample work combining art and writing) *Ballpoint pens for writing *Writing may be typed by the teacher and mounted with artwork
Time for sharing stories and reflections.	
Students retell rain forest information and finish their K-W-L chart. The teacher abstracts information from the chart to make an eight-page booklet for children to illustrate.	*Completed K-W-L chart *Eight-page booklet
As time and interest allows, children work together to create a torn/cut-paper mural of a rain forest.	*Fadeless butcher paper *Paper, scissors, glue

Figure 9–3 *Continued*

Collecting Questions

Another method for thematic organization is to put up a large piece of white butcher paper or free up a bulletin board. Children may use this area to write questions, jot notes, and record information. A variation of this idea is to provide a large sheet of paper or some easel-sized tablet paper for small groups.

Literature at the Heart of It All

I build my thematic studies around literature: children's picture books and nonfiction as well as poetry. I feel it is important for me to incorporate carefully chosen books and materials to support the content areas we are studying. These resources are a great foundation. They also give children vicarious experiences; they help them put themselves in the story situations.

When I taught the rain forest unit, I brought in books about tropical rain forests in both Australia and South America. One of the skills I most want to teach in my classroom is combining critical thinking and creative thinking. Literature books, nonfiction materials, and the discussions they evoke help me achieve this.

Teaching with themes gives children a lot of choices about their learning. It provides for individual, collaborative, and large-group activities and lots of opportunities to think things through and problem solve creatively.

The Great Kapok Tree: **A Great Opportunity for Smart Thinking**

Several years ago, before rain-forest conservation was a well-known topic, a new picture book I read was a catalyst for a wonderful class discussion, resulting in some breakthrough ideas. When I shared *The Great Kapok Tree: A Tale of the Amazon Rain Forest* (Cherry 2000) with my first graders, they were mesmerized. This was one of the first materials on this subject for children. Lynne Cherry's picture book tells the story of a Brazilian rain forest and a man who has been sent to cut down a large kapok tree. The worker reflects about whether he should actually chop down the tree. He labors a while and then takes a nap before accomplishing the task. Various rain forest creatures and a young boy whisper in the man's ear as he sleeps, giving him reasons he should not cut down the tree, an action that would destroy their world.

I stopped reading the book after the sleeping man had received all the animals' messages and asked my kids what they thought he should do. Many children said that the man had to cut down the tree to make money for his family. Other students were upset that the tree would be destroyed and noted that the animals would no longer have homes. However, most of the children could not think of a solution for the problem. The class was evenly divided about what should be done.

Just as we were at an impasse, one child said, quite simply and concisely: "The man should *not* cut down the tree. He should pick those beautiful flowers and nuts from the rain forest and sell them in the town. Then he would have money for his family. And the tree would be saved." Another child thought that the man should become an artist and make paintings of the trees and animals. "People could like the paintings. He could sell them and the trees and plants would not die, and this would protect the rain forest," he said.

I was so impressed with children's thoughts and words that I wrote them down in a notebook. This was a period of time when rain-forest products were not yet sold in stores, and there were few materials on the subject. I realized that children had hit on some possible solutions to a very great problem.

This experience reminds me that when we need to think outside the box, we should ask kids for *their* ideas!

Teaching with Themes

There are several themes I feel are important to teach my first graders. I may not get to all of the topics each year, so I pick and choose. In general, the more time I spend with a thematic unit, the more activities we can tie in to it, and the more I feel the children get out of it. I choose the projects that we are most excited about and that focus the most on skills we are working on. Related children's literature books, art activities, and lots of time for personal writing and reflection are always important parts of each unit. (Please see the References for a sampling of books I use for specific units.)

Here is a list of some thematic units I have taught. Of course, I do not teach *all* of these themes in one year. It is great to have variety from year to year.

- Seasons

- Holidays in General

- Fall Holidays

- Winter Holidays

- Spring Holidays (I may just teach a lesson or two about a special holiday or celebration rather than a thematic unit. I now substitute many seasonal activities for some of the holiday lessons I previously taught.)

- All About Me/Self-Respect (A great theme for starting the year. I circle back to it periodically with different materials and activities.)

- Family

- Friends

- The Neighborhood and Community

- People Who Live and Work in the Community

- City and Country

- Our World/Cultural Diversity

- Transportation

- Habitats: Rain Forest, Mountains, Ocean

- Animals and Living Things

- Plants

- Sea Life

- Earth Day, Planet Earth, Our Environment

- Weather

- Teeth and Dental Health

- Fire Safety

- Health and Safety

- Mail/Writing

- Celebrations

- Courage

Several of these units can be combined into one area of study, such as community and the people who work there, habitats and the people and animals living in them, and so on. I try to tailor thematic units to the curriculum we need to cover as well as the time blocks available.

Allow Time for the Unexpected

Flexibility is very important. I watch my kids carefully and run a unit as long as children seem interested and seem to be getting something out of it. Sometimes we need to stop what we are doing to make time for a different activity of greater importance. This happened in my classroom the day one of my children saved his mother's life.

I became aware of this event when Joey brought in an award for bravery given to him by his parents. Early in the morning, before school, Joey's mother had an asthma attack. She was home alone with Joey and was barely able to breathe or speak. Joey dialed 911, and according to the paramedics and the doctor, he did indeed rescue his mother. We were all in awe as Joey described the event to us.

I transcribed Joey's words and made them into a book for him to illustrate (this was his idea; see Figure 9–4). We included his bravery award with the text. After asking Joey's parents for permission, I telephoned a local newspaper, and it ran a beautiful article about this child and his mother.

After this event, it became apparent that other children, at first extremely proud of Joey, needed to be acknowledged for brave things *they* had done. They wrote about *their* courageous acts, and we also created a class bulletin board and a class book. Their title for both was *We Are All Brave!* I worked up a brief theme plan and brought in a lot of fairy tales—stories in which characters go through adversity and triumph because of their courage and struggles. We sang, "Scared and Not Scared," a song on the record *Small Voice Big Voice* by Dick Lourie and Jed. I

Figure 9–4
*Excerpt from
Joey's book about
saving his mother.*

And she gotted hungry.
And I am a HERO because
I saved my mommy!

read *Some Things Are Scary* by Florence Parry Heide (2003). I also read such books as *Little Tim and the Brave Sea Captain* by Edward Ardizonne (2000); *Swimmy* by Leo Lionni (1973); and *The Story of Jumping Mouse,* a Native American legend retold and illustrated by John Steptoe (1989).

Children were all honored for surmounting problems such as fear of spiders, leaving mom in the morning to go into the classroom when the bell rang, and not wanting to turn off the lights at night. In just a few days of exploring this theme, I sensed great feelings of satisfaction and fulfillment from the kids, as well as some real growth in self-respect.

Seasons and Celebrations

As the poet William Cole says in the introduction to his poetry anthology *Poems for Seasons and Celebrations* (1961), the seasons are "the earth's celebrations." Holidays are the times *we* choose to celebrate.

School districts across the country hold a variety of philosophies about celebrating holidays in school, with some districts allowing a large diversity of celebrations, and others, none at all. I work in a school district with children from many cultures who speak a multitude of languages. I feel that helping children become knowledgeable about a variety of holidays from many cultures, especially those of children in my class, helps them become culturally literate. It also validates children's heritage. I also believe in an emphasis on family and family celebrations.

Teachers in districts discouraging the teaching of holiday curriculum may focus instead on the holidays we can *all* celebrate, in every district throughout the country: the seasons. We can enjoy these together as we observe the changes in nature throughout the year. I keep this as a recurrent theme we study all year long. Knowledge about Earth, growing things, birds and animals, and the seasons, is part of the first-grade science curriculum (in fact, it's part of the curriculum in all grades). And this wonderful area of study can connect powerfully with the language arts and art as well as science and math. An overview of one of my seasonal units follows.

Summer and Fall

We start school in late summer, and we note the changes in our environment in the next few months as days grow shorter and colder and trees lose their leaves. In the San Francisco Bay area, we have Indian summer through late October, so we are able to experience warmer weather and then note the changes that autumn brings. The kids and I take a science walk near the beginning of the school year and sketch the trees and other details of the landscape. A later walk shows us changes in the environment, including the contrast between evergreens and deciduous trees with bare branches. In October and November we gather fallen leaves and use them for a variety of integrated literature and art projects. We also create beautiful drawings as well as torn-paper compositions of trees and landscapes we have seen.

Children learn vocabulary words for science concepts, as well as for art, as they *look,* try to express themselves, and learn about the elements of design they used to create their tree drawings. We talk about the *lines* of the tree trunk moving from the roots upward, and when we move our eyes around the tree, we see its *form.* We talk about *texture*: how the tree trunk feels—smooth or rough, hard or soft. And as we observe the tree and its branches, limbs, twigs, and leaves, all reaching skyward, we see interesting *spaces* and *patterns.* Children are excited about this unit of study because they can investigate with their own eyes and other senses as well.

We enjoy picture books such as *Red Leaf, Yellow Leaf* by Lois Ehlert (1991) and *Sky Tree: Seeing Science Through Art* by Thomas Locker (2001). *Fall* by Ron Hirschi (1991) is another favorite book. I also like to share *Gather Up, Gather In* by M. C. Helldorfer (1994).

Sharing Our *Own* Observations

We absorb these books and stories together and share our artwork and personal observations from nature. Karina holds up her carefully crafted drawing, complete with her own writing, and spontaneously hugs her work. She says, "It's good to love a tree." Other kids enthusiastically agree.

Fall also lends itself to the study of animals and birds, as they get ready for the seasonal changes winter brings. The following are some favorite related books.

> *Nuts to You!* by Lois Ehlert (1993)
> *Owl Moon* by Jane Yolen (1987)
> *Red Fox Running* by Eve Bunting (1996)
> *When Winter Comes* by Nancy Van Laan (2000)
> *Frog and Toad All Year* by Arnold Lobel (1984)

(See the References for a more complete list of some of our other favorite books.)

We learn poetry and songs about autumn, about trees, leaves, birds, and animals. The children illustrate poetry charts and enjoy fall poems. We dance and sing and recite poetry, sometimes dropping real leaves. Then we make leaf prints, attaching the leaves to the final art. (See Figure 9–5. For directions for making leaf prints, please see the Appendix, pages 217 to 218.)

Figure 9–5
*Adrian makes a
leaf print.*

Leaf-Print Poetry Charts

Since real, dried leaves are fragile, and easily come apart when attached
to leaf poems, leaf prints are an ideal way to illustrate poetry charts. I
use twenty-four-by-thirty-six-inch manila tagboard. I print a poem with
permanent black pen, and children illustrate the chart with leaf prints.
Charts can be illustrated with a torn-paper collage too. Children also
create their own individual leaf prints.

Here are some of our favorite poems to learn and create on charts:

"One by One the Leaves Fall Down," from *Nibble, Nibble* by
  Margaret Wise Brown
"Down!, Down!" by Eleanor Farjeon (1951)
"The Night Is a Big Black Cat" by G. Orr Clark (1983)
"Like a Leaf or a Feather" by Beatrice Shenk de Regniers (1958)

Showcasing the Leaf Prints

I feel that making leaf prints is a very satisfying project on many levels.
It gives children a chance to use found seasonal materials to create their
own beautiful art. The art reflects our experiences with gathering leaves

143

and learning poetry, and it showcases our new knowledge about the Earth and its seasons.

Children take away from these sessions their remembrances of our brief walks to sketch and forage outdoors, the poetry and songs they have committed to memory, knowledge about the natural world, and the completed leaf prints that are artifacts of the whole experience. They also have time to think, converse, and write about their activities and their own observations.

Making leaf prints is one of my favorite activities to do with children, partly because the art looks the same whether done by a child or an adult. No one can believe that first graders created these works of art! This alone is a great boost to self-esteem.

Seasons Are an Important Area of Study

If I taught in a district where I could not celebrate holidays, I would be sure to include, as I do now, many literature, art, and science lessons relating to seasons. I teach many seasonal and holiday activities in writing, literature, and art that integrate well with many areas of the curriculum.

Here is a brief sampling of some of these seasonal art activities. The lessons can be matched with picture books to integrate art and literature.

- Poetry calendars—Use any calendar template. I use eleven-by-fourteen-inch copy paper and run off the calendars with a printed poem or nursery rhyme on each page for children to illustrate. The calendar takes up the bottom two-thirds of the paper. I use this project with *A Child's Calendar* by John Updike (1999) and *Month by Month a Year Goes Round* by Carol Diggory Shields (1998).

- Leaf prints can be used as covers for our poetry calendars.

- Torn- or cut-paper suns, leaves, umbrellas or clouds, or snowmen can be made from construction paper and hung from yarn or fishing line. Use with books such as *A Circle of Seasons* (poetry) by Myra Cohn Livingston (1982); *Welcome Back, Sun* by Michael Emberley (1993); *The Cloud Book* by Tomie dePaola (1985); *Rain, Rain Rivers* by Uri Shulevitz (1988); and *The Snowman* by Raymond Briggs (1986).

- Owls (and other birds and animals) made from torn paper, with clay-print or torn-paper eyes. Leaf-printed paper may be torn into owl shapes and then finished with the torn-paper eyes. If holidays are celebrated, Thanksgiving turkeys can be made the same way. To make clay-print eyes, children form plasticine clay balls and then flatten them on a table. Pinch up a handle for holding the ball. Draw a design in the clay using a pencil. To print these balls, paint with tempera and then press them down on paper. I use this project with Jane Yolen's picture book *Owl Moon* (1987) and *Owl Babies* by Martin Waddell (1996). Torn-paper animals with clay-print eyes can be used with such books as *All Kinds of Babies* by Millicent E. Selsam (2000), *Dick Bruna's Animal Book* by Dick Bruna (1976), and *Foolish Rabbit's Big Mistake* by Rafe Martin (1991).

- Mural of the environment—a culmination of our Earth Day/environment studies. This activity involves many levels of learning, as described in the next section.

A Thematic Study of Our Environment

When we study our environment, we talk about planet Earth, "the blue planet," and I share Patricia Lauber's book *Seeing Earth from Space* (1990). Lauber has compiled photographs taken by astronauts from space, and she makes a plea to us all to treasure our planet. The children remark about how blue and beautiful Earth looks, and we spend a lot of time discussing pollution and things we can do to help keep our world clean. (See Chapter 8, pages 122 to 123, for some reflections students had after viewing children's art from China on this theme.) Some other books I like to share as part of this unit follow.

- *The World That Jack Built* by Ruth Brown (1991)

- *Common Ground: The Water, Earth, and Air We Share* by Molly Bang (1997)

- *A River Ran Wild: An Environmental History* by Lynne Cherry (2002)

- *The People Who Hugged Trees: An Environmental Folktale* by Deborah Lee Rose (2001)

■ *Hey! Get Off Our Train* by John Burningham (1994)

■ *Crocodile Smile: 10 Songs of the Earth as the Animals See It* by Sarah Weeks (2003)

As a culminating activity at the end of our study, I invite children to create *their* ideas about an unpolluted, healthy world. Last year's class produced a beautiful cut-paper mural of a meadow, lake, and forest as well as a small community. This work was complete with families, birds, animals, and other living things. Kids created pieces of the whole scene, and we moved them around on butcher paper on the floor until we had the composition the way we liked it.

After we glued and discussed our mural, which depicted a fine and healthy world to live in, I read Ruth Brown's book *The World That Jack Built* (1991). This cumulative story, modeled after *The House That Jack Built,* begins with a beautiful world and ends with the scene of a ruined meadow, brown sky, and polluted waters and trees next to a factory. After I read, the children had a lot to say about what went wrong in the story. After many heated, indignant comments, the kids decided to "trash" part of our mural so that we could see the comparisons between the sort of world we want to live in and one we could end up inhabiting if we aren't careful. (See Figure 9–6.)

Figure 9–6
Our mural of the environment, showing a beautiful world on the left and a polluted one on the right.

The children and I collected bits of classroom trash to attach to part of the mural. The kids also covered part of our beautiful artwork by sponge-painting it with black and brown paint to represent pollution.

We were all very upset as we looked at what we had done. The final mural—one of high contrast between a great place to live and a dying world—stimulated a lot of discussion and a class poem. I jotted down the children's words and read them back to them. The poem ended poignantly with one child's lament: "And the baby birds never even got to have a life!"

On a similar theme last Earth Day, my friend Kristi Yee created a wonderful peace mural, titled "Peace Is . . . ," with her kindergarten class. She first read her children *The Peace Book* by Todd Parr (2004), and allowed time for a lot of discussion. Kristi said, "The book helped kids understand this very abstract concept [peace]. And then when children painted, and expressed to me their own creative thoughts, they made this very abstract idea concrete through their art and oral language."

The peace mural created by Kristi's class has been displayed at the California Kindergarten Conference and several other venues. (See Figure 9–7.)

Field Trips: Great Culminations for Thematic Units

In the same way that murals pull learning together, field trips are terrific learning experiences: wonderful for community building and a great grand finale for a unit of study. They give children the big picture and opportunities to observe, talk, and reflect as well as apply knowledge. (For more about field trips, see *Everything You Need to Know to Teach First Grade* [Dragan 2003].)

The third-grade teacher team at my school has refined the art of field trips to a science. Part of the teachers' rationale is that our students are from many other countries and locales and need a sense of place—an overall idea about where they are now living. The classes take many trips throughout the Bay Area, from San Francisco and Sausalito to Pacifica and points south. They get to visit many locations and gain a strong appreciation of the natural world.

Figure 9–7

Part of Kristi's kindergarten's peace mural, showing one five-year-old's thought: "Peace is liking the world."

Another focus for these events is language development for all children, but particularly for English learners. As Rebecca Fishman said, "Our kids get so excited about seeing these places that they blurt out language spontaneously, naming animals and plants, constructing sentences, and using a multitude of new vocabulary words. Kids start to really care about the places they visit and begin to understand environmental concerns. They frequently bring their families back to these locales on weekends."

Rebecca always brings a digital camera and downloads photos to the shared third-grade computers so that students can incorporate personal pictures into their follow-up writing projects.

Each year these teachers write proposals for grants and organize ten trips that highlight third-grade curriculum. They ask parents to help supply transportation, and they take a study trip each month. Gail Kossowsky, one of the creators of the field trip project, said, "Other teachers ask us how we can stand the stress of taking so many trips. But it's easy, because after the first trip or two, expectations are established. Everyone knows what we've been focusing on, what to expect, and how to behave. All the kids are motivated to learn!"

Gail explained that the third-grade teacher team spends each month on specific areas of study in the classroom, stressing language development for the English learners, as well as vocabulary, science, and social studies. "We integrate curriculum wherever we can," she said. "Trips are the reward for all that learning. Kids can apply what they have studied."

Cregg Ramich, another member of the team, told of the excitement of studying a unit and then taking kids to actually experience what they have just been learning. "We study wildflowers, plants, and animals of San Bruno Mountain," he said. "And then we take our students up there. They run around, finding and naming the plants, and are astonished at what they know! It's a really joyful and rewarding experience." The third-grade students actually have a chance to see some of the endangered species on the mountain: the mission blue butterfly and the Callippe silverspot butterfly.

When the kids return to school, they make a mural about the plant and animal life of San Bruno Mountain. This field experience also influences their later study of the Ohlone Indians. San Bruno Mountain is the location of one of the largest and oldest prehistoric Native American cultural sites in the San Francisco Bay Area, an Ohlone shell mound dating to 3200 B.C.E.

Julie Blair, also a member of this third-grade teacher team, told me about another highlight: the spring tide pool trip. "Kids just can't believe they are actually *seeing* the tide pool plants and animals they have been studying and researching. They gain knowledge that will stick for life!"

A Year's Worth of Trips

Here is a partial list of the third-grade field trip destinations and study themes. There is some variation year to year, depending on which facilities and sites are available and which units of study the teachers decide to pursue.

Field Trip Location	*Theme of Study*
Redwood Grove	Ohlone Indians
Hidden Villa	Plants and the environment
Theater performance	Theme varies each year
Whale Bus	Marine mammals
Año Nuevo	Elephant seals
Planetarium in San Francisco	Solar system
Peninsula Humane Society	Pet care and overpopulation
Fitzgerald Marine Reserve	Tide pools
Marsh Muck—Coyote Point	Wetlands
San Bruno Mountain Park	Native wildflowers

Out and About with First Graders

Like their third-grade counterparts, first graders also need many opportunities to get out into the world for engaging learning. Aside from a more elaborate trip to an aquarium, zoo, or museum, we frequently take a number of walking trips in the nearby neighborhood. Here are some of our favorite destinations:

- The public library
- A local tortilla factory
- A panadería (Mexican bakery)
- The fire department
- The police station
- City hall
- The post office

We do many art, writing, and building projects after these trips: class quilts, printmaking, community model making, and class books. We take some photographs on each trip and include them in personal and group writing projects.

Assemblies

Another way to bring kids special knowledge, create tie-ins with content being studied, and encourage language skills and other learning is to organize school assemblies and connect them with further classroom activities. Our local South San Francisco Fire Department always does a terrific program, presenting interactive skits to help children learn how to check a door for heat before opening it, how to crawl out of bed if a room is smoky, and so on. Fire department personnel come to school to give programs on personal safety as well.

Wild Things in the Lunchroom

This month my children enjoyed a wonderful program put on by Wild Things, a Northern California organization that brings endangered animals into schools. In an assembly format in the cafeteria, Gabe and Barbie Kerschner showed primary-grade kids several injured birds and animals, now restored to health as much as possible but unable to return to the wild. The children loved meeting Hooter, the barn owl; Koomba, a bush baby from Africa; Phyllis Quiller, a North American porcupine; and Billabong, a ten-month-old red kangaroo from Australia. Other hits were a feisty mountain lion named Canyon and Izog, a hundred-pound, twenty-two-year-old North American alligator.

My kids were in awe as they were introduced to fascinating facts and absorbing observations of these animals. Billabong delighted them the most by hopping around the lunchroom! And on their way out of the assembly, the children could actually touch Izog the alligator's snorkel-like nose, see close up and personal its long white tongue muscle and the extra membrane over its eyes, and get a good look at the strongest jaw in the animal kingdom. (See Figure 9–8.)

Figure 9–8
Marco checks out the alligator, Izog.

These were experiences to talk about and marvel over for the rest of the day and beyond—the kind of memories to remember and build on! And we will build on them, in our classroom, with a variety of related extension activities. That way meaning will become clear for everyone.

Contests and Competitions

Bringing contests into the classroom is another good way to involve students. This year I taught poster art using the fire department's smoke alarm contest theme, and seven of my first graders won at least a second- or third-prize ribbon. The task was to create clear, meaningful posters showing the importance of smoke alarms. One child won a district grand prize and was invited to the fire department for lunch. Some special activities at the event were a tour of the fire station and a chance to slide down the fire pole with a firefighter. Six other children won a local Art Takes a Bus Ride competition and will have their artwork displayed on San Trans buses.

In-Class Field Trips

In-class field trips are a great alternative to more expensive bus trips when funds are tight. Recently, my children enjoyed a classroom workshop given by Mia Klett from the Laurence Hall of Science, University of California at Berkeley. The topic was animal clues.

Children sat in a semicircle on the rug to watch Mia enact a story about a little girl looking for animal clues in the woods. With Mia's help, the doll representing the child sorted through leaves on a mat in front of the room. She found and talked about items such as feathers, bones, and shed snakeskin. Children were then invited to carefully sort (just as scientists do) some materials in bins in order to find animal clues. Small groups of students worked together to discover items such as feathers, bones, a small skull, and a snakeskin.

Children then sat on the floor in small circles. Mia told them animal stories, and then the groups took turns visiting with live creatures: a snake, a rat, a rabbit, and a ring-necked dove. Students were able to hold the animals by providing a "nest" in their laps or a perch on their fingers.

At the end of the workshop, children were able to easily identify three sets of animal footprints and talk about several things they had learned.

The animals they met firsthand intrigued my first graders. The kids gained a lot of information and *loved* getting to sort through forest debris like scientists. Many of them chose to begin some writing about their experiences during writers workshop. I read related picture books and taught some songs and poems. We also did several cut- and torn-paper collage art projects related to the workshop and created our own woodland mural. Art extended and enhanced these experiences and provided a format for talking about the activity as well.

I feel that the integrated science, writing, and art extended the workshop experience and cemented learning. Many children were writing, reading, and talking about these animals for weeks.

From Subway Maps to Llamas

Some other in-class field trips we have enjoyed are a visit from Matthew's father, Ben Edelhart, who shared maps, coins, and anecdotes about his trip to London. Children particularly loved reading the subway maps and hearing stories about the Tower of London and the royal crown jewels.

Gina Lazzari, the "Tooth Lady," taught children about brushing, flossing and rinsing through music, modeling, and an interactive play. And Mary Troop, teacher and zoo volunteer, fascinated my kids with her anecdotes about working at the petting zoo in San Francisco. Mary brought in animal photos, samples of hair and feathers, extensive knowledge, and funny stories about the wide variety of animals in her care, especially the spitting llamas. (See Figure 9–9.)

The Power of Working with Themes

Teaching with themes can fill many needs. Themes can help us grow emotionally and intellectually. And they can add zing and excitement to our learning endeavors. Thematic units are ways to create memories together and have authentic learning experiences. The heightened intensity and variety of hands-on activities help make learning fun and concepts make sense. We remember things better when we group concepts for learning and make connections. And it's good to have things we look forward to in our days together.

Figure 9–9

Kelcie's thank-you letter to Mary Troop.

Thematic studies support language learning by providing inter-related activities and materials that spark kids' interests, fuel their questions, and *infuse* them with the need to chat, discuss, imagine, and wonder. Children learn English in meaning-centered ways, through context supported by real things: manipulatives, books, maps, videos, audiocassettes, examples and models, poetry and songs. They have time to do research, make discoveries, and interview experts in the field. Students gain fluency because they use language for authentic communication, and they are excited to talk about their experiences.

Winston Churchill once said, "I love learning, I just hate being taught." I believe Churchill was referring to the excitement of active, self-selected learning as opposed to passive, imposed types of experiences. Students enjoy learning through themes because *they* have some input and some ownership of the thematic study projects. They participate in meaning-making activities. They get to *do* things, explore, problem solve, and think of new ideas. In their fire to know things—make meaning from words and sense of concepts and talk about all of it—kids learn a lot. They are really engaged. In essence, they have been teaching themselves.

Writing and Publishing with English Language Learners

Words are wonderful. By writing them and putting them together, I could make them say whatever I wanted to say. It was a kind of magic.

—Clyde Robert Bulla, *A Grain of Wheat: A Writer Begins*

I'm writing about recess, and I love them!

—Joey

The year I was ten years old I fell off a galloping horse and remained unconscious while my friend Marcia flooded my face with a canteenful of water. Months later, after struggling with an agonizing fear of riding, I made a comeback by going on a weeklong pack trip into the mountains and riding a beautiful black horse bareback across a meadow. These were powerful experiences for me. I visualized them over and over in my head, reveled in them, and finally drew them with pencil, pen, and crayons. This still wasn't enough for me: I used my visualizations and vivid memories, as well as my drawings, for reference. Then I struggled to write everything down and get it right.

These mind pictures, as well as my art, were dress rehearsals for my writing. When I floundered in my written descriptions, I looked at the pictures I had created as well as the images in my head. These helped me paint the whole glorious achievement with words. I believe this was the first time I had ever written something just for myself. I got the idea and struggled to do it because writing down my story seemed so important, a way to make things more truly real. And I discovered that I could live the experience all over again when I wrote and drew.

The combination of my drawings and my writing rounded out the horseback-riding adventures for me and made them the most they could be. I couldn't say which was the most important means of expression: I needed both words and images to make it all come alive.

Getting Out of the Way So That Children Can Write

I believe that my students flourish when they have opportunities to write down and illustrate things of importance to *them*. They know that one way to maximize a special experience is to draw it, paint it, and write it down. One of the things I can do to most help them is model writing myself, do minilessons, and show both interest in and enthusiasm about their work. I believe it is important to respect the learner-writer and to let the child take the lead in figuring out what to spend time developing.

Being Part of the Writing Club

I want my first graders to get the feel of being published early in the school year. I think this helps propel them to write and share. At the beginning of the year I ask children to "write *their* way" by putting words on paper, even just making marks and drawings, writing any way they can. Children may also, if they prefer, dictate their stories to me, or if they can, write in their own language. If I don't speak a child's language, I write down what he says phonetically and read it back to him. He is then able to make corrections by repeating any words that don't sound right. I realize that the words I scribe are not written correctly, but at least the gist of the child's story is down on paper. I can read it back, using my makeshift phonetic spellings, and the child can feel a sense of accomplishment in expressing himself and being understood. Illustrations then help make meaning clear to others. I believe this strategy honors both the child's story and the home language. And it reinforces the idea that I, too, can write things down my way and have a record of something important even though I am new to the language.

Early one school year when I typed these beginning stories, the children took turns sitting in the author's chair to "read" their work and share their illustrations. (See Figure 10–1.) It was a wonderful beginning and children were astounded by what they had accomplished. I realized that I wanted to be part of this sharing, too. I had with me my advance copy of my own newly published book, *Everything You Need to Know to Teach First Grade* (2003). After the group author sharing, I asked the class, "Would you like to see *my* book?"

The children were not just polite, but wild to see my work. And they were enthusiastic, too, when they saw my picture on the cover with some of their now second-grade cousins, friends, and neighbors. "Oh!"

Figure 10–1
*Monserrat reads
her writing while
sitting in the
author's chair.*

they said. "You're an author too, just like *we* are! We can be authors together!" This was a special club I had been invited to join and I was truly touched and honored. Although I present my books at workshops and conferences, never will sharing my own writing be as sweet an experience.

Using Art to Help Children Get Started Writing

The problem is the same with both English learners and English-speaking children in early elementary grades: how to get new writers to put words (or letters, images, or scribbles that are comprehensible to them) down on paper. So we begin with art.

Art is another language for literacy. Many children in early elementary grades are at ease with drawing and have spent many hours using crayons, marking pens, and pencils before they even got to school. According to the official website of Binney and Smith Company (maker of Crayola products, www.crayola.com), the average child in the United States will wear down 730 crayons by his tenth birthday. For many children, drawing is a familiar and comforting activity. Linking drawing with writing is a way to help children start putting words down on paper. Drawing leads to the creation of stories and frees children to make meaning and create through both images and the integration of art and writing.

I stress with my students how lucky they are to be able to draw. I explain to children that many adults are afraid to draw or say they do not know how. (They can check this out on their own!) I tell children my theory that if they keep drawing throughout their lives, they will never lose this skill. I like to blur the line between drawing and writing. I ask my beginning writers to get their stories down on paper using any ways that work for them.

Now What? Let's Get Some Writing Going!

When I begin writers workshop, I model writing and do shared writing each day on a large tablet. The children dictate to me, they help me spell words, and I scribe for them. We illustrate our work. We soon do some interactive writing, during which children share the pen with me and take turns doing some of the writing. I prefer to use shared writing with the whole group and interactive writing with smaller groups because children will have more turns to write with me. These activities support language learners as well as the rest of my class.

A logical progression from these modeled writing lessons is to do written conversations, a wonderful technique I learned from Pat Gallagher and Gloria Norton's book *A Jumpstart to Literacy: Using Written Conversation to Help Developing Readers and Writers* (2000).

Written conversations were devised as a one-to-one way to write with a child on a topic of special interest. The child picks the topic. I offer my writing companion the opportunity to write with me and give him or her a choice of writing implements. Usually my student uses a pen and I use one with a thicker point in a different color. In this way each writer's work is visually distinct.

Variations of the Written Conversation

Since I first began working with children on writing (and drawing) written conversations, I have become an even stronger believer in the power of this technique. I have also been extending the ways I do this with children in order to work with many students at a time. The optimum amount of children for me would be a group of four to six, or possibly eight. This is a good-sized group that enables me to give a lot of support to struggling writers and language learners. However, I frequently continue to make written conversations an option for my entire class at the same time. Some children choose to continue writing and illustrating their own stories by themselves instead of writing with me. Since beginning writers are slow to get things down on paper, some days I work with all the children who want to do written conversations. I am able to get to everyone, although not in as much depth as I would wish. Other days I concentrate on children who need more help, more scaffolding.

I keep a hanging folder for each student in a writers workshop box decorated with puff paint, a gift from Mario Penman, my principal. During writers workshop each student is free to work on yesterday's filed story (or another work in progress in the folder), a poem, a written conversation, or something new. Children may use lined paper or white or colored copy paper. Many colors of copy paper are available. This adds a little interest. And once you get that color of paper you want, you may as well write on it! I fold down the top of these papers to create a space one-third the size of the whole piece of paper. This part of the paper is for drawing. The bottom two-thirds is for writing. If children need more space, we tape (scroll-style) or staple on another piece of paper. Each child has a ballpoint pen to use. This works better than pencil since children can draw a line through their errors and still see what their thinking was.

Because children may be waiting for me, I ask them to think of their own topics and begin drawing and writing. When I work with a child, I ask her to read her writing to me. I respond with comments to convey interest or questions I might have. We chat briefly about the artwork as well. Then I answer in writing and read my words back to the child. In my writing, when it's my turn, I try to weave in words the student might need. An alert student writer notices this and corrects his spelling in the next part of the writing, when it is his turn. I do not point mistakes out to the children. (I never say, "Look, this is how you spell *dragon,*" for example.) I say something like, "You might find some clues for words you want to spell if you look at my writing." And then I read aloud what I have written.

When I first wrote with a student I will call Juan Carlos, a second language learner, he kept insisting that I tell him how to spell words. He was frantic to have me spell for him. I told him to listen and write the sounds he could hear and that it did not matter right now if things were not spelled perfectly. We could fix his spelling later. After a couple of very nervous turns writing back and forth with me, Juan Carlos realized that he could find some of the words he needed right there in my answers to him. The realization helped him get rid of his anxiety and write several sentences.

This was a major breakthrough for a child who had come to me from another school district, beginning first grade for the third time! I was able to get him moved to an appropriate grade placement and special help, but not immediately. In the meantime, these written conversations were a way Juan Carlos could succeed and gain some confidence and self-esteem.

Creating a Personal Word Bank

Some children have very involved drawings and may be a little stuck about getting words or letters on paper, especially if they are language learners. If they wish, I *label* things with these children: I look carefully at the drawing, admire it, and ask the child to tell me about the picture.

Then, with the child's permission, I will print the words in appropriate parts of the drawing, sometimes adding little arrows that point from the words to the picture. Now this new writer-illustrator has her very own word bank to use in writing her story. This facilitates vocabulary development and helps children make some headway in their struggle to get their words on paper. (See Figure 10–2.)

I learn a great deal about the kids in my class when we write back and forth like this. When I wrote with Brenda, I also learned about the Latin American legend of the tooth rat, a figure much like our tooth fairy. (See Figure 10–3.)

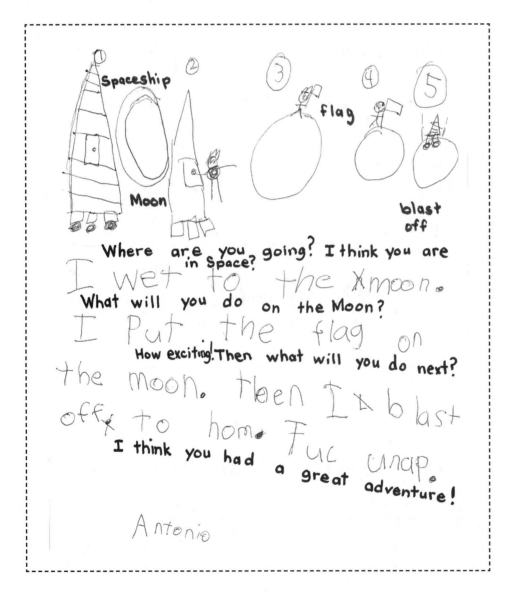

Figure 10–2
Written conversation word bank.

Figure 10–3
Brenda writes to me about the tooth rat.

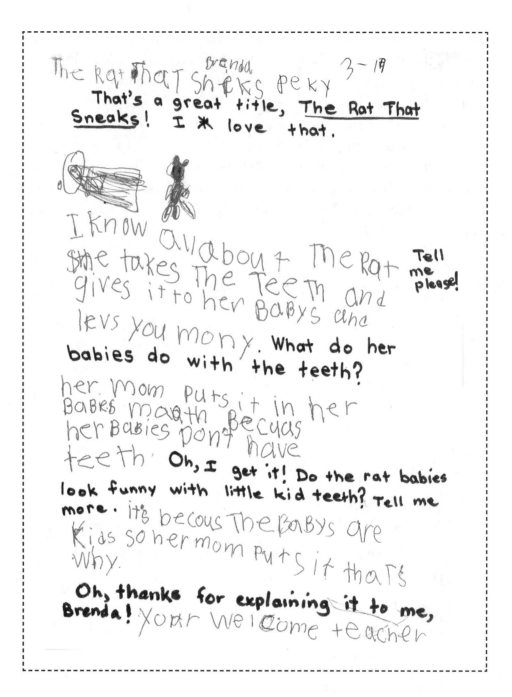

The Rat That Sneks peky   Brenda   3-19
That's a great title, The Rat That Sneaks! I * love that.

I know all about The Rat   Tell me please!
she takes The Teeth and gives it to her Babys and levs you mony. What do her babies do with the teeth?
her mom puts it in her Babes maath Becuas her Babies Dont have teeth. Oh, I get it! Do the rat babies look funny with little kid teeth? Tell me more. it's becous The BaBys are Kids so her mom puts it thats why.

Oh, thanks for explaining it to me, Brenda! Yoar welcome teacher

Pictures Nudge the Writing Along

When children do written conversations with me, some are sequential and work on either writing or drawings first. Most work on drawings and writing simultaneously, and the pictures they are making give insights and vision to what they are trying to get down on the page. The kids are relaxed as they create their drawings, and this facilitates their thinking and reduces anxiety about writing. I believe many of them are surprised as well as delighted at what they are able to accomplish when they draw and write this way. They have taken a gentle and moderate risk, and for most of them it works!

Picture Making

There is a lot of power in picture making. Children can develop pictures in tandem with stories. Art and words work together to help them create a satisfying whole with both a text and visuals—a complete experience. Students need to visualize and understand the story if they are to create illustrations that match the text. These pictures in their minds bring it all alive and are one of the main reasons that people read in the first place.

When we write, pictures in our minds and those we make on the paper can help us create meaning. These illustrations evolve along with the story. Pictures are akin to words and give a different dimension to the things we are trying to say. They are *another way* of thinking, extending ourselves, and making meaning. And they can be a big help for self-expression when words fail us or we are in the process of acquiring them.

When we use pictures we can see what we're saying, or what written text is saying to us. Pictures give us the opportunity to *be* in the text and respond to it in a new way. Extending and stretching ourselves in our use of pictures helps us become stronger at painting pictures with words. Pictures can be words we visualize.

Admiring the Authors and Illustrators

At the end of each writing period, the class shares stories and illustrations on the rug. Usually there is time for three or four children to read and show their work. This is the part of writers workshop that makes it all happen, because most children *want* to take that chance and share their efforts.

I conference with children and we read their written conversations. I encourage children to look through their written conversation collections and choose a story to tell and write. Eventually some of these pieces of writing develop into completed stories.

Word Folders

I have a word wall in my classroom, but I felt that my students needed some kind of reference tool right under their noses. I stapled two pages of word wall words inside a file folder, one page on the left, one on the right. All spaces on the folder are used. In this way, kids could stand the folder up, giving them some privacy if they wished, and more easily find words they needed. This small tool helps all children write more and better, no matter what their language level.

ELLs Need Some Extra TLC

I always have a few language learners (and sometimes others) who get very tangled up and frustrated as they try to write and make sense of English. First of all, I rarely ask a child to write about a specific topic. This kind of requirement is very difficult for children who are learning English. Another thing I do to help those in need is call them over one or two at a time and have them tell me what they are writing, what they want to say. Then I sit with them as they write it down word for word. I remind them to listen for sounds, put down the sounds they hear, and keep going.

One child was writing pages of hieroglyphics. When I sat with him, we took deep breaths and slowed down. He would tell me his whole thought, and we would count the words in his sentence. Then I guided him through putting down each word. I did not change anything or correct anything. That would have totally shut him down. But working this way, with a tiny bit of support, word by word, this little boy managed to write a five-line story. This was a big breakthrough for him.

Personal Interviews

Another technique I rely on heavily for getting writing going in my classroom is conducting personal interviews. We do simple interviews, shared writing style, at the beginning of the school year so that one child a day gets a chance to be the special person we get to know.

Other interviews evolved later in the school year when I noticed that my students had many passionate and fascinating personal interests. This was evidenced from books they chose, discussions we had, things they would bring from home, and special tidbits children chose to tell me.

Alejandro's great interest for weeks was sand painting. He had been making paintings at home using a commercial sand-painting kit, and he brought me a painting one day. He was very excited about the paintings he had made and talked a lot about them. We wrote a class story about his experiences, shared writing style, on a large tablet. While Alejandro told the group what he had done and his classmates asked questions, I scribed for them. The kids helped me write the sand-painting directions, spelling some of the words as we went along. When the writing was finished, we read it together and corrected it. Alejandro clarified things that were unclear and then did illustrations to go with his how-to story.

For several days Alejandro continued to talk about his experiences with sand painting. He was still working on more paintings at home. Although Alejandro had command of some English, he was struggling to express himself. This didn't stop him from talking because he was so involved in communicating his experiences with this new exciting craft and sharing with all of us.

I invited Alejandro to bring his painting kit to school and to *show* us how he painted with sand. He sat in front of the children and demonstrated. They had a few questions. He then drew them a sequential drawing showing how he created his paintings, step-by-step. And he seemed to rapidly become more fluent each day that went by.

Interviews Are About Asking Questions

I finally realized that I was overlooking a great way to help children practice both oral and written language, as well as missing out on a way for them to share their deep personal experiences and interests. I asked Alejandro if he would like to share his sand-painting kit with us again, and he brought it the next day. Then I had a heart-to-heart talk with my group.

I explained to my class that once upon a time I had been a newspaper reporter and that I loved to ask people questions and then write stories about them. When I asked the kids whether they were interested in doing the same thing, the response was overwhelmingly positive. We had a little discussion about the difference between asking questions and making comments, and then practiced asking questions. We also talked about different ways to take notes and made our own list for reference.

Ways of Taking Notes

Notes could be

- A picture

- A sequence of pictures

- Beginning letters or parts of words (a kind of shorthand or secret code)

- A mixture of words and pictures

- Writing—some sentences and perhaps some pictures about the really important parts of the story

- Special words and phrases

- A list

- Anything else that helps you record and remember the story

I outfitted my students with brand-new sharpened pencils. I sharpened their multitudinous supply of old pencils as well. I also gave each child a brand-new spiral-bound notebook. We all sat on the carpet and Alejandro set up his supplies on a small table in front of us. Then we gave Alejandro the floor.

As the children asked questions, I took quick notes on the large tablet off to the left of Alejandro. I recorded the group's questions and Alejandro's answers. Children stuck for words could look at my messy notes, but most seemed involved in working through their own ways to record information.

Alejandro's demonstration of the previous day was still fresh in their minds, so the children jumped right in with their questions. I was floored with the depth of some of the things they wanted to know. At the end of the interview, Ricky asked my favorite question: "How do you feel about your art?" On hearing this, Alejandro stood up tall, took a deep breath, looked up, and gestured widely with both arms. "Great, just great," he said. And we could see that this was true.

Interview Follow-Ups

When the interview was concluded, children went back to their seats to write. They had choices about what to pursue—they could write about Alejandro, about some part of the sand-painting interview, continue working on writing that they had previously worked on, or begin something new. When we met back at the rug at the end of the period to share our work, several children had done some interesting writing about Alejandro's sand paintings. Jazlyn had a list, quite a few students had brief stories, and others had mixtures of stories and notes. Most of the children had very involved illustrations to help tell their tales.

One by one other children asked to be interviewed. Before the year was out everyone had been interviewed, a few children several times. There was no daily schedule, although I did have an ongoing list of children who were waiting for their turn. Interviews happened when the children let me know they were ready. Here is a small sampling of interviews, recorded by me.

Sarai's Interview

Sarai's Title: Sarai's Magic Ballerina Shoes

Background: Sarai does not use English easily. On this day she came to school proudly wearing a ballerina necklace and hugging a ballerina book. She asked to be interviewed. I spoke to her beforehand in English and Spanish to see whether she needed any help or any vocabulary words. She seemed quietly confident about what she wanted to say. I had the idea that she felt supported by wearing the ballet-shoes charm, one she seemed convinced had magical powers.

I was impressed that Sarai was empowered by her fascination with the new charm and book to practice some things she wanted to say and then ask to speak in front of the class. She had given her presentation a lot of thought, she had worked on it at home (her own idea!), and she was ready.

To begin her interview Sarai addressed the group. "I'm gonna wear ballerina shoes and a dress for Halloween." Then she pointed to her necklace and the book that went with it.

Q: Where do you buy that [the ballet-shoes necklace]?

A: K-Mart. With a book.

Q: You wanna be a ballerina when you grow up?

A: Yes.

Q: What does the book do?

A: You need to put this necklace on to read the book. [*I believe Sarai thought the necklace would help her out with a lot of skills. She wore it proudly and serenely.*]

Q: Does the necklace go with the book?

A: Yes.

Q: The necklace is magic? [*The children caught on to Sarai's demeanor, that this was no ordinary necklace.*]

A: Yes.

Q: How?

A: Magic if you can spell a word. Magical. If I say a word and it likes it.

Q: If you wear the ballerina necklace you know how to spell stuff?

A: Yes.

Q: Do you like to have stuff for being a ballerina?

A: Yes.

Q: How many does it cost?

A: $2.99.

Q: That's not so much. You could say the magic words?

A: [*The answer came with a secretive smile.*] I don't wanna do it here.

At the end of the interview I read Sarai's ballerina book to the group.

Sarai gave us the gist of what she wanted to say but was not able to express all the details of her more involved ideas. I had the impression that her ideas were evolving, and she didn't want to spoil the magic by nailing them down.

The children did not know quite how to question Sarai to help her to say more. They seemed to intuit a lot of what she wanted to express and nudged her on a bit to try to explain things. They gave her ideas as well. Sarai was quite pleased with herself when the interview was over. We were all proud of her too.

Ricky's Interview   Ricky asked to be interviewed. He is very fluent in both English and Spanish. I am just including a portion of his interview here.

Ricky's Title: Ricky's Baby-Sitting Job

Background: Ricky told us he had a job. He asked to be interviewed about it. He took this job very seriously, so much so that he was a little insulted that I had forgotten what his interview would be about. Ricky explained to us that "[his] mom has this friend and [he takes] care of the kid. It's a baby."

> Q: [*From a startled listener*] What? You alone?
>
> A: Actually, I do the bottle. My mom does the diaper.
>
> Q: What do you do with the baby?
>
> A: I play with him. And I talk to him. And I give him his bottle. He follows me around.
>
> Q: How do you feel about the baby?
>
> A: Like I'm bigger.

Ricky went on at length to tell of the games he played with the baby and all he did to take care of him. He had wonderful command of himself and smooth control of the group. At times I felt as if I were watching a miniature talk show host. (See Figure 10–4.)

Figure 10–4
*Ricky conducts his
interview.*

Edgard's Interview

Edgard's Title: Teaching Brother to Walk

Background: The whole class was aware that Edgard had been very excited about teaching his brother to walk. He asked to be interviewed about this experience. Unfortunately, a few children were ahead of him in the interview lineup. I realized later that I sometimes needed to alter the interview order and let the class have the opportunity to interview a child who was at the height of excitement and the need to share.

Although Edgard had been given lots of time in class to talk about this experience with his brother, it had been difficult for him to wait for his interview. I felt that the resulting interview didn't have the punch and excitement it would have had if Edgard had been able to conduct it the day he had wanted to do it. I think my class would have understood if I had explained this and asked if he could go ahead of three or four children. Their interview material was not as "dated."

Q: When your brother was little, he knows how to walk?

A: No. We've been showing him how.

Q: You like him a lot?

A: Yes, even if he falls down.

Q: Did you hold your brother's little hand to help him?

A: When I grab his hand, he gets up and crawls away from me!

Q: How do you teach him how to walk?

A: He just cries until I hold his hand and then he cries for me and I then I hold his hand and he starts to walk to me.

Q: Was it hard?

A: Not really.

Q: Do you like to teach your brother to walk?

A: Not all the time. I'm bored when he's going in circles. When he crawls in the kitchen I try to pick him up. He starts to cry and goes away.

Q: Does your brother like you?

A: Yeah, 'cause I don't play rough with him. When I walk him he goes in front of me. But sometimes he puts one feet on my face and bangs on my face.

Edgard has a large vocabulary and speaks well in both English and Spanish. Only occasionally does he make grammatical errors or run into problems expressing himself.

Jazlyn's Interview

Jazlyn's Title: Jazlyn Dances Hula

Background: The class was aware that Jazlyn and her sister were taking hula lessons. They had seen Jazlyn perform in the school talent show a month before. Jazlyn is an English speaker who speaks some Tagalog.

Q: When you are performing is it fun?

A: Yes. Embarrassed though.

Q: Do you like doing hula hoops?

A: I'm doing hula. It's a dance. In Hawaii they dance hula.

Teacher aside: Doing the interviews and being interviewed gives children a chance to practice patience and to give explanations when they feel they are being misunderstood. I believe children become not just aware of diverse cultural traditions but also more flexible and tolerant as a result of these experiences.

Q: When you were onstage you were as tall as your sister.

A: [*Jazlyn nodded her head briefly.*]

Q: How did you learn hula?

A: The hula teacher taught us how.

Q: When you were onstage were you proud?

Q: Happy?

A: Yes.

Q: You're not from Hawaii?

A: No. Sacramento.

Q: Do your teacher love hula?

A: I thi-ink.

Q: Where did you buy the suit of hula?

A: You mean the skirt? The parayo? My grandma.

Although Jazlyn has a good command of English and a good vocabulary, she uses oral language sparsely. The children sensed this but did not really know how to get more details out of her. The interview was ended a little prematurely when the lunch bell rang. We were not able to get back into the experience after the lunch break, and since our school year was ending, Jazlyn's interview had to end at this point. However, she and the rest of the class seemed satisfied.

One of the things I noticed in Jazlyn's interview was the children's creativity and flexibility in using language. For example, when Maria didn't know how to describe the garb that a hula dancer wears, she came up with something that made sense to her: "the suit of hula."

Another thing that touched me as I listened to the children conduct their interviews and made my own notes was the total climate of interest and respect created by my first graders.

Typed Interviews

I typed each of the children's interviews, including the questions asked and the answers. Children had a collection of them to illustrate and to practice reading. Because these were so personal, they were popular reading material. (See Figure 10–5.)

Interviews as Language Assessments

These classroom interviews gave me a lot of information about how the children speak and think and write. I noticed that many of them were speaking in incomplete sentences. I also noticed that many just spoke in the present tense, and some mixed tenses. Several needed help with words and sentence structures for asking questions.

I filed this information away to use for help in coming up with lessons that would work on specific skills without spotlighting individual children's needs and their difficulties with language. I never want to correct a child's language. First of all, that doesn't work. And more importantly, the children would no longer feel free to take risks to express themselves meaningfully their way, from their hearts.

For more about using interviews in the classroom, please see Paula Rogovin's books *Classroom Learning, a World of Learning* (1998) and *The Research Workshop: Bringing the World into Your Classroom* (2001). There is also a video available: *Classroom Interviews in Action* (Rogovin 1998).

Figure 10–5
Juan's typed and illustrated interview.

Class Interview with Juan: April 26
Juan's First Championship

Q: What's your sport? **Soccer.**
Q: Is soccer your favorite sport? **Yes.**

Q: When you play, do you get all the hits?

Yes. When we play a hard team they always hit me and Cesar and Juanito because we are the best.

Q: What are hits?
Like when they hit with feet, like kick with soccer shoes when I pass the ball. They want me to break my feet.

Q: Do you have a lot of fun with your friends?
Yes ' cause we always get in first place. I play with Chivas. I used to play with Vipers.

Q: Did you win the championship? **Yeah.**

Q: Do they ever give you a yellow or red card? **Almost. The red card would get us out. And we don't play for one game. They wanted to give us a yellow card once 'cause we were yelling to our team 'cause they didn't play the procedure. One time the man had a red card in his hand. We said "Uh-oh! Sorry!" And he said, "Okay."**

Q: Do you have a good kick? **I have a good kick. But sometimes if the ball is hard I can't kick it hard.**

Q: Do you like winning? Are you proud? **Yes.**
Q: Are you good at soccer? **Andrea, you already saw!**
Are you good? **Yes!**
Q: How good? **So much!**

Making Books

Another favorite way to stimulate children to write is to show them how to make pop-ups and other kinds of books. There is magic here when the two-dimensional becomes three-dimensional. It doesn't matter whether we use rulers, prerun copies with pop-up boxes, or just cut them ourselves roughly on the spot.

173

The first time I did this with my children this year was during one of those moments when *this* project was just what we needed to do. There was no preplanning on my part, so I cut two pop-up boxes, showing my class how to cut them, make folds, push the boxes inside the folded paper, and then glue a cover on the book. (See the Appendix, page 220, and the References for directions and recommended books. For some other pop-up ideas, see *Everything You Need to Know to Teach First Grade* [Dragan 2003].)

It was a rainy-day recess, and everyone was bored, but the moment I shared the pop-up how-to, there was a feeling of intense and passionate wanting to know! Everyone completed the pop-up background, with boxes, and I helped glue this paper to a cover sheet. We brainstormed things we could glue onto the pop-up box. Marco was the first one to get it. He cut out a small house, stuck it against a pop-up box, and moved it back and forth, saying, "It's come alive, it's come alive!"

Writing Inspiration Hits

Children made the books quickly. They were still in various stages of completion when children began writing their own stories in them. These kinds of projects are irresistible. As soon as children make a book, they *want* to put a story in it, and *nothing* holds them back.

When this activity catches on in your classroom, there will be no stopping the pop-up and story production, and written and oral language will flourish!

CHAPTER 11

Putting It All Together with Puppetry, Masks, and Drama

Puppets are fortunate—they can do and say things a live performer wouldn't touch with a stick.

—From a 1969 proposal for *The Muppet Show*

Children can turn anything into anything. For this gift we call them magical . . . born alchemists of the spirit. But they are more than this: They are the first real inventors—and each child in her own time invents the world all over again, as if it had never been made before.

—Richard Lewis

Erwin, as I will call my new student, left his home on a small rural farm in Mexico and joined our class midyear. Although I used both English and Spanish when communicating with him, and paired him with multilingual buddies who sat on each side of him, Erwin had no previous experience with English and rarely spoke Spanish. From the first day his usual response was to nod . . . slightly. Erwin was a real challenge for me because it became obvious that he was uncomfortable speaking and interacting with others. He really seemed to want to blend right into the woodwork.

It was important to me help Erwin become comfortable in our classroom and to facilitate his crucial transition from home to school. It became obvious from his body language and facial expressions that this

175

assimilation process must be pretty traumatic. Later knowledge of both Erwin's personality and his home situation confirmed this fact. I tried to figure out ways to ease his transition into our classroom and tempt him to interact with me and with his fellow students. I watched him for clues.

The Arts to the Rescue!

As I soon found out, Erwin had a real affinity for small, detailed drawings. On his first day in our class, he drew a tiny pen drawing of a sad-looking child in the midst of a happy, busy group. I couldn't help believing that the drawings showed Erwin himself, feeling lost and alone in the midst of a class full of other children who all knew each other. Erwin's drawings taught me that it was important for him to have a sketchbook and pen at hand all the time. Drawing and sketching was obviously an effective way for him to feel centered, and to communicate, and it was one of the things he needed to have available to survive and thrive. Another aid for Erwin was puppetry.

You Can't Have Too Many Puppets

I have a large collection of puppets at school, and I frequently show children how to *make* a variety of puppets as well. I use these assorted creatures frequently in the classroom: to share news, to get attention, for comic relief, and for giving interesting lessons. Sometimes these puppets speak for me and sometimes they speak for the children. They are a great break from pressure and enable us all to let off steam through the words of someone (or something!) else. Once in a while when I have a class full of "wild things," I stop and chew out a puppet. The kids are typically both riveted and relieved. After all, *they* aren't the ones in trouble! We all get a much-needed laugh, and behavior and focus seem to improve when this happens.

Using puppets that talked and played for him enabled Erwin to briefly come out from behind his defenses and enjoy himself. He spoke in his home language and some bits of emerging English through these creatures.

Erwin is probably going to remain a child who does not socialize much and, as I've learned from researchers Fillmore and Snow (2002), this type of student is slower to acquire language than students who enjoy taking part in social activities. But the chance to use talking toys helped Erwin make some language progress as well as enjoy interacting with other children in meaningful activities. He was also quite good at making and inventing puppets, and this skill gave him his own special place in our classroom.

Puppets can be complicated, but many are extremely simple to make. Children like making them, and this is a satisfying and easy way for them to extend their supply of toys.

Mouth Puppets

Mouth puppets are a quick way to get kids and puppets talking. A simple folded piece of paper becomes a talkative critter when animal details are added. It can also become a book character or self-portrait. To make this puppet, follow these simple directions.

Materials

- Twelve-by-eighteen-inch construction paper (or nine-by-twelve-inch construction paper)

- Paper scraps

- Good "junk": sequins, glitter, fabric pieces, pipe cleaners, pom-poms, yarn, rickrack, and so on

- Paper plates (optional for body)

- White glue

Procedure

Fold the puppet paper in thirds the long way. I may prefold and then unfold the papers so that very young children can follow my directions and have a chance at creating the correct basic puppet structure. With second graders and above, I let the children do all the folding.

I always point out to students that when we fold something in thirds, the first edge is folded over and two parts *the same size* as the folded-over part remain unfolded. (See Figure 11–1.)

I ask students to fold the other edge over, matching it to the fold we already created so that the paper is now folded in three equal parts.

Figure 11–1

How to fold a mouth puppet.

These puppets yak and yak—
they get a lot of talk going!

Materials

Twelve-by-eighteen-inch or nine-by-twelve-inch construction
   paper or copy paper
Good scraps
Glue or glue stick

Procedure

1. Fold paper in thirds the
   long way. (Teacher may
   prefold paper and then open
   it flat. Kids find it easier to fold
   it this way the first time.)

2. Fold in half, with the open
   edges on the bottom.

3. Fold open ends to the center.
   This forms two pockets and
   a mouth. Stick thumb in
   bottom pocket and first
   three fingers in top pocket.
   Move fingers and thumb
   to make the puppet talk.

4. Add all kinds of scraps and items like feathers, sequins,
   and so on.

This paper, still folded in thirds, is now folded in half, top to bottom, with the folded edge on top. Now fold each open edge up to the middle, making four parts. This makes a zigzag and creates two pockets for a puppet mouth.

I demonstrate this procedure as I speak to the class, but I also have samples at each folded stage taped to the whiteboard for reference. (I am a native English speaker, but *I* have trouble making sense of spoken directions like these unless I see a visual that goes with the words. Children just learning English will have even more difficulties!)

When the child puts his fingers in one pocket made by the folded paper and his thumb in the other pocket, he can move and talk the puppet's mouth. Children enjoy personalizing their puppets by adding details:

- Puppet features: paper scraps, wiggle eyes, buttons, foil, pom-poms, fake fur, yarn, felt or fabric scraps

- Puppet body (optional): attach a paper plate, paper scraps or fabric

Children like to make these creatures talk. And it gives *them* practice too!

Make That Junk Come Alive!

One of my favorite classroom puppets evolved from a discussion with my kids at the beginning of a puppet-making unit. I wanted to prove to them that just about anything can be turned into a puppet. I grabbed a yellow plastic mug from a cupboard, stuffed some yarn in it, letting it overhang parts of the cup, and added features cut from felt scraps. I held the puppet by the mug handle and began to talk. As I did, the puppet's personality began forming right before our eyes! *She* became a very demanding, exotic, bossy character that the children named Madame Spaghetti. At a later date, I used a glue gun to secure the yarn and felt hair and features. This creature lived in our classroom for the rest of the year and was a consistent favorite with the kids!

Sock Puppets

We made sock puppets in the classroom with wooden skewers attached to move the knotted fabric arms. (I first cut off pointed skewer ends with scissors.) One of the most enthusiastic puppeteers, moving his creation wildly and speaking through it with a loud, clear voice, was Erwin, who usually had a little group of children working with him or taking part in his projects.

Sock puppets are easy to make. Materials are easy to come by, because everyone always has single unmatched socks!

Materials

- Unmatched socks, one per puppet

- Polyester foam filling (crunched-up paper scraps from the recycling bin may also be used)

- Rubber bands

- Wooden chopsticks or meat skewers (with points removed) from the supermarket

- Good junk: felt scraps, fabric scraps, yarn, wiggle eyes, pipe cleaners, and so on

Procedure

Fill the socks with polyester foam filling or other materials, and close them up with twisted rubber bands. Twist ties from the supermarket may also be used to secure the stuffed sock.

Create a puppet head by wrapping a narrow piece of fabric or cut sock material (about six inches long) around the sock partway down from the toe. Twist or knot this, leaving ends dangling to make arms. The area above the sock arms is the puppet head.

Attach a wooden chopstick or meat skewer (with points removed) to each arm by knotting the fabric around the wooden dowel, and you can make this puppet gesture as you talk for it. Add all kinds of scraps to create its personality!

Other Puppets

Here is a brief sampling of other simple and meaningful puppets for children to make (See Appendix, pages 221 and 222, for directions). Also, check out the book *The Muppets Make Puppets* by Cheryl Henson and the Muppet Workshop (1994) for a large variety of creative puppet ideas.

- Photo puppets: Cut out photos of children by cutting carefully around the outline of the person in the photo. Adhere photos to manila tagboard or cardboard. These may be laminated to prolong their use. Attach the photos to kraft sticks for very personal puppets.

- Small puppet theaters: Open a paper lunch bag and cut a hole in *one* side two or three inches from the bottom. Attach small paper cutout puppets to kraft sticks *at their heads*. Lower puppets into the bag feet first, and move sticks to make them perform. The scene may be viewed through the hole in the bag. Adjust the size of the cutout stage opening for better viewing. The outside of the bag may be decorated to create an interesting theater that reflects the puppet show theme. This is a great way for children to respond to specific pieces of literature. (See Figure 11–2.)

Figure 11–2
Assorted puppets.

■ Styrofoam puppets: Stick a kraft stick, chopstick, or dowel into a Styrofoam ball. Add all kinds of things: pinned-on felt features, feathers, and so on. Bodies may be added from fabric or felt. A low-temperature glue gun may be needed to attach items to the Styrofoam. Children show *me* what they want to attach, and *I* do the gluing. It is helpful to have extra glue guns and some adult volunteers available for this project. (See Figure 11–2.)

■ Paper roll ring puppets: These are easily made from a small ring cut from a paper towel roll (cut by the teacher, of course). Decorate the ring with features, hair, and so on. Hold one hand upright and drape a handkerchief, tissue, or piece of fabric over the top. Secure this with the paper roll ring. An easy, fast puppet to make. (See Figure 11–2.)

Body Puppets

Large paper grocery bags are the perfect base for creating supersized puppets. Children start with the bag flap side up, bag opening down. They create cut construction paper heads and features and glue them on the bag flap. Paper or wallpaper clothing and strips of crepe paper for arms and legs may be added. The kids love to trace and cut out their own hands and feet to make extra-detailed puppet figures.

To make these puppets wearable, attach a piece of yarn in the center of the bag flap and tie the bag around the puppeteer's neck. Staple a large rubber band into the end of each crepe-paper arm and leg. Just fold the crepe paper over the rubber band and staple, and this will provide a way to attach the crepe-paper limbs to the child's arms and legs.

We create these puppets to represent book characters, famous people in history, and workers in the community, not to mention ourselves. Children love to prop them up at desks in the classroom to greet parents on Back-to-School Night! (See Figure 11–3.) This puppet idea comes from Nancy Renfro, author of *Bags Are Big! A Paper Bag Craft Book* (1987).

Masks

Masks, much like puppets, give users a break from presenting their real faces. Masks are great things for students to hide behind when reading or performing. This can be especially helpful for language learners, who

often need a boost in confidence. (For a simple mask template and directions for making masks, see the Appendix, pages 223 and 224.) These masks can be decorated to represent any book character, historic figure, or culture. Animal masks and contemporary masks can be made this way too.

Construction paper or manila tagboard (old file folders) is just about all that is needed for masks. Stick on cut papers, use crayons to draw features, or put on any good junk or craft supplies to add to the fun. Masks can be attached to tongue depressors so that students can hold them in front of their faces, or they can be tied on with yarn or string.

The first project is a simple eyehole mask. Cut it out and add all kinds of interesting junk, including simple paper scraps. This mask pattern (see page 223) does not need to be tied on since flaps loop over ears. I show students how to layer paper by adding a piece of construction paper and then attaching an even smaller piece in such a way that the first paper leaves a colored border around the second one.

Another simple mask is formed from nine-by-twelve-inch or twelve-by-eighteen-inch construction paper. The first step is to create a mask base by cutting an oval from the paper. I ask my students to just cut off the corners of the paper. This makes a rough oval, and we still have some paper left to work with!

Figure 11–4
Assorted masks.

Now the mask is decorated with paper scraps, wallpaper, oil pastels, and so on. Geometric designs may be added to the mask. Cut out eye slits or holes.

When the mask is decorated, cut one-inch slits in the mask, as shown in Figure 11–4. Overlap the paper and staple. Now the base is three-dimensional. Children can attach a tongue depressor for a handheld mask or attach string to each side and tie the mask around their head.

Variation: Use manila tagboard for the mask base. Kids can decorate the mask with crayon designs. Brush over designs with a tempera wash—a mixture of one-half water, one-half tempera paint.

Other items can be added to enliven completed masks: sequins, glitter, feathers, raffia, yarn, and so on.

Meet the Mask or Puppet

An important component of these activities is the follow-up sharing time, when students get the chance to introduce their masks or puppet figures. A lot of good descriptions and vocabulary development evolve from these discussions. Kids are excited to talk and show off what they have made. These activities stretch their oral language and listening skills, build class community, and provide tempting opportunities for spontaneous use of language.

Drama

We have all kinds of drama experiences in class to liven things up and help learning take place. Children love to pretend, to become someone or something else. One of our favorite experiences is to just act things out informally. I reread a favorite story, and children play the roles of chosen parts. They speak the lines of the story any way they wish, and I feed them lines as well, if they want help. The result is a rough performance, but one that is very much enjoyed. One year children must have played Maurice Sendak's book *Pierre: A Cautionary Tale in Five Chapters and a Prologue* (1991) at least three times a week for three or four months. They never seemed to tire of it, and performances got better and better. For more information on this technique, see *Literacy from Day One* (Dragan 2001).

Children had a wonderful drama experience last year when we went on a field trip and they visited a "medieval castle." They were able to dress up, use cooking tools from days gone by, and act out a scene in an ancient castle kitchen. (See Figure 11–5.)

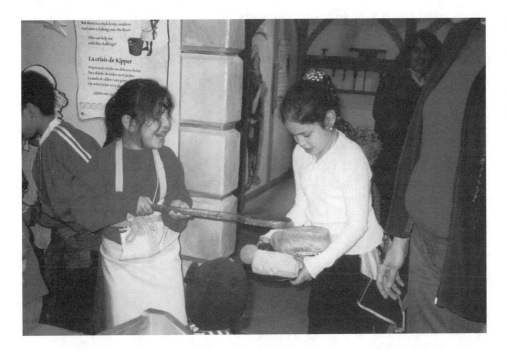

Figure 11–5
Rebecca and Kassy "cook" in a medieval castle kitchen.

Tableau

I also use an activity called tableau or tableau vivant. This method is the representation of a scene by a group of students posing silently and motionless. When we do tableau, children choose to play parts from a familiar text. They huddle up in a little group with an excerpt from a piece of literature. Then they decide how to play the scene, and they work collaboratively to plan a group pose.

When the tableau is ready, each actor takes a pose and freezes. Each participant takes on the role of one character. When I, as the magic director, tap a cast member with my magic wand, that child speaks the truth as she sees it and explains the scene from that particular character's point of view. Children also like to take turns being the magic director.

These performances are easy and quick, and they reflect comprehension and understanding of a written work as well as drama techniques. Students also get good practice in collaborative activities as well as lots of opportunities to talk over scenes to decide on the meaning of a literature excerpt and how best to convey it.

Puppet Theater Alternatives

I have a class puppet theater but have found in the past that children aren't sure how to use it, even though we practice. A typical puppet show used to consist of a few puppets hitting each other and making a few negative remarks. This wasn't terribly entertaining, and it was pretty hard on the puppets. This type of show also seemed to celebrate the kind of behavior we were trying to eliminate, not showcase.

Now I use the puppet theater for TV or radio dramas. These are great ways for children to practice reading aloud. When children go "on the air" at Radio Station B.O.O.K., they read to entertain an audience. Kids soon learn that they had better be pretty practiced and interesting readers to keep audience members in their seats! (See Figure 11–6.)

Figure 11–6
*Brenda reads to an
audience at Radio
Station B.O.O.K.*

Puppetry, masks, and dramatic activities are special ways to engage
with a story, to enter into the hearts of literary characters as well as the
hearts of the children we teach. These activities are also a wonderful,
exciting stimulus for acquiring language, and they give our students
ways to practice language on their own and with friends.

CHAPTER 12

Connecting with Families

Parents are the first, the best, and the most reliable teachers of their children. . . . A school that validates a student's home life and shows an appreciation for his or her parents or caregivers goes a long way toward building the student's sense of identity and self-esteem.

—Alma Flor Ada

Children Help with Family Communication

Ruchi looks puzzled as she stands next to the stroller where her baby brother babbles and waves his hands. She talks with her mother in Hindi and then speaks to her teacher in English. Everyone is a little confused, but then some parts of the conversation become clear. Ruchi is doing an important job: facilitating communication between her mother and her teacher.

Like Ruchi, María is six years old and has been helping her parents by translating for them ever since she can remember—probably at least since kindergarten or even preschool. Even though Ruchi and María have minimal command of English, they are able to provide important links between their families and teachers, storekeepers, and other English speakers in the community. Both children understand the rudiments of what is needed to help their parents. There may be a lot of fumbling and back-and-forth conversations between the child, the parents, and the teacher or person in the neighborhood. But most of the time, if everyone is patient, some meaning and understanding can be achieved. This is not an ideal situation, but it is a common one. A lot can be accomplished if everyone involved feels that the other parties are working to understand. These attempts to communicate go a long way toward developing good relationships between parents and teachers.

Forging Family Connections

We can all make a difference in the lives of our children and their families as we work together to help our students become lifelong learners. The first step is to create strong home–school connections with our children's families. Sometimes parents who do not speak English or do not speak it well may be reluctant to talk with their children's teachers. Many parents bring their children to school and pick them up afterward. My time before school is limited since I want to keep my focus on my students. I can manage just a small amount of time with a parent or two. The time after school is much more workable for me.

As children leave in the afternoon I sometimes see parents who look as if they wish to approach me but may not know how to speak to me. The trick for me is to approach them and just assume that we can connect. A lot of our communication may be done through gestures or showing things, or rudimentary language, as with Ruchi's and María's families, but this is a beginning.

Often parents will help with this crucial home–school link by bringing another adult to ask their questions and help translate. Older siblings can frequently be of help if they have learned some English.

Parent Conferences

Although I meet parents at our Back-to-School Night, our early October parent conferences are crucial links between home and school. They help us all see the big picture: how we can best work together to help each student learn and grow.

Getting kids ready for parent conferences is important work as well. I meet with children individually to talk with them before their parents come. I ask children about their progress and their feelings about how they are doing. I also ask if there is anything they would like me to tell their parents. When students have this preview of what is going to be said, it relieves a lot of anxiety. The kids are also welcome to attend the conferences.

I give students time to work on their portfolios—folders of special work they want to share. I make audiocassettes as well. Early in the year, I make one whole-group cassette recording of a couple of songs and poems to share when I meet with each parent. At the March parent conferences, parents are invited to listen to tapes of their own children reading. I give these tapes to families who would like to keep them.

Students also enjoy sharing phonics phones with their families. These are specially made devices to help children hear themselves read, segment, and blend words. These inexpensive tools are very helpful for practicing reading and for hearing the sounds of words when writing them. (Please see Resources, page 227, for source information.)

School Family

This process of working to connect with students' parents is all part of becoming a school family. The children know I care about them and their families, and they care about mine too. Early this year, when a truck hit my mother as she crossed in a crosswalk with her walker, my children were quite concerned. They made her drawings and notes at home and brought her small treasures. They seemed to have assigned themselves their own homework: making things for my mother. Almost every child came to school with a note or small picture, some repeatedly over a lengthy period of time. And this idea did not come from me!

One day during my mother's recuperation, María came to school with a crumpled and lumpy sealed envelope. These words were printed on top: "Givit tyuo Mom dan opendis le yor mom." (Give it to your Mom. Don't open this. Let your Mom.) Inside the envelope (I didn't open it!) was a clump of tangled pink beads (once a bracelet) and a folded paper airplane laboriously decorated with the word *Siderela* (Cinderella). My mom got a big kick out of this gift and was very touched. I was moved as well. And I also was delighted, because this was the first time María had created some original writing on her own, for her own important self-expression.

Another one of my sweet children, who spoke almost no English, handed me a brand-new baby doll one day and said, "For your mother."

This was one of the first times Beatríz had attempted to speak to me in English. The doll was probably her only Christmas present. I didn't want to take Beatríz's baby, but I didn't want to hurt her feelings either. "Shall I let my mother play with the doll today and bring it back to you tomorrow?" I asked her in English and again in Spanish. Beatríz beamed and nodded. The next day she gave me a brilliant smile and hugged her doll happily when I returned it to her.

First Teachers

One of the things I endeavor to stress with my students' families is the importance of the child's family and extended family in the learning process. Some of our parents have had limited formal education and want many more opportunities for their children. Some people may also feel a bit uncomfortable about the task of helping their offspring succeed academically. One of my most crucial jobs is to help validate the importance of the parent as the child's first teacher. I also want to convey my respect for every child's first language and culture.

I speak to parents about ways they can support children's learning at home. The first thing I stress is the importance of read-aloud time, in English or the child's home language. Some parents may be unable to read in English and reluctant to read in their native language. I have had several parents tell me they thought they shouldn't read to their child in a language other than English since their child was learning English. These parents needed to be reassured that reading to children in their home language is a *wonderful* thing to do! It helps children develop their first language and teaches skills that will transfer to English as well. And there's nothing like the joyful experience of being read to by someone you love.

Many children are fortunate to have several generations available to read aloud to them: grandparents, parents, brothers, sisters, cousins, aunts, and uncles. I ask that *everyone* read to the children, and talk with them, listen to them, and tell them special family stories. All of this promotes literacy—and humanity—in the most beautiful ways. (See Figure 12–1.)

For more about reading aloud to children, please see *Literacy from Day One* (Dragan 2001).

Figure 12–1
Tiana and her Uncle George love sharing stories together.

Helping Children Value Family Learning and Family Language

A special goal of mine each year is to help my first graders value the things they can learn from their families. Once in a while at school I begin a discussion and brainstorm with my children some great things they have learned at home. The kids love to share these stories and I think talking about home learning helps validate it!

Occasionally, parents tell me that their son or daughter will no longer willingly speak their home language. Often parents and grandparents are quite distressed about this. I try to mediate the situation by telling children how important it is that they keep up their language skills so that they can talk to members of their families.

I tell about how much harder it is for me to talk with my mother, who is deaf, when I do not keep up with practicing sign language. And I tell them my dad's story about not being able to speak with or understand his grandmother from Fife, Scotland, when he was a little boy. Fife has its own vernacular, called Fife tongue. At the time my dad was small, this dialect was very hard for outsiders to understand. My father was always sorry that no one in his predominantly Irish family could help him learn enough to bridge that Fife language barrier.

At times, my encouragement may be all that is needed to get children working on keeping up their home language skills (as well as working on language acquisition!). I do work on this subtly in the classroom throughout the year, by reading some stories in Spanish and English and even Tagalog. There are several phonetically written picture books that enable me to read Tagalog that also have the matching text in English. And of course, I rely heavily on the pictures. I think my approval of and interest in speaking and reading other languages help children see value and worth in maintaining their own.

I also like to share incidents in my own life when I have surprised Spanish or Italian speakers on trips by being able to converse and unexpectedly join into conversations no one thought by looking at me that I would possibly be able to understand. I tell my kids about people's gasps of surprise, and that this was like having secret powers no one thought I had. All these extra skills we have are powerful and can make a big difference in the directions in which our lives take us.

A Little Language Goes a Long Way

Ho Sun was my new Korean student. She entered school near the beginning of the school year, but I had no advance notice, and thus I had not gathered any helpful background information about her language and culture. Had I known ahead of time, I could have attempted to locate a volunteer Korean translator and looked up information on the Internet and in the library. I would also have tried to obtain a few Korean picture books and a picture dictionary (see Resources, page 222, for sources). Since Ho Sun spoke no English, nor did her parents, there was no possibility of my new student doing any translating for me.

When I spoke with Ho Sun's mother after school—or tried to—I learned that she spoke a few words of English. We used those up rapidly. The two of us mimed and gestured, and I showed her some of the work her daughter would be doing. Although we didn't really understand each other, the main feeling was one of caring and goodwill. And that was somehow enough, for a start.

I spoke with a Korean priest I know who shared with me some Korean writing and a few phrases I could say. I learned to write both Ho Sun's and her little sister Hee Sun's names in Korean calligraphy. I practiced saying phrases such as "Welcome," "How are you?" "Hello," "Good-bye," and "Thank you" in Korean. The following week when I sent home the parent conference appointment forms, I wrote Ho Sun's name in calligraphy. Her mother checked the box to indicate she would attend the conference. She wrote an arrow next to her daughter's name, and the word "Wonderful!" I loved this, but my favorite moment occurred when she came into the classroom for her appointment. When I greeted her in Korean, this quiet and composed lady actually screamed. Then she gave me a big hug.

I felt pleased with my attempts to welcome Ho Sun and her family through the use of Korean phrases and calligraphy. A side effect of working to speak to both children and their parents in their home language is helping families—especially children—*value* their language and realize that other people in the world value it too.

Making the Parent-Student-Teacher Conference Work

Although Ho Sun could not speak English, she was able to be an important part of our parent-student-teacher conference. She showed her work and some of the books we were reading and explained things to her mother in her home language. I felt it was a very successful meeting. The following year when I had Hee Sun in class, Ho Sun was able to translate for me. But Hee Sun held her own. She shared her work with her mother and explained it in Korean and a little English. The girls' mother had learned some English, which made things easier as well. More than actual language, the *willingness* of people to try to understand each other made good things happen!

Family Homework

One way to celebrate families and cultural diversity is to provide opportunities for families to write and draw together and share something personal from their culture: a recipe, a game, a special toy or artifact or experience. A collection of this work may be put together for a class book or reproduced for families.

Of course, the easiest way is to just assemble the work as it comes back to school, make a cover, and bind the book. Children enjoy sharing their family experiences. For a more sophisticated offering, work can be typed, illustrated, and put together to make a book for each family. This decision depends on time and availability of paper and copy machines. I find sometimes that it is well worth doing things the more simple way because they get done in a timely fashion. Children can take turns taking a *Family Book* home to share. (See Figure 12–2.)

Family Literacy Club

At my school several teachers work together to present family literacy events for children and parents. Typically we hold meetings after school, targeting one grade level at a time. We usually begin with a series of meetings for first-grade parents, and then a kindergarten series, and then a second-grade series. When time allows, we plan a program for upper-grade students and parents as well. Occasionally, we hold an evening event, since not every interested parent is free during the day.

Evening programs are especially fun because we set up literacy centers in the multiuse room for children to attend with their parents. Here is a brief list of some of the centers we have put together:

- Read-aloud center, with a couch, cozy lamp, and lots of books

- Word and phonics games, outlined with tape on the floor of the room

- Bookmaking centers

- Family dioramas and writing

- Center for writing family stories together

- Board games to reinforce literacy skills

FAMILY HOMEWORK FOR JANUARY 30.
A Special Celebration in Our Family
 Please return Monday, if possible. Thank you!

TAREA DE LA FAMILIA POR 30 DE ENERO.
Una Celebracíon en nuestra familia
 Favor de devolverla el lunes, si es posible. ¡Gracias!

We celebrate Easter, and my Birthday together.
We color easter eggs and have an easter egg hunt.
The whole Family has a BBQ and we all eat. We then
have the pinatas, cake, and then I open my presents.

Figure 12–2 *Jazmin's family homework page.*

Figure 12–3
Juan and Maria love picking out a book to keep.

- Word center with shaving cream and cookie sheets for tracing letters, practicing letter sounds, and writing words

- Center for making lists together

- Center for collecting words in a special word book

Each session has a specific literacy focus. It would also work to have one evening or afternoon session with several centers on a single topic, such as making books. A highlight of each session is the gift of a book for every child. (See Figure 12–3). For more about setting up family literacy programs, see *Everything You Need to Know to Teach First Grade* (Dragan 2003).

Using Families as a Resource

Connecting with families is one of the most powerful things we do to help our students succeed. And siblings can be some of the best resources of all. I occasionally meet with a few brothers and sisters—sometimes at parent conferences—to ask for their brief assistance with children in my class. I show these older students some quick, simple read-aloud

Figure 12–4
Alfonzo and his big sister head home together.

tips; how to choral-read (read aloud *with* a brother or sister, while pointing to the words, letting the younger child say what words he or she can); how to work on math problems with manipulatives, such as pennies or dried beans; and so on. I suggest a tutoring or read-aloud time limit of about ten to fifteen minutes and say that they can use a kitchen timer to keep track of the time. In this way, family helpers won't feel burdened.

As educators, we struggle against many odds to make it possible for our children to learn and thrive; it is worth making the effort to explore all avenues of help. In the words of our twenty-sixth president, Theodore Roosevelt, "Do what you can, where you are, with what you have."

"I Like" Self-Portrait Template
Inverview Grid
Thought Balloon
Celebration Banners
"Who Took the Cookie from the Cookie Jar?" Booklet Template
Hundreds Day Kites
Kite Pattern
Artistic License
Scene or Museum Boxes
Poetry Frame
Mandala
"I Was Born to" Booklet Template
K-W-L Chart
Web Template 1
Web Template 2
Leaf Prints
Eight-Page Booklets
Eight-Page Pop-Up Books
Simple Hand Puppets
Cup Theaters or Habitats with Puppets
Mask Template
Masks

"I Like" Self-Portrait Template

200

Interview Grid

Name _____ **Date** _____

Home Language	Age	Favorite color
Language Level	Birthday	Favorite food
Family	Friends	Favorite game
Favorite toy	Favorite thing to do	
Teacher Notes: Listening	Speaking	
Reading	Writing	

Thought Balloon

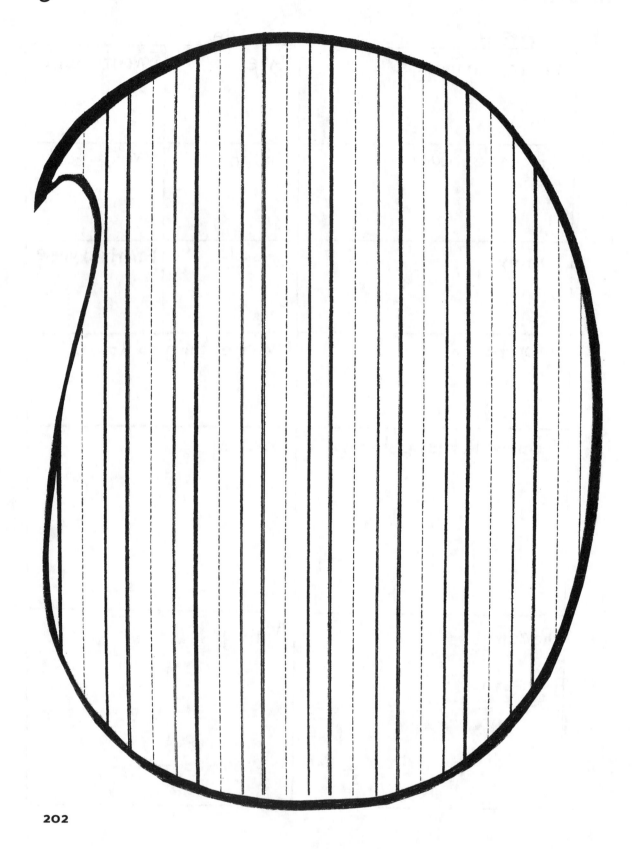

202

Celebration Banners

Use with *Children Just Like Me: Celebrations!* by Anabel and Barnabas Kindersley (New York: DK Children, 1997). Share the book and discuss celebrations in many parts of the world. Children love sharing their own celebrations!

Materials

Twelve-by-eighteen-inch construction paper in an
    assortment of colors
Six-inch squares of white construction paper (or nine-by-
    twelve-inch pieces)
Marking pens and/or crayons
Stapler
Optional: tissue strips, cut thin

Procedure

1. Discuss celebrations, especially children's own special days. I like to send home a paper asking parents to sit with children and write about a special family celebration together on a piece of white construction paper. The child illustrates the paper. These papers become a class display and sometimes a class book.

2. Each child draws one or more celebrations and glues the paper or papers to the twelve-by-eighteen-inch paper. Fold the top over for hanging.

3. The bottom can be scalloped or cut in decorative points or children's own invented designs. Tissue streamers may be added. These are very festive and meaningful to the kids. The more freedom they have in making their creations, the better!

Personal writing may be displayed on the back of the banners.

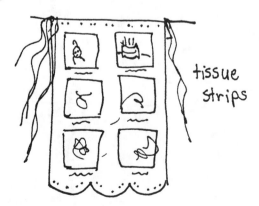

tissue strips

"Who Took the Cookie from the Cookie Jar!" Booklet Template

Who took the cookie from the cookie jar?

Who took the cookie from the cookie jar?

_____ took the cookie from the cookie jar!

Not me! Couldn't be!

Who Took the Cookie from the Cookie Jar?

Written and Illustrated by

Then who?

Hundred's Day Kites

This kite is a very versatile project. Make with red copy paper for Chinese New Year or Valentine's Day. Vary the color and design to suit any theme.

Materials

Copy paper, one piece per kite
Straws, one per kite
Length of light string, one to two yards per kite
Crepe-paper strips, one per kite (Cut folded crepe
    paper into 1½-inch strips.)
Marking pens, crayons, or colored pencils
Transparent tape
Paper punch
Optional: kite pattern

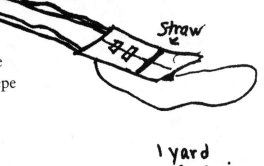

Procedure

1. Fold a piece of copy paper in half the long way ("hot dog" fold).

2. Make a three-fourth-inch or one-inch fold on the folded edge, as shown.

3. Open the paper, leaving the one-inch fold still folded. Tape the paper with two or three pieces of transparent tape on the front. This joins the front panel, leaving a "pleat"

Continues

Hundred's Day Kites (Continued)

4. Decorate the kite with marking pens, crayons, or colored pencils. Stamp with marking pens in ten groups of ten pictures for Hundreds Day decorations.

5. Refold the paper so that the pleat is even in the middle of the kite. Tape a straw to the top side of the kite, about 3½ inches down from the top edge. Trim the straw to fit the kite.

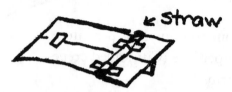

6. With a paper punch, make two holes in the pleated part of the kite, one on each side of the straw. One hole should be 1¾ inches from the top of the paper. The other hole should be 4¼ inches from the top of the paper.

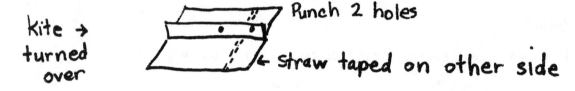

7. Tie one end of the length of light string to each hole in the kite to form a loop. Cut one full strip of crepe paper (1½ inches wide) in half. Attach both strips to the bottom of the kite with transparent tape. Run and fly—no fail!

Note: More string may be used. A second length of string can be attached to the string loop.

Kites may be decorated during the assembly process or when they are completed. Vary color and decorations to suit themes, literature books, holidays, and celebrations.

Kite Pattern

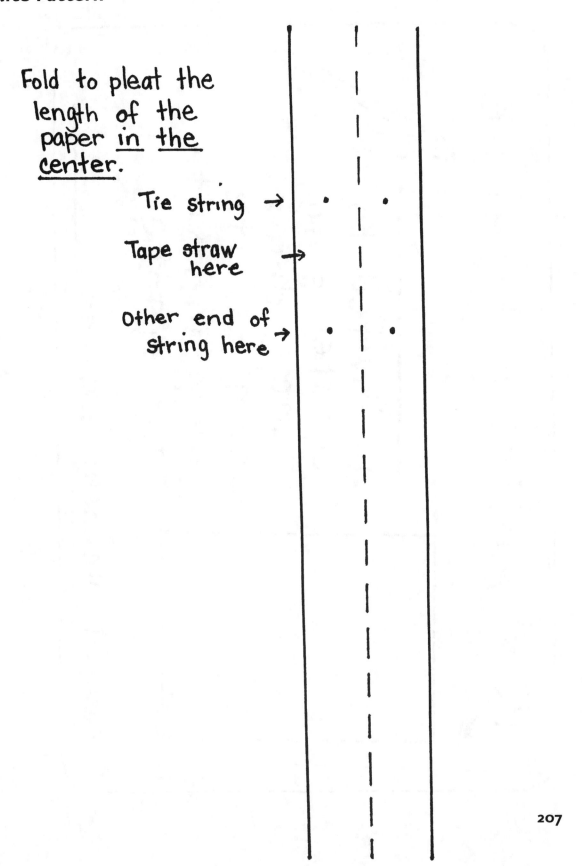

Fold to pleat the length of the paper <u>in</u> <u>the</u> <u>center.</u>

Tie string →

Tape straw here →

Other end of string here →

207

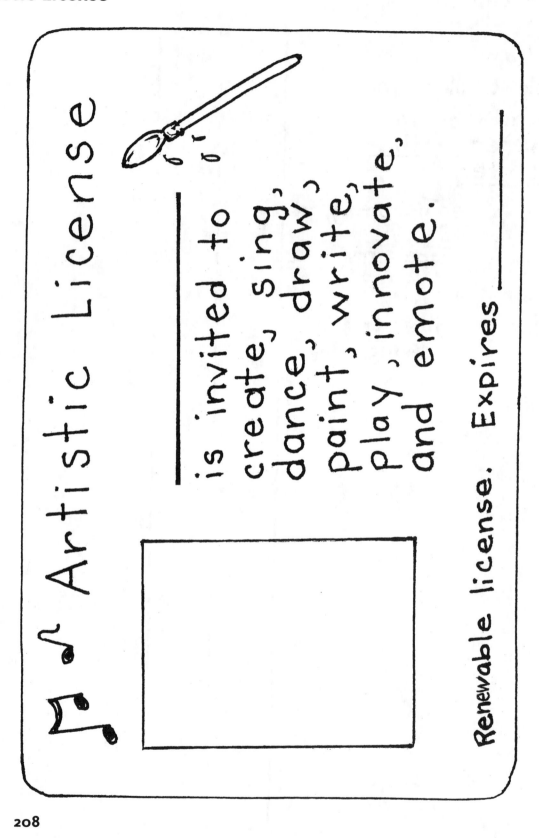

Artistic License

♪ ♫ Artistic License

_____

is invited to create, sing, dance, draw, paint, write, play, innovate, and emote.

Renewable license. Expires _____

Scene or Museum Boxes

This craft project can be a personal museum or a thematic one focused on individual interests or scenes from literature books. Photo art, magazine cutouts, and all kinds of two- and three-dimensional materials may be attached or put on display. At the beginning of the school year, my class sometimes chooses to create a box for each letter of the alphabet, with pictures and words attached. Other years children opt to make personal, individual museum boxes.

Materials

Twelve-by-eighteen-inch construction paper
Glue or stapler
Crayons, pens, paper scraps, old magazines
Personal photos or photocopies of photos
Personal items if children wish

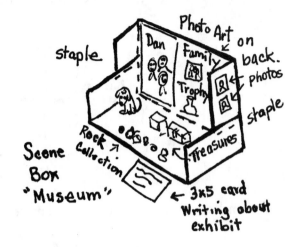

Brainstorm with students the concept of a museum. I share museum books such as *Let's Go to the Museum,* by Lisl Weil (1989); *Visiting the Art Museum,* by Laurene Krasney Brown and Marc Brown (1990); and *Make Your Own Museum,* a kit by Belioli (1999).

Students may decorate their museums to show off their own interests, abilities, favorite activities, foods, and so on. They may use crayons, pens, paper scraps, magazine pictures, and other items.

Optional: Allow students to bring small items from home, such as photos, small knick-knacks, and so on.

Be sure to allow time daily for children to add to and visit the museums. This activity will generate a lot of conversation, helping children to really get to know each other.

Students may also write or dictate information to be placed on three-by-five-inch cards to explain their creations.

Continues

Scene or Museum Boxes (Continued)

Procedure for Making Box

Teachers may wish to prefold these boxes for younger students.

1. Fold a piece of construction paper in half the long way. Open paper.

2. Fold three-inch flaps on each end, and cut as shown.

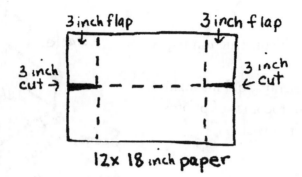

3. Bend at folds and staple to assemble, overlapping sides and bottom.

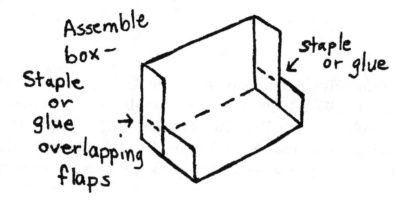

Poetry Frame

Mandala

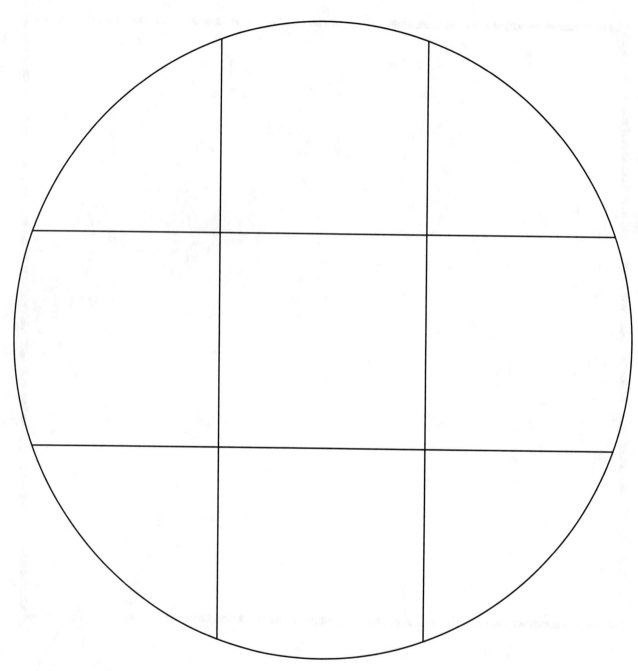

Design Symbols:

"I Was Born to" Booklet Template

I was born to _____.

I was born to _____.

I Was Born to _____

Written and Illustrated by _____

I was born to _____.

213

K-W-L Chart

K	W	L
Knows	Wants to Know	Learned

Web Template 1

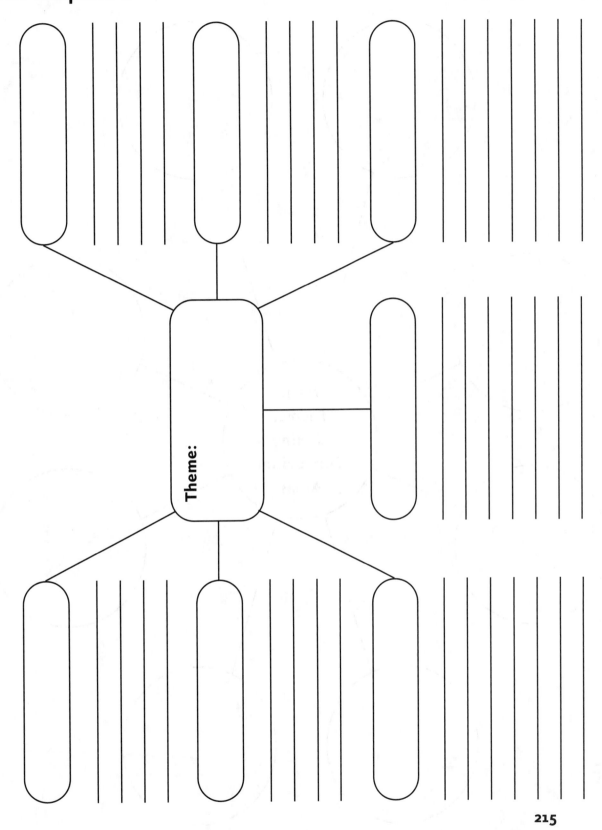

Theme:

215

Web Template 2

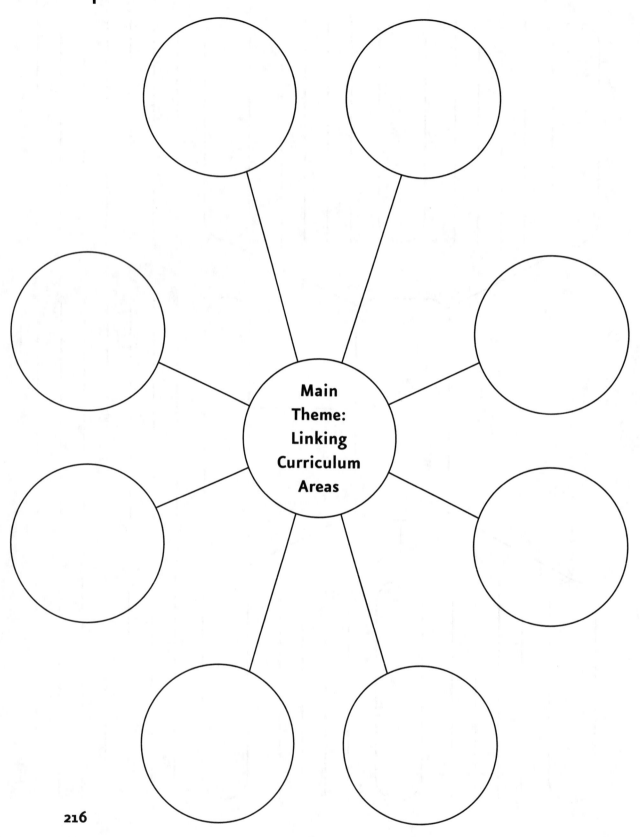

Main Theme: Linking Curriculum Areas

Leaf Prints

To make leaf prints, you need a few leaves; middle-sized leaves are just right. Save that old telephone book when your new one comes. Put the leaves you collect between the pages. Newsprint absorbs moisture and the sheer weight of all those pages will help the leaves dry nice and flat.

I store the telephone book between seasons. However, I don't save pressed leaves long. It's best to print leaves within a week or two, before they become too crumbly to use.

Materials

Leaves that have been pressed flat in an old telephone book

Newspapers to cover the work area

Newspaper pages, cut in halves or fourths (Use to cover painted leaves while making prints.)

Tempera paint on paper plates or in recycled margarine tubs (I put out red, orange, yellow, blue, and brown paint.)

Paintbrushes

Twelve-by-eighteen-inch construction paper in assorted colors (prefer black, purple, magenta, orange, and dark blue paper for this project)

Paper towels

Empty half-gallon milk carton, with top cut off, for storing brushes

Setup

I prefer to do leaf prints with just two to four children at a time. Other students may be doing different projects with leaves, independent reading, sketching in sketchbooks, or a multitude of other activities.

I cover a table with newspapers and then set up painting places. Each place has a couple of sheets of newspaper to work on, with a folded paper towel on the top right and a paintbrush resting on the towel. (Put the towel and brush on the left for lefties.) I put the telephone book, with some extra leaves inside, in the center of the table. I also place leaves to print and four or five paper plates with tempera paint in the center as well. I keep extra paper towels and a wastebasket nearby.

I like to leave the tempera out on the plates for a half hour or so before printing. This isn't crucial, but it thickens the paint and makes it a little tacky, which is more suitable for making prints.

Continues

Leaf Prints (Continued)

Paper plates and paint may be wrapped in the newspapers and tossed out at the end of the printing session without making a mess. Leaves, even used ones as long as they're *dry,* can be collected in the pages of the telephone book. The sink is nearby. Resting in it is a half-gallon milk carton with the top cut off. This is a great place to put dirty brushes.

Procedure

Children choose a piece of colored construction paper to print on and put their name on the back. I show them how to place a leaf vein side up on newspaper, and paint the leaf with one or more tempera colors. I demonstrate how to wipe the paintbrush clean with a paper towel before I change paint colors.

Next the children place the painted leaf on construction paper, paint side down. They cover the leaf with a piece of newspaper or a ripped-out telephone book page and press. Throw away the piece of newspaper, with the paint folded inward. (I do this messy part. It keeps our printing area clean while children are focused on creating.) I demonstrate how to lift up the leaf to "pull" the print.

Children may print until they are satisfied with their finished product. It's usually only necessary to paint the leaf once or twice to fill the construction paper with prints or create a pleasing composition. Some of the most interesting finished prints have only light tracings of leaves, with not much paint residue. These partial prints have great texture.

Leave the final leaf-print paper to dry. Cut *dry* leaf-print papers to ten inches by eighteen inches. I do this trimming on the paper cutter. The scraps I cut off are one inch by twelve inches; we staple or glue these on top and bottom of the printed paper to trim the leaf print. These strips are an easy way to frame the prints and turn the artwork into a "canvas." The result is very sophisticated-looking.

When the leaf-print papers and leaves are dry, children may wish to have a leaf—the printing tool—pinned on their print. I use a straight pin. Leaf poetry may also be attached on either side of the leaf-print artwork.

1 inch by 12 inch contrasting trim

10 inch by 18 inch background paper

How to Make an 8-Page Book
from a Single Piece of Paper

Fold paper as shown:

1.  "Hot dog" fold. Open.

2.  "Hamburger" fold. Open.

3. Fold both edges to center fold.

↑ center fold

4. 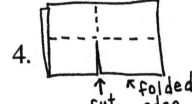 Open and cut.

↑ cut   ↖ folded edge

5. Open and refold.

fold↓ cut↓ cut↓ fold↓

6. 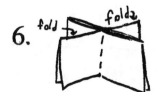 Push in ends and fold up. Presto: a booklet!

fold↓ fold↓

219

Eight-Page Pop-Up Books

Eight-page books may have as many as three pop-up pages. Pop-up boxes are cut on *inside folds* as shown. Cut boxes and refold. Push pop-up boxes through to the front side of the book.

Unfold booklet

1.
back cover →

front cover →

book pop-up

box pop-up (fold, then cut!)

face, globe, snowman, etc.

Fold and cut each pop-up. Fold on pop-up dotted lines. Refold book. Push out pop-ups.

Cut pop-up boxes on inside folds. Do *not* cut a pop-up box in the cover fold. (This is an *outside fold*.)

2.

Fold over to cut pop-ups
↓

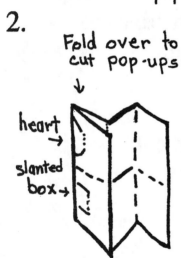

heart →

slanted box →

All kinds of pop-up boxes can be cut into folds: book shapes, box shapes, hearts, faces, and so on. Just be sure to leave the box *attached* or you will have holes!

Simple Hand Puppets

Materials:

Piece of fabric, tissue, or handkerchief,
  one per craft
Paper rolls cut in slices about 1½ inches
  wide (by adult, ahead of time), one per craft
All kinds of good junk: foil, sequins, feathers,
  buttons, scissors, white glue, and so on

Procedure

1. Each child finds a piece of fabric or handkerchief to place over her or his hand, with fingers pointing up. Place the paper roll over two or three fingers to form the puppet's head.

2. Now decorate the puppet. This is very simple and lots of fun. The puppet comes apart when the child removes his or her hand but it is easy to reassemble.

Cup Theater or Habitat with Puppets

This puppet theater craft has a pop-up
puppet. Children love to personalize these.
The theater and puppets are a great way to respond
to any piece of literature, personal event, or
holiday. A box may be used instead of a cup.

Paper cup base

Materials

Paper or foam cups, one per project
Paper puppets
Popsicle sticks or straws, one long straw per puppet
Paper scraps
Scissors
Glue or transparent tape
Crayons and marking pens

Procedure

1. Poke a hole in the center of the bottom of the cup
   (or box).

2. Insert the stick or straw. Make a puppet and attach
   it with transparent tape or glue to the top of the
   straw.

3. Pull the straw down to make the puppet disappear;
   push it up to make the puppet reappear.

4. The container may be decorated to create a habitat
   for the puppet: a goldrush town, fairy tale castle,
   and so on.

City scene on a cup

Variation: A book may be used instead of a cup or box. Stand the book upright, and have
the puppet perform over the top of the cover. The book may be used with the cover showing
or with pages of the story and specific illustrations showing.

Mask Template

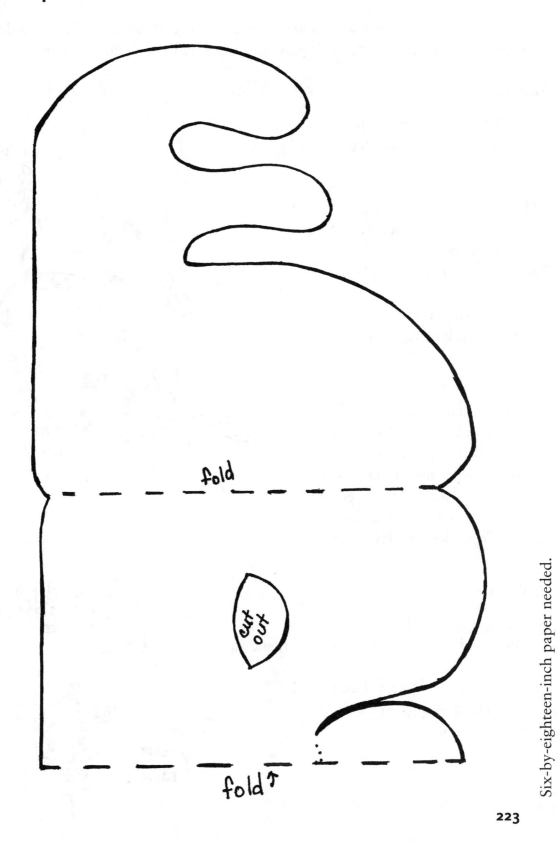

Half-Mask Pattern—Use on manila tagboard or construction paper base.

fold

cut out

fold ↑

Six-by-eighteen-inch paper needed.
Decorate with scraps, feathers, pens, and so on.

223

Masks

Masks give students a chance to act out anonymously, borrowing another face. Children who may not wish to speak much often find masks a great way to perform and play.

Materials

Nine-by-twelve-inch or twelve-by-
  eighteen-inch construction paper
Stapler
Scissors
Glue
Paper scraps and any other available
  decorative items
Tongue depressors for handheld
  masks
Yarn for tie-on masks
Optional: raffia or yarn for hair

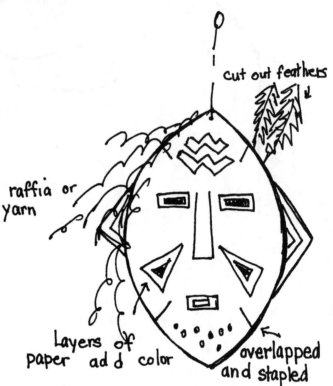

cut out feathers

raffia or yarn

Layers of paper add color

overlapped and stapled

Procedure

1. Create a mask base from construction paper. To create the base, cut an oval from paper. (*Note:* Other shapes may also be cut.) Add details with paper scraps, wallpaper, oil pastels, and so on. Geometric designs may be added to the mask.

2. Cut out eye slits.

3. Cut four slits as shown. Overlap the paper where slits are cut, and staple.

   Overlap; glue, or staple; add slits

   Now the mask is three-dimensional. Add a tongue depressor for a hand-held mask.

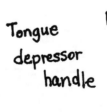

Tongue depressor handle

224

Resources

Professional Organizations

International Reading Association (IRA)
800 Barksdale Road, PO Box 8139, Newark, DE 19714-8139
Online: www.reading.org

National Council of Teachers of English (NCTE)
1111 West Kenyon Road, Urbana, IL 61801-1096
Phone: 877-369-6283 Online: www.ncte.org

Teachers of English to Speakers of Other Languages, Inc. (TESOL)
700 South Washington Street, Suite 200, Alexandria, VA 22314
Phone: 703-836-0774 Fax: 703-836-7864 or 703-836-6447
Email: info@tesol.org (general information) Online: www.tesol.org

National Association for Bilingual Education (NABE)
1030 Fifteenth Street, NW Suite 470, Washington, DC 20005
Phone: 202-898-1829 Fax: 202-789-2866 Email: nabe@nabe.org

Professional Magazines

The Hornbook Guide to Children's and Young Adult Books. Published twice a
    year by The Horn Book, Inc., 56 Roland Street, Suite 200, Boston, MA 02129

The Horn Book Magazine. Published six times a year by The Horn Book, Inc.

The Horn Book Guide Online—www.hornbookguide.com

Book Links. Published six times a year. PO Box 615, Mt. Morris, IL 61054-7566
Phone: 888-350-0950 Fax: 815-734-5858 Online (new orders): blnk@kable.com

School Library Journal. 245 West Seventeenth Street, New York, NY 10011
Phone: 800-959-1066

Instructor Magazine. Published eight times a year.
Phone: 800-544-2917 or 800-959-1676 (Magazineline)
Online: www.scholastic.com/Instructor or www.magazineline.com

Arts and Activities. Published ten times a year.
Phone: 619-819-4520 Online: www.artsandactivities.com

School Arts and Activities. Published nine times a year.
Phone: 800-533-2847

Classroom Book Club

Scholastic Book Club. Phone: 800-SCHOLASTIC (800-724-6527)

Magazines for Children

Highlights for Children. Online: www.highlights.com

National Geographic World. National Geographic Society, Washington, DC 20036

Ranger Rick. National Wildlife Association, 8925 Leesburg Pike, Vienna, VA 22184
Online: www.nwf.org/nwf

Zoobooks. Wildlife Education Ltd., 12233 Thatcher Court, Poway, CA 92064-6880
Online: www.zoobooks.com

Commercial Products Mentioned in the Text

Post Office Boxes for a Class Mail Center   Calloway House has a large variety of
   fiberboard organizers, such as the post office boxes I use in my classroom.

Calloway House, Inc., 451 Richardson Drive, Lancaster, PA 17603-4098
Phone: 800-233-0290 Fax: 717-299-6754

Adhesive Material for Hanging Charts   I use Fun Tac reuseable adhesive to hang
   artwork and put artwork together (affixing parts of a mural on background
   paper, affixing illustrations to charts, and so forth). Similar products are available at teacher supply stores and hardware stores.

DAP Inc., 2400 Boston Street, Suite 200, Baltimore, MD 21224-4775
Phone: 800-543-3840, x2804 or 888-327-8477 Online: www.DAP.com

Phonics Phones $48 per case, twenty-four phonics phones per case

CANDL Foundation, PO Box 18623, Huntsville, AL 35804
Phone: 800-633-7212 Online: www.phonicsphone.org

Puppets

Folkmanis, Inc: Furry Folk and Folktales, 1219 Park Avenue, Emeryville, CA
    94608
Online: www.folkmanis.com

Other Classroom Supplies

Lakeshore Learning Materials, 2695 E. Dominguez St., Carson, CA 90810
Phone: 800-421-5354 Online: www.lakeshorelearning.com

Art Education Prints and Transparencies

AllPosters.com
Phone: 888-654-0143

Davis Art Images

50 Portland Street, Worcester, MA 01608-2013
Toll Free: 800-533-2847, x253 Fax: 508-831-9260
Email: das@davis-art.com

Shorewood Art Prints

Crystal Productions
PO Box 2159, Glenview, IL 60025
Toll Free: 800-255-8629 Fax: 800-657-8149
Email: custserv@crystalproductions.com

Children's Bilingual Dictionaries
and Language Resources

Keyes, J. R. 1998. *The Oxford Picture Dictionary for Kids* (English/Spanish
    Edition). London, UK: Oxford University Press.
Turhan, S. 2003. *Milet Picture Dictionary* (Chinese-English). London, UK: Milet
    Publishing Ltd.
———. 2003. *Milet Picture Dictionary* (Farsi-English). London, UK: Milet
    Publishing Ltd.
———. 2003. *Milet Picture Dictionary* (Korean-English). London, UK: Milet
    Publishing Ltd.
    Note: Milet publishes bilingual dictionaries in many languages.
See also ESL bilingual online link: www.milet.com/dictionaries.asp

Catalogs and References for Books About Other
Cultures and Bilingual Resources

African-American Books for Children
Online: www.bookladder.com

Asian American Curriculum Project, Inc.
529 East Third Avenue, San Mateo, CA 94401
Phone: 650-375-8286 or 800-874-2242 Fax: 650-375-8797
Email: www.aacpinc@asianamericanbooks.com

Mariuccia Iaconi Book Imports (Spanish and English language books
    for children K–12)
970 Tennessee Street, San Francisco, CA 94107
Phone: 800-955-9577 or 415-821-1216 (Bay Area) Fax: 415-821-1596
Email: mibibook@pacbell.net Online: www.mibibook.com

Shen's Books
40951 Fremont Boulevard, Fremont, CA 94538
Phone: 800-456-6660 Fax: 560-668-1057
Online: www.shens.com

References

Chapter 1

Professional Books

Ada, A. 2002. *A Magical Encounter: Latino Children's Literature in the Classroom*. 2d ed. Needham Heights, MA: Allyn & Bacon.
Krashen, S. 2003. *Explorations in Language Acquisition and Use*. Portsmouth, NH: Heinemann.

Children's Books

Ada, A. 1995. *My Name Is María Isabel*. Illus. K. Thompson. Reprint ed. New York: Aladdin.
Ajemera, M., et al. 2001. *Children from Australia to Zimbabwe: A Photographic Journey Around the World*. Revised ed. Washington, DC: Shakti for Children.
Aliki. 1998. *Marianthe's Story: Painted Words, Spoken Memories*. New York: Greenwillow.
Browne, A. 2003. *The Shape Game*. New York: Farrar, Straus and Giroux.
Burningham, J. 2003. *Would You Rather?* Reprint ed. New York: Seastar.
Garza, C. L. 1990. *Family Pictures/Cuadros de familia*. San Francisco: Children's Book.
Kindersley, A., and B. Kindersley. 1995. *Children Just Like Me*. New York: DK Children.
Krauss, R. 1989. *A Hole Is to Dig*. Illustrated by M. Sendak. Reprint ed. New York: HarperTrophy.
Milne, A. A. 1989. *Pooh's Library: Winnie-the-Pooh, The House at Pooh Corner, When We Were Very Young, Now We Are Six*. Illus. E. Shepard. Reissue ed. New York: Dutton.
Ross, D. 1972. *I Love My Love with an A*. London, UK: Faber and Faber.
Schwartz, A. 2003. *What James Likes Best*. New York: Atheneum/Richard Jackson.

Sendak, M. 1991. *Pierre: A Cautionary Tale in Five Chapters and a Prologue.* Reprint ed. New York: HarperTrophy.
Wolfe, G. 2004. *Look! Body Language in Art.* London, UK: Frances Lincoln Children's.

Children's Books for Self-Esteem

Bottner, B. 1997. *Bootsie Barker Bites.* Illus. P. Rathmann. New York: Paper Star.
Burningham, J. 1993. *Avocado Baby.* Reissue ed. New York: HarperCollins.
Carlson, N. 1990. *I Like Me!* Reprint ed. New York: Penguin Putnam.
———. 1999. *ABC I Like Me!* New York: Puffin.
Curtis, J. L. 2002. *I'm Gonna Like Me: Letting Off a Little Self-Esteem.* New York: Joanna Cotler.
Deacon, A. 2002. *Slow Loris.* La Jolla, CA: Kane/Miller.
Henkes, K. 1991. *Chrysanthemum.* New York: Greenwillow.
Jordan, D., with R. Jordan. 2003. *Salt in His Shoes.* New York: Aladdin.
Kraus, R. 1994. *Leo the Late Bloomer.* Reissue ed. New York: HarperCollins.
Lester, H. 1999. *Hooway for Wodney Wat.* New York: Houghton/Walter Lorraine.
Lewis, E. B., illus. 2005. *This Little Light of Mine.* New York: Simon & Schuster Books for Young Readers.
Lionni, L. 2002. *Frederick and His Friends: Four Favorite Fables.* Book and CD ed. New York: Knopf.
Rathmann, P. 1997. *Ruby the Copycat.* New York: Scholastic.

Children's Recordings for Self-Esteem

Archambault, J., and D. Plummer. 1997. *Baby Eagles Standard Book.* Denver, CO: SRA/McGraw-Hill.
———. 1999. *I'm a Can-Do Kid and Other Self-Esteem Building Songs & Activities.* Huntington Beach, CA: Creative Teaching.
———. 2000. CD. *Grandmother's Garden (Magical Miracle Me).* Huntington Beach, CA: Youngheart Music, Inc.
Thomas, M. and Friends. 1983. CD. *Free to Be . . . You and Me.* Colart, Producer. New York: Arista.

Books on Sign Language

Charlip, R., and M. B. Miller. 1987. *Handtalk.* New York: Aladdin.
Flodin, M. 1991. *Signing for Kids.* Berkeley, CA: Berkeley Publishing/Perigee.
Kramer, J., and T. Ovadia. 2001. *You Can Learn Sign Language.* New York: Troll.
Rankin, L. 1996. *Handmade Alphabet.* New York: Picture Puffins.

Chapter 2

Professional Books

Asher, J. 2000. *Learning Another Language Through Actions.* Los Gatos, CA: Sky Oaks.
Cary, S. 2004. *Going Graphic: Comics at Work in the Multilingual Classroom.* Portsmouth, NH: Heinemann.

Dragan, P. B. 2003. *Everything You Need to Know to Teach First Grade.* Portsmouth, NH: Heinemann.

Freeman, Y. S., and D. E. Freeman. 1998. *ESL/EFL Teaching: Principles for Success.* Portsmouth, NH: Heinemann.

Peregoy, S. F., and O. F. Boyle. 2004. *Reading, Writing and Learning in ESL: A Resource Book for K–12 Teachers, MyLabSchool Edition.* 4th ed. Needham Heights, MA: Allyn & Bacon.

Rogovin, P. 2004. *Why Can't You Behave?* Portsmouth, NH: Heinemann.

Children's Books

Aardema, V. 1998. *Borreguita and the Coyote.* New York: Dragonfly.

Fox, M. 1998. *Tough Boris.* Reprint ed. New York: Voyager.

———. 2001. *Whoever You Are.* New York: Voyager.

Henkes, K. 2000. *Wemberly Worried.* New York: Greenwillow.

Hoffman, M. 1991. *Amazing Grace.* New York: Dial.

Kraus, R. 1994. *Leo the Late Bloomer.* Reissue ed. New York: HarperCollins.

Steptoe, J. 1989. *The Story of Jumping Mouse.* New York: HarperTrophy.

Children's Multimedia

The Black Stallion. 1979. VHS. Director, C. Ballard. Santa Monica, CA: MGM.

Chapter 3

Professional Books and Papers

Fillmore, L. Wong 1991. "Second Language Learning in Children: A Model of Language Learning in Social Context." In *Language Processing by Bilingual Children,* ed. E. Bialystok. Cambridge: Cambridge University Press.

Krashen, E., S. Krashen, and T. Terrell. 1983. *Natural Approach* (Language Teaching Methodology Series). New York: Pergamon Press.

Krashen, S. 2003a. *Explorations in Language Acquisition and Use.* Portsmouth, NH: Heinemann.

———. 2003b. *The Power of Reading.* 2d ed. Portsmouth, NH: Heinemann.

Samway, K. D. and D. McKeon. 1999. *Myths and Realities.* Portsmouth, NH: Heinemann.

Wittgenstein, L. 2003. Calendar. *365 Daily Thoughts and Inspirations About Teachers.* Huntington Beach, CA: Avalanche.

Children's Books

Ahlberg, J., and A. Ahlberg. 1999. *Each Peach Pear Plum.* New York: Penguin.

Frasconi, A. 1972. *See and Say.* New York: Harcourt.

Hort, L. 2003. *The Seals on the Bus.* New York: Owlet Paperbacks.

Martin, B. Jr. 1991. *Polar Bear, Polar Bear, What Do You Hear?* Illus. E. Carle. New York: Henry Holt.

———. 1992. *Brown Bear, Brown Bear, What Do You See?* Illus. E. Carle. New York: Holt.

———. 1996. *"Fire! Fire!" Said Mrs. McGuire.* New York: Harcourt.

———. 2002. *Oso pardo, oso pardo, ¿qué ves ahí?* Board Book. Reprint ed. New York: Holt.

Martin, B. Jr., and J. Archambault. 2000. *Chicka Chicka Boom Boom*. New York: Aladdin.

Oxenbury, H. 2003. *Farmer Duck*. Board ed. Cambridge, MA: Candlewick.

Spier, P. 1988. *People*. New York: Doubleday.

Van Laan, N. 1992. *Possom Come A-Knockin'*. New York: Dragonfly.

———. 1995. *The Big Fat Worm*. New York: Random House.

Wood, A., 1991. *The Napping House*. Illus. D. Wood. New York: Harcourt.

Zelinsky, P. 1990. *The Wheels on the Bus*. Pop-up ed. New York: Dutton.

Children's Nonfiction

Freedman, R. 1998. *Kids at Work: Lewis Hine and the Crusade Against Child Labor*. Photog. L. Hine. Reprint ed. New York: Clarion.

Kindersley, A., and B. Kindersley. 1995. *Children Just Like Me*. New York: DK Children.

———. 1997a. *Celebrations: Festivals, Carnivals, and Feast Days from Around the World*. Collingdale, PA: Diane.

———. 1997b. *Children Just Like Me: Celebrations!* New York: DK Children.

Children's Chapter Books

Dahl, R. 1998. *Matilda*. Reissue ed. New York: Puffin Books.

L'Engle, M. 1973. *A Wrinkle in Time*. Reissue ed. New York: Yearling.

Paterson, K. 1987. *Bridge to Teribithia*. Reissue ed. New York: HarperTrophy.

Rowling, J. K. 2004. *Harry Potter*, Paperback Boxed Set Books 1–5. New York: Scholastic.

Children's Books: Participation Books

Aardema, V. 1992. *Bringing the Rain to Kapiti Plain: A Nandi Tale*. New York: Dial.

Ahlberg, J., and A. Ahlberg. 1999. *Each Peach Pear Plum*. New York: Penguin.

Alborough, J. 1997. *Where's My Teddy?* Cambridge, MA: Candlewick.

Brown, M. W. 1997. *The Important Book*. New York: HarperTrophy.

Burningham, J. 1990. *Mr. Gumpy's Outing*. Reissue ed. New York: Holt.

Carlstrom, N. W. 1996. *Jesse Bear, What Will You Wear?* New York: Aladdin.

Charlip, R. 1993. *Fortunately*. New York: Pearson.

Emberley, B. 1987. *Drummer Hoff*. Illus. E. Emberley. New York: Simon & Schuster.

Fox, M. 1992. *Hattie and the Fox*. New York: Pearson.

Gag, W. 1996. *Millions of Cats*. Reissue ed. New York: Paper Star.

Hoberman, M. A. 1982. *A House Is a House for Me*. Reissue ed. New York: Puffin.

Hort, L. 2003. *The Seals on the Bus*. New York: Owlet Paperbacks.

Krauss, R. 1989. *The Carrot Seed*. Illus. C. Johnson. New York: HarperCollins.

Mahy, M. 1987. *17 Kings and 47 Elephants*. New York: Dial.

Martin, B. Jr. 1991. *Polar Bear, Polar Bear, What Do You Hear?* Illus. E. Carle. New York: Holt.

———. 1992. *Brown Bear, Brown Bear, What Do You See?* New York: Holt.

———. 1996. *"Fire! Fire!" Said Mrs. McGuire*. New York: Harcourt.

Martin, B. Jr., and J. Archambault. 2000. *Chicka Chicka Boom Boom*. New York: Aladdin.

Merriam, E. 1994. *Train Leaves the Station*. Illus. D. Gottlieb. New York: Holt.

Numeroff, L. 1997. *If You Give a Mouse a Cookie*. New York: HarperTrophy.

Rosen, M. 2003. *We're Going on a Bear Hunt*. Illus. H. Oxenbury. New York: Aladdin.

Sendak, M. 1991. *Chicken Soup with Rice: A Book of Months*. New York: Pearson.

Tabak, S. 1999. *Joseph Had a Little Overcoat*. New York: Viking (Penguin Putnam).

Van Laan, N. 1992. *Possom Come A-Knockin'*. Illus. G. Booth. New York: Knopf.

———. 1995. *The Big Fat Worm*. Illus. M. Russo. New York: Knopf.

———. 1988. *Sheep in a Jeep*. Illus. M. Apple. Boston: Houghton Mifflin.

Wood, A. 1991. *The Napping House*. Illus. D. Wood. New York: Harcourt.

Zolotow, C. 2000. *Do You Know What I'll Do?* Illus. J. Steptoe. Revised ed. New York: HarperCollins.

Chapter 4

Professional Books

Cary, S. 1997. *Second Language Learners*. Strategies for Teaching and Learning Professional Library. Portland, ME: Stenhouse.

———. 2000. *Working with Second Language Learners: Answers to Teachers' Top Ten Questions*. Portsmouth, NH: Heinemann.

Dragan, P. B. 2003. *Everything You Need to Know to Teach First Grade*. Portsmouth, NH: Heinemann.

Graham, C. 1979. *Jazz Chants: Rhythms of American English for Students of English as a Second Language*. New York: Oxford University Press.

———. 2003a. *Jazz Chants*. New York: Oxford University Press.

———. 2003b. *Jazz Chants*. CD. New York: Oxford University Press.

Warren, J. 1983. *Piggyback Songs: New Songs Sung to the Tunes of Childhood Favorites*. Boone, IA: Totline.

Children's Books

Ada, A. F., and F. I. Campoy. 2003. *Pío Peep! Traditional Spanish Nursery Rhymes*. English adapt. A. Schertle. New York: HarperCollins.

Aliki. 1998. *Marianthe's Story: Painted Words, Spoken Memories*. New York: Greenwillow.

Beall, P. C., et al. 2002. *Wee Sing Around the World*. Book, CD, and cassette. New York: Price, Sloan, Stern.

Brown, P. 1978. *Hickory*. New York: HarperCollins.

Bunting, E. 1990. *How Many Days to America: A Thanksgiving Story*. Reprint ed. New York: Clarion.

Choi, Y. 2001. *The Name Jar*. New York: Knopf Books for Young Readers.

Edwards, M. 2001. *Pa Lia's First Day*. Tarzana, CA: Rebound by Sagebrush.

Hoa, N. 1989. In *Angel Child, Dragon Child*. (See Surat).

Hoffman, M. 2002. *The Color of Home*. New York: Phyllis Fogelman.

Joosse, B. 1995. *The Morning Chair*. New York: Clarion.

Langstaff, J. 1991. *Oh, A-Hunting We Will Go*. Illus. N. W. Parker. New York: Aladdin.

Lass, B., and P. Sturges. 2000. *Who Took the Cookies from the Cookie Jar?* New York: Scholastic.

Park, F., and G. Park. 2002. *Good-Bye, 382 Shin Dang Dong*. New York: National Geograpic.

Recorvits, H. 2003. *My Name Is Yoon*. New York: Farrar, Straus and Giroux.

Surat, M. M. 1989. *Angel Child, Dragon Child*. Reading Rainbow book. New York: Scholastic Paperbacks.

Wilkes, S. 1994. *Un día tuvimos que huir*. London: Evans Brothers.

Children's Recordings

Langstaff, J. 2002. *John Langstaff Sings the Jackfish, and Other Songs for Singing Children*. CD. New York: Revels Records.

———. 2004. *Songs for Singing Children*. CD. New York: Revels Records.

Langstaff, N., and J. Langstaff. 1986. *Sally Go Round the Moon and Other Revels Songs and Singing Games for Young Children*. New York: Revels Records.

A Sampling of *Reading Rainbow* Videos

The videos are available from:

Great Tapes for Kids, PO Box 954, Middlebury, VT 05753
Phone: 800-KID-TAPES (888-543-8273) or 802-462-2623

Amazing Grace
Angel Child, Dragon Child
Bicycle Man
Bringing the Rain to Kapiti Plain
Galimoto
Linnea in Monet's Garden
Mufaro's Beautiful Daughters
Tar Beach
Uncle Jed's Barbershop

Chapter 5

Professional Books

Carson, J. 1984. *Tell Me About Your Picture: Art Activities to Help Children Communicate*. Palo Alto, CA: Dale Seymour.

Graves, D. 2004. *Teaching Day by Day: 180 Stories to Help You Along the Way*. Portsmouth, NH: Heinemann.

Owocki, G., and S. Bredecamp. 1999. *Literacy Through Play*. Portsmouth, NH: Heinemann.

Children's Books

Anholt, L. 2003. *The Magical Garden of Claude Monet*. New York: Barron's Educational Series.

Axelrod, A. 1997. *Pigs Will Be Pigs: Fun with Math and Money*. Reprint ed. New York: Aladdin.

Barton, B. 1990. *Building a House.* Reissue ed. New York: HarperTrophy.

Bjork, C. 1987. *Linnea in Monet's Garden.* New York: R & S.

Browne, A. 2001. *Willy's Pictures.* Boston: Walker.

Conrad, P. 1995. *The Tub People.* New York: HarperTrophy.

Day, A. 1988. *Frank and Ernest.* New York: Scholastic.

Everitt, B. 1995. *Mean Soup.* New York: Voyager.

Gibbons, Gail. 1987. *Fire! Fire!* New York: HarperTrophy.

Hurd, T. 1998. *Art Dog.* New York: HarperTrophy.

Hyman, T. S. 1983. *Little Red Riding Hood.* New York: Holiday House.

Lester, H. 1990. *Tacky the Penguin.* Reprint ed. Boston: Houghton Mifflin.

Lobel, A. 2002. Frog and Toad Book Set. New York: Scholastic.

Martin, B. Jr. 1999. *"Fire! Fire!" Said Mrs. McGuire.* Reprint ed. New York: Voyager.

Mayhew, J. 2004. *Katie's Picture Show.* New ed. New York: Orchard.

McLerran, A. 1992. *Roxaboxen.* Illus. B. Cooney. New York: Pearson.

Paulsen, G., and R. W. Paulsen. 1998. *The Tortilla Factory.* Reprint ed. New York: Voyager.

Sassa, R. 2001. *The Stray Dog: From a True Story.* New York: HarperCollins.

Schneider, H. 2000. *Chewy Louie.* New York: Scholastic.

Sendak, M. 1991. *Pierre: A Cautionary Tale in Five Chapters and a Prologue.* Reprint ed. New York: HarperTrophy.

Shaw, N. 1995. *Sheep Out to Eat.* Reprint ed. Boston: Houghton Mifflin.

Steig, W. 1990. *Doctor DeSoto.* Reissue ed. New York: Farrar, Straus and Giroux.

Zion, G. 1997. *Harry, the Dirty Dog Treasury—Three Stories.* New York: Barnes & Noble.

Zolotow, C. 1985. *William's Doll.* Illus. W. P. duBois. Reprint ed. New York: HarperTrophy.

Children's Books: English as a Second Language

Burningham, J. 2002. *Would You Rather?* Zurich, Switzerland: North-South/ SeaStar.

Levine, E. 1995. *I Hate English.* New York: Scholastic.

Wildsmith, B. 1997. *Brian Wildsmith's Amazing World of Words.* Brookfield, CT: Millbrook.

Folk and Fairy Tales

Aardema, V. 1998. *Borreguita and the Coyote: A Tale from Ayutla, Mexico.* Illus. P. Mathers. Reprint ed. New York: Random House.

dePaola, T. 1981. *Fin M'Coul: The Giant of Knockmany Hill.* New York: Holiday House.

———. 2002. *Adelita: A Mexican Cinderella Story.* New York: Putnam.

Galdone, P. 2001. *Nursery Classics: A Galdone Treasury.* New York: Clarion.

Kellogg, S. 1987. *Chicken Little.* Reprint ed. New York: HarperTrophy.

Knutson, B. 2004. *Love and Roast Chicken: A Trickster Tale from the Andes Mountains.* Minneapolis: Carolrhoda.

Marshall, J. 1993. *Red Riding Hood.* New York: Puffin.

McDermott, G. 1988. *Anancy the Spider: A Tale from the Ashanti.* New York: Holt.

———. 1993. *Raven: A Trickster Tale from the Pacific Northwest.* New York: Harcourt.

————. 2001. *Jabuti the Tortoise: A Trickster Tale from the Amazon*. New York: Harcourt.

Sierra, J. 1996. *Nursery Tales Around the World*. New York: Clarion.

Slobodkina, E. 1988. *Caps for Sale: A Tale of a Peddler, Some Monkeys and Their Monkey Business*. New York: HarperCollins.

Stevens, J. 1995. *The Three Billy Goats Gruff*. New York: Harcourt Brace.

Wattenberg, J. 2000. *Henny Penny*. New York: Scholastic.

Wiesner, D. 2001. *The Three Pigs*. New York: Clarion.

Zelinsky, P. O. 1986. *Rumplestiltskin*. New York: Puffin.

Children's Books with Math Themes—Hundreds Day

Cuyler, M. 2000. *100th Day Worries*. Illus. A. Howard. New York: Simon & Schuster.

Harris, T. 2000. *100 Days of School*. Illus. B. G. Johnson. Brookfield, CT: Millbrook.

Kasza, K. 1989. *The Wolf's Chicken Stew*. New York: Putnam.

Pinczes, E. 1999. *One Hundred Hungry Ants*. Illus. B. MacKain. Boston: Houghton Mifflin.

Ryan, P. M. 1996. *One Hundred Is a Family*. Illus. B. Huang. New York: Hyperion.

Slate, J. 1998. *Miss Bindergarten Celebrates the 100th Day of Kindergarten*. Illus. A. Wolff. New York: Dutton.

Sloat, T. 1995. *From One to One Hundred*. New York: Puffin.

Wells, R. 2000. *Emily's First 100 Days of School*. New York: Hyperion.

Children's Books: Kites

Compestine, Y. C. 2003. *The Story of Kites*. New York: Holiday House.

Demi, H. 2000. *Kites: Magic Wishes That Fly Up to the Sky*. New York: Dragonfly.

Lin, G. 2004. *Kite Flying*. New York: Dragonfly.

Yolen, J. 1998. *The Emperor and the Kite*. New York: Putnam.

Children's Recordings

Diamond, C. 1985. *10 Carrot Diamond*. CD. Richmond, B.C., Canada: Hug Bug Music.

————. 1998. *Charlotte Diamond's Musical Treasures: A Songbook with Activities for Teachers and Families*. Richmond, B.C. Canada: Hug Bug Music.

————. 2000. *Charlotte Diamond's World*. CD. Richmond, B.C., Canada: Hug Bug Music.

McCracken, R., and M. McCracken. 1999. *The Tiger Sings on CD*. Blaine, WA: Glitchless Productions.

Chapter 6

Professional Books and Programs

Andrzejczak, N., Project director. 2003. Project RAISE: Elements and Applications—A New View. Visual Integration to Enhance Writing. Lake Elsinore, CA: Project RAISE.

Asher, J. 2000. *Learning Another Language Through Actions*. Los Gatos, CA: Sky Oaks.

Dragan, P. B. 2001. *Literacy from Day One*. Portsmouth, NH: Heinemann.

———. 2003. *Everything You Need to Know to Teach First Grade*. Portsmouth, NH: Heinemann.

Owocki, G. 1999. *Literacy Through Play*. Portsmouth, NH: Heinemann.

Wiertsema, H. 2002. *101 Movement Games for Children*. Berkeley, CA: Publishers Group West.

Poetry

Carle, E., illus. 1999. *Eric Carle's Animals, Animals*. Comp. L. Whipple. New York: Puffin.

Cole, J. 1984. *A New Treasury of Children's Poetry*. New York: Doubleday.

de Regniers, B. S., ed. 1988. *Sing a Song of Popcorn: Every Child's Book of Poems*. Reprint ed. New York: Scholastic.

George, K. O. 2005. *Fold Me a Poem*. New York: Harcourt.

Hopkins, L. B., ed. 2005. *Days to Celebrate: A Full Year of Poetry*. New York: Greenwillow.

Kennedy, X. J., and D. M. Kennedy. 1992. *Talking Like the Rain*. Boston: Little, Brown.

Kuskin, K. 2003. *Moon, Have You Met My Mother? The Collected Poems of Karla Kuskin*. New York: HarperCollins/Laura Geringer.

Larrick, N. 1990. *Mice Are Nice*. New York: Philomel Books.

Lobel, A. 1988. *Whiskers and Rhymes*. New York: Morrow.

Moore, L. 1992. *Sunflakes: Poems for Children*. New York: Clarion.

Prelutsky, J. 1986. *Ride a Purple Pelican*. Illus. G. Williams. New York: Morrow.

———. ed. 2000. *The Random House Book of Poetry for Children*. Illus. A. Lobel. New York: Random House.

Watson, C. 1987. *Father Fox's Pennyrhymes*. Reprint ed. New York: HarperTrophy.

———. 1992. *Catch Me and Kiss Me and Say It Again*. New York: Puffin.

Children's Books

Bryan, A. 2003. *Beautiful Blackbird*. New York: Atheneum.

McDermott, G. 1996. *Zomo the Rabbit: A Trickster Tale from West Africa*. New York: Voyager.

———. 2001. *Jabuti the Tortoise: A Trickster Tale from the Amazon*. New York: Harcourt.

McPhail, D. 1999. *Those Can-Do Pigs*. Reprint ed. New York: Puffin.

Van Allsburg, C. 1985. *The Polar Express*. Boston: Houghton Mifflin.

Children's Recordings

Bryan, A. 2004. *Ashley Bryan's Beautiful Blackbird and Other Folktales*. CD. Audio Bookshelf.

Diamond, C. 1985. *10 Carrot Diamond*. CD. Richmond, B.C., Canada: Hug Bug Music.

———. 2000. *Charlotte Diamond's World*. CD. Richmond, B.C., Canada: Hug Bug Music.

Langstaff, J. 1996. *Songs for Singing Children*. CD. New York: Revels Records.

———. 2002. *John Langstaff Sings the Jackfish, and Other Songs for Singing Children.* CD. New York: Revels Records.

Palmer, H. 1960. *Learning Basic Skills Through Music.* CD.

———. 2000. *Easy Does It: Activity Songs for Basic Motor Skill Development.* Record (Ar581). Educational Activities. (See Discount School Supply Catalog, 800-627-2829.)

Raffi. 1996a. *Baby Beluga.* CD. Rounder/Pgd.

———. 1996b. *The Singable Songs Collection.* CD. Rounder/Pgd.

Smithsonian Folkways Children's Music Collection. 1998. Various artists. CD. Smithsonian/Folkways.

Chapter 7

Professional Books and Articles

Avery, C. 2002. *And with a Light Touch: Learning About Reading, Writing, and Teaching with First Graders.* 2d ed. Portsmouth, NH: Heinemann.

Dragan, P. B. 2001. *Literacy from Day One.* Portsmouth, NH: Heinemann.

Fisher, B., and E. F. Medvic. 2000. *Perspectives on Shared Reading: Planning and Practice.* Portsmouth, NH: Heinemann.

Fountas, I. C., and G. S. Pinnell. 1996. *Guided Reading: Good First Teaching for All Children.* Portsmouth, NH: Heinemann.

Fox, M. 2001. *Reading Magic: Why Reading Aloud to Our Children Will Change Their Lives Forever.* New York: Harvest.

Hall, D., and P. Cunningham. 2002. *Month by Month Phonics for First Grade: Systematic, Multilevel Instruction.* Greensboro, NC: CarsonDellosa.

Holdaway, D. 1984. *The Foundations of Literacy.* Portsmouth, NH: Heinemann.

Lewis, V., and W. M. Mayes. 2004. *Valerie & Walter's Best Books for Children: A Lively, Opinionated Guide,* Revised Edition. New York: Avon.

Marriott, D., and J. Kupperstein, eds. 2001. *What Are the Other Kids Doing While You Teach Small Groups?* Huntington Beach, CA: Creative Teaching.

Miller, D. 2002. *Reading with Meaning: Teaching Comprehension in the Primary Grades.* Portland, ME: Stenhouse.

New York Times Obituary for Bill Martin, Jr. Aug. 13, 2004.

Routman, R. 2002. *Reading Essentials: The Specifics You Need to Teach Reading Well.* Portsmouth, NH: Heinemann.

Spann, M. B. 2001. *The Scholastic Big Book of Word Walls: 100 Fresh & Fun Word Walls, Easy Games, Activities, and Teaching Tips to Help Kids Build Key Reading, Writing, Spelling Skills and More!* New York: Scholastic.

Taberski, S. 2000. *On Solid Ground: Strategies for Teaching Reading K–3.* Portsmouth, NH: Heinemann.

Trelease, J. 2001. *The Read-Aloud Handbook.* 5th ed. New York: Penguin.

Children's Books

Bradby, M. 1995. *More than Anything Else.* Illus. C. K. Soentpiet. New York: Orchard/Jackson (Scholastic).

Carrick, D. 1990. *The Wednesday Surprise.* Illus. E. Bunting. New York: Scott Foresman.

Cohen, M. 1989. *When Will I Read?* New York: Aladdin.

Henkes, K. 2004. *Kitten's First Full Moon.* New York: Greenwillow.

Hoberman, M. 2002. *You Read to Me, I'll Read to You: Very Short Stories to Read Together.* Illus. M. Emberley. Boston: Megan Tingley, Little, Brown.

LeSeig, T. 1965. *I Wish That I Had Duck Feet.* New York: Random House.

McPhail, D. 1997a. *Edward and the Pirates.* Boston: Little, Brown.

———. 1997b. *Santa's Book of Names.* Boston: Little, Brown.

Mora, P. 2000. *Tomas and the Library Lady.* Illus. R. Colon. New York: Dragonfly.

Shannon, D. 2004. *A Bad Case of Stripes.* New York: Scholastic.

Sierra, J. 2004. *Wild About Books.* New York: Knopf.

Simmons, J. 2000. *Come On, Daisy/Eja, Dejzi!* English and Arabic ed. London, UK: Miller.

Small, D. 1988. *Imogene's Antlers.* Reprint ed. New York: Dragonfly Books.

Turner, P. S. 2004. *Hachiko: The True Story of a Loyal Dog.* Boston: Houghton Mifflin.

Willems, M. 2004. *Knuffle Bunny: A Cautionary Tale.* New York: Hyperion.

Chapter 8

Professional Books

Baer, G. 1972. *Paste, Pencils, Scissors, and Crayons.* New York: Parker.

CAEP Committee of the 1990 Institute. 2003. *Chinese Children: Art on the Environment.* Beijing, China: CEEC-SEPA of China.

Carson, J. 1984. *Tell Me About Your Picture: Art Activities to Help Children Communicate.* Palo Alto, CA: Dale Seymour.

Dragan, P. B. 2003. *Everything You Need to Know to Teach First Grade.* Portsmouth, NH: Heinemann.

Dvorak, R. R. 1985. *Drawing Without Fear.* Palo Alto, CA: Dale Seymour.

Hart, K. 1988. *I Can Draw! Ideas for Teachers.* Portsmouth, NH: Heinemann.

Hubbard, R. 1989. *Authors of Pictures, Draughtsmen of Words.* Portsmouth, NH: Heinemann.

Lehman, B. 2004. *The Red Book.* Boston: Houghton Mifflin.

Marantz, S. S. 1992. *Picture Books for Looking and Learning: Awakening Visual Perceptions Through the Art of Children's Books.* Phoenix: Oryx.

Romberg, J., and M. Rutz. 1972. *Art Today and Every Day: Classroom Activities for the Elementary School Year.* New York: Prentice Hall.

Schuman, J. M. 2002. *Art From Many Hands: Multicultural Art Projects.* Worcester, MA: Davis.

State of California. 2005. *Standards for the Visual and Performing Arts.* Sacramento: State of California.

Thompson, K. B., and D. S. Loftus. 1994. *Art Connections: Integrating Art Throughout the Curriculum.* New York: Goodyear.

Children's Books

Brown, T., and Junior League of San Francisco. 1981. *The City by the Bay: A Magical Journey Around San Francisco.* San Francisco: Chronicle.

Jakobsen, K. 2003. *My New York: New Anniversary Edition.* New York: Megan Tingley.

Lucas, D. 2004. *Halibut Jackson*. New York: Knopf.

Otsuka, Y. 1981. *Sujo and the White Horse*. New York: Viking.

Reynolds, P. H. 2005. *The Dot*. Cambridge, MA: Candlewick.

———. 2004. *Ish*. Cambridge, MA: Candlewick.

Sis, P. 2000. *Madlenka*. New York: Farrar, Straus and Giroux.

Art History/Appreciation

Blizzard, G. 2002. *Come Look with Me: Enjoying Art with Children*. West Palm Beach, FL: Lickle Publishing.

Johnson, K., and J. O'Connor. 2002. *Henri Matisse: Drawing with Scissors*. New York: Grosset & Dunlap.

Kohl, M. A., and K. Solga. 1996. *Discovering Great Artists: Hands-On Art for Children in the Styles of the Great Masters*. Bellingham, WA: Bright Ring.

Matisse, H. 1947. *Jazz*. New York: George Braziller, Inc.

Metropolitan Museum of Art. 2002. *Museum ABC*. Boston: Little, Brown.

Micklethwait, L. 1993. *The Child's Book of Art: Great Pictures First Words*. New York: DK.

———. 2004. *I Spy Shapes in Art*. New York: Greenwillow.

Children's Art Activity Books

Blake, Q., and J. Cassidy. 1999. *Drawing for the Artistically Undiscovered*. Palo Alto, CA: Klutz.

Editors of Klutz. 2001. *Drawbreakers: A Drawing Book That We Start and You Finish*. Palo Alto: CA: Klutz.

Hurd, T., and J. Cassidy. 1992. *Watercolor for the Artistically Undiscovered*. Palo Alto, CA: Klutz.

Irvine, J. 1988. *How to Make Pop-Ups*. Illus. B. Reid. New York: Morrow.

———. 1992. *How to Make Super Pop-Ups*. New York: Morrow.

Kistler, M. 1988a. *Drawing in 3-D*. New York: Fireside.

———. 1988b. *Mark Kistler's Draw Squad*. New York: Fireside.

Children's Books with Art Themes and Model Illustrations

Anderson, H. C. 1999. *The Ugly Duckling*. Illus. J. Pinkney. New York: Morrow.

Andrews-Goebel, N. 2002. *The Pot That Juan Built*. Illus. D. Diaz. New York: Lee & Low.

Anholt, L. 1994. *Camille and the Sunflowers: A Story About Vincent Van Gogh*. New York: Barrons.

———. 1996. *Degas and the Little Dancer: A Story About Edgar Degas*. New York: Barrons.

———. 1998. *Picasso and the Girl with a Ponytail: A Story About Pablo Picasso*. New York: Barrons.

———. 2000. *Leonardo and the Flying Boy: A Story About Leonardo da Vinci*. New York: Barrons.

Bang, M. 1987. *The Paper Crane*. New York: Morrow.

Bjork, C. 1985. *Linnea in Monet's Garden*. Illus. L. Anderson. New York: R & S.

Carle, E. 2002. *A House for Hermit Crab*. New York: Aladdin.

Cohn, D. 2002. *Dream Carver*. Illus. A. Cordova. San Francisco: Chronicle.

Greenberg, J., and S. Jordan. 2003. *Action Jackson.* Illus. R. A. Parker. Brookfield, CT: Millbrook.

Hurwitz, J. 1993. *New Shoes for Silvia.* New York: Morrow.

Keats, E. J. 1981. *The Snowy Day.* New York: Viking.

Lionni, L. 1995. *Matthew's Dream.* New York: Knopf.

Winter, J. 1994. *Diego.* Illus. J. Winter. New York: Knopf.

———. 1997. *A Color of His Own.* New York: Dragonfly.

———. 1998. *My Name Is Georgia.* New York: Silver Whistle.

———. 2003. *Frieda.* Illus. A. Juan. New York: Scholastic/Arthur A. Levine.

Chapter 9

Professional Books and Materials

Cary, S. 1997. *Second Language Learners.* Strategies for Teaching and Learning Professional Library. Portland, ME: Stenhouse.

Dragan, P. B. 2003. *Everything You Need to Know to Teach First Grade.* Portsmouth, NH: Heinemann.

National Geographic. 1994. Video. *Really Wild Animals: Totally Tropical Rainforest—South America.*

———. 1994. Video. *Really Wild Animals: Wonders Down Under—Australia.*

Children's Books

Ardizonne, E. 2000. *Little Tim and the Brave Sea Captain.* New York: Harper-Collins.

Baker, J. 1988. *Where the Forest Meets the Sea.* New York: Greenwillow.

Bang, M. 1997. *Common Ground: The Water, Earth, and Air We Share.* New York: Blue Sky.

Briggs, R. 1986. *The Snowman.* New York: Random House.

Brown, R. 1991. *The World That Jack Built.* New York: Dutton.

Bruna, D. 1976. *Dick Bruna's Animal Book.* New York: Price Stern Sloan.

Bunting, E. 1996. *Red Fox Running.* New York: Clarion.

Burningham, J. 1994. *Hey! Get Off Our Train.* Reprint ed. New York: Dragonfly.

Cherry, L. 1994. *El gran capoquero: un cuento de la selva.* New York: Harcourt.

———. 2000.*The Great Kapok Tree: A Tale of the Amazon Rain Forest.* Reprint ed. New York: Voyager.

———. 2002. *A River Ran Wild: An Environmental History.* Reprint ed. New York: Voyager.

Cole, W. 1961. *Poems for Seasons and Celebrations.* New York: Putnam.

dePaola, T. 1985. *The Cloud Book.* New York: Rebound by Sagebrush.

de Regniers, B. S. 1958. *Something Special.* New York: Harcourt.

Ehlert, L. 1991. *Red Leaf, Yellow Leaf.* New York: Harcourt.

———. 1993. *Nuts to You!* New York: Harcourt.

Emberley, M. 1993. *Welcome Back, Sun.* Boston: Little, Brown.

Farjean, E. 1951. *Eleanor Farjean's Poems for Children.* New York: Lippencott.

Heide, F. P. 2003. *Some Things Are Scary.* Cambridge, MA: Candlewick.

Helldorfer, M. C., et al. 1994. *Gather Up, Gather In: A Book of Seasons.* New York: Viking.

Hirschi, R. 1991. *Fall.* New York: Cobblehill.

Jenkins, S. 2004. *Actual Size*. Boston: Houghton Mifflin.

Lauber, P. 1990. *Seeing Earth from Space*. New York: Orchard.

Lionni, L. 1973. *Swimmy*. New York: Dragonfly.

Livingston, M. C. 1982. *A Circle of Seasons*. New York: Holiday House.

Lobel, A. 1984. *Frog and Toad All Year*. Reprint ed. New York: HarperTrophy.

Locker, T. 2001. *Sky Tree: Seeing Science Through Art*. New York: HarperTrophy.

Martin, R. 1991. *Foolish Rabbit's Big Mistake*. New York: Sandcastle.

Morris, J. 1993. *Australian Bats*. Maleny, QLD, Australia: Greater Glider Productions.

———. 1996. *Australian Frogs, Amazing Amphibians*. Maleny, QLD, Australia: Greater Glider Productions.

———. J. 1997. *Green Air*. Maleny, QLD, Australia: Greater Glider Productions.

———. 2003. *Silly Baby Magpie*. Maleny, QLD, Australia: Greater Glider Productions.

Parr, T. 2004. *The Peace Book*. New York: Megan Tingley.

Prelutsky, J. ed. 1983. *The Random House Book of Poetry for Children*. New York: Random House.

Rose, D. L. 2001. *The People Who Hugged Trees: An Environmental Folktale*. New York: Roberts Rinehart.

Selsam, M. E. 2000. *All Kinds of Babies*. New York: Scholastic.

Shields, C. D. 1998. *Month by Month a Year Goes Round*. New York: Dutton.

Shulevitz, U. 1988. *Rain, Rain Rivers*. New York: Farrar, Straus and Giroux.

Steptoe, J. 1989. *The Story of Jumping Mouse*. New York: HarperTrophy.

Updike, J. 1999. *A Child's Calendar*. New York: Holiday House.

Van Laan, N. 2000. *When Winter Comes*. New York: Atheneum/Anne Schwartz.

Waddell, M. 1996. *Owl Babies*. Board ed. Boston: Candlewick.

Weeks, S. 2003. *Crocodile Smile: 10 Songs of the Earth as the Animals See It*. Book and CD ed. New York: Laura Geringer.

Yolen, J. 1987. *Owl Moon*. New York: Philomel.

Recording
Lourie, D. and Jed. 1973. *Small Voice, Big Voice*. New York: Folkways Records.

Chapter 10

Professional Books
Bissix, G. 1980. *Gnys at Wrk: A Child Learns to Write and Read*. Cambridge: Harvard University Press.

Bridges, L. 1997. *Writing as a Way of Knowing*. Portland, ME: Stenhouse.

Calkins, L. M. 1994. *The Art of Teaching Writing*. Portsmouth, NH: Heinemann.

Ernst, K. 1993. *Picturing Learning*. Portsmouth, NH: Heinemann.

Gallagher, P., and G. Norton. 2000. *A Jumpstart to Literacy: Using Written Conversation to Help Developing Readers and Writers*. Portsmouth, NH: Heinemann.

Graves, D. 1994. *A Fresh Look at Writing*. Portsmouth, NH: Heinemann.

———. 2003. *Writing: Teachers & Children at Work, 20th Anniversary Edition*. Portsmouth, NH: Heinemann.

Johnson, P. 1993. *Literacy Through the Book Arts*. Portsmouth, NH: Heinemann.

———. 1997. *Pictures & Words Together: Children Illustrating and Writing Their Own Books*. Portsmouth, NH: Heinemann.

————. 1998. *A Book of One's Own: Developing Literacy Through Making Books.* Portsmouth, NH: Heinemann.

Rogovin, P. 1998. *Classroom Interviews in Action.* Video. Portsmouth, NH: Heinemann.

————. 1998. *Classroom Learning, a World of Learning.* Portsmouth, NH: Heinemann.

————. 2001. *The Research Workshop: Bringing the World into Your Classroom.* Portsmouth, NH: Heinemann.

Routman, R. 2004. *Writing Essentials: Raising Expectations and Results While Simplifying Teaching.* Book and DVD ed. Portsmouth, NH: Heinemann.

Children's Books

Ada, A. F. 2001. *With Love, Little Red Hen.* Illus. L. Tryon. New York: Atheneum/Simon & Schuster.

Ahlberg, A., and J. Ahlberg. 1986. *The Jolly Postman or Other People's Letters.* Boston: Little, Brown.

Cronin, D. 2000. *Click, Clack, Moo: Cows That Type.* Illus. B. Lewin. New York: Simon & Schuster.

————. 2002. *Giggle, Giggle, Quack.* New York: Simon & Schuster.

Heide, F. P., and J. H. Gilliland. 1990. *The Day of Ahmed's Secret.* Illus. T. Lewin. New York: Lothrop.

Teague, M. 2002. *Dear Mrs. La Rue: Letters from Obedience School.* New York: Scholastic.

Waber, B. 2002. *Courage.* Boston: Houghton Mifflin/Walter Lorraine.

Williams, V. B. 1999. *Stringbean's Trip to the Shining Sea.* New York: Mulberry.

Books About Making Pop-Ups and Other Books

Carter, D. A., J. Diaz. 1999. *The Elements of Pop-Up: A Pop-Up Book for Aspiring Paper Engineers.* Pop-up ed. New York: Little Simon.

Irvine, J. 1988. *How to Make Pop-Ups.* Illus. B. Reid. New York: Morrow.

————. 1992. *How to Make Super Pop-Ups.* New York: Morrow.

Klutz. 2002. *Making Mini Books.* Palo Alto, CA: Klutz.

Children's Pop-Up Books

Bates, K. L., and R. Sabuda. 2004. *America the Beautiful: A Pop-Up Book.*

Zelinsky, P. 2000. *The Wheels on the Bus.* Pop-up ed. New York: Dutton.

————. 2003. *Knick-Knack Paddywhack!* Interactive moving parts book. New York: Dutton.

Chapter 11

Professional Books

Dragan, P. B. 2001. *Literacy from Day One.* Portsmouth, NH: Heinemann.

Fillmore, L. W., and C. E. Snow. 2002. "What Teachers Need to Know About Language." In *What Teachers Need to Know about Language,* ed. C. Adger, C. Snow, and D. Christian, Washington, DC: Center for Applied Linguistics.

Renfro, N. 1984. *Puppetry, Language, and the Special Child.* Austin, TX: Nancy Renfro Studios.

How-to Craft Books

Henson, C., and The Muppet Workshop. 1994. *The Muppets Make Puppets: How to Make Puppets Out of All Kinds of Stuff Around Your House.* Boulder, CO: Workman.

Kennedy, J. E. 2004. *Puppet Mania: The World's Most Incredible Puppet Making Book Ever.* Cincinnati, OH: North Light.

Renfro, N. 1984. *Puppet Shows Made Easy.* Spiral ed. Austin, TX: Nancy Renfro Studios.

———. 1987. *Bags Are Big! A Paper Bag Craft Book.* Austin, TX: Nancy Renfro Studios.

Children's Books

Sendak, M. 1991. *Pierre: A Cautionary Tale in Five Chapters and a Prologue.* Reprint ed. New York: HarperTrophy.

Chapter 12

Professional Books

Ada, A. F. 2002. *A Magical Encounter: Latino Children's Literature in the Classroom.* Needham Heights, MA: Allyn & Bacon.

Dragan, P. B. 2001. *Literacy from Day One.* Portsmouth, NH: Heinemann.

Taylor, D. 1998. *Family Literacy: Young Children Learning to Read and Write.* Portsmouth, NH: Heinemann.

Children's Books

Baker, J. 2004. *Home.* New York: Greenwillow.

Cannon, J. 1993. *Stellaluna.* New York: Harcourt Brace.

Chen, C. 2004. *Guji Guji.* La Jolla, CA: Kane/Miller.

Cooke, T. 1997. *So Much.* Illus. H. Oxenbury. Reprint ed. Cambridge, MA: Candlewick.

Dorros, A. 1997. *Abuela.* Illus. E. Kleven. Reprint ed. New York: Pearson.

Fox, M. 1994. *Koala Lou.* New York: Voyager.

Garza, C. L. 1990. *Family Pictures/Cuadros de familia.* San Francisco: Children's Book.

———. 2000. *In My Family/En mi familia.* San Francisco: Children's Book.

Henkes, K. 2002. *Grandpa and Bo.* Reissue ed. New York: Greenwillow.

Hest, A. 1999. *In the Rain with Baby Duck.* Reprint ed. Cambridge, MA: Candlewick.

Hoban, R. 1993. *A Baby Sister for Frances.* Illus. L. Hoban. Reprint ed. New York: HarperTrophy.

Joosse, B. 1993. *Mama, Do You Love Me?* San Francisco: Chronicle.

Kraus, R. 1986. *Whose Mouse Are You?* Illus. J. Aruego. New York: Aladdin.

Mitchell, M. K. 1998. *Uncle Jed's Barbershop.* Illus. J. Ransome. New York: Aladdin.

Mora, P. 1984. *Pablo's Tree*. New York: Simon & Schuster.

Polacco, P. 2001. *The Keeping Quilt*. New York: Aladdin.

Ringgold, F. 1996. *Tar Beach*. New York: Dragonfly.

Root, P. 2003. *The Name Quilt*. New York: Farrar, Straus and Giroux.

Rosenberg, L. 1997. *Monster Mama*. Illus. S. Gammell. New York: Putnam.

Rylant, C. 1993. *When I Was Young in the Mountains*. Illus. D. Goode. New York: E. P. Dutton.

———. 2001. *The Relatives Came*. Illus. S. Gammell. New York: Atheneum.

Soto, G. 1996. *Too Many Tamales*. New York: Pearson.

Spinelli, E. 1992. *Thanksgiving at the Tappletons'*. New York: HarperCollins.

Steig, W. 1988. *Sylvester and the Magic Pebble*. Reissue ed. New York: Aladdin.

Steptoe, J. 2001. *In Daddy's Arms I Am Tall*. New York: Lee & Low.

Viorst, J. 1988. *I'll Fix Anthony*. Illus. A. Lobel. New York: Aladdin.

Waddell, M. 1994. *Can't You Sleep, Little Bear?* Cambridge, MA: Candlewick.

———. 2002. *Owl Babies*. Reprint ed. Cambridge, MA: Candlewick.

———. 2004. *Tiny's Big Adventure*. Cambridge, MA: Candlewick.

Wells, R. 1987. *Hazel's Amazing Mother*. New York: Dial.

Williams, V. 1984. *A Chair for My Mother*. New York: Scott Foresman.

Woodson, J. 2004. *Coming Home Soon*. New York: Putnam.

Zolotow, C. 1990. *Mr. Rabbit and the Lovely Present*. Illus. M. Sendak. New York: HarperCollins.

———. 2004. *A Father Like That*. Revised ed. New York: HarperCollins.

Other References

Cultural Diversity

Dooley, N. 1992. *Everybody Cooks Rice*. Minneapolis: Reprint ed. Carolrhoda.

Fox, M. 2001. *Whoever You Are*. Reprint ed. New York: Voyager.

Frasconi, A. 1972. *See and Say*. New York: Harcourt.

Gray, N. 1991. *A Country Far Away*. New York: Orchard.

Hanamaka, S. 1999. *All the Colors of the Earth*. New York: HarperTrophy.

Hooks, B. 2004. *Skin Again*. New York: Jump at the Sun Hyperion.

Jackson, E. 2003. *It's Back to School We Go! First Day Stories from Around the World*. Brookfield, CT: Millbrook.

Knight, M. B. 1995. *Talking Walls*. Reprint ed. New York: Tilbury House.

Lewin, T. 2000. *Market!* Reprint ed. New York: HarperTrophy.

Morris, A. 2000. *Families*. New York: HarperCollins.

Rohmer, H. ed. 1999. *Honoring Our Ancestors: Stories and Pictures by Fourteen Artists*. San Francisco: Children's Book.

Ross, D. 1972. *I Love My Love with an A*. London, UK: Faber and Faber.

Schuett, S. 1997. *Somewhere in the World Right Now*. Reprint ed. New York: Dragonfly.

Stojic, M. 2002. *Hello World! Greetings in 42 Languages Around the Globe*. New York: Cartwheel Books/Scholastic.

Swope, S. 2001. *The Araboolies of Liberty Street*. New York: Farrar, Straus and Giroux.

Folk and Fairy Tales

Aardema, V. 1998. *Borreguita and the Coyote: A Tale From Ayutla, Mexico.* Reprint ed. New York: Dragonfly.

Ada, A. F. 1996. *La lagartija y el sol/The Lizard and the Sun.* New York: Dragonfly.

———. 1997. *Medio pollita/Half-Chicken.* Reprint ed. New York: Dragonfly.

Bierhorst, J. 1987. *Doctor Coyote: A Native American Aesop's Fable.* New York: Macmillan.

Coburn, J. 1996. *Jouanah: A Hmong Cinderella.* Fremont, CA: Shen's.

———. 2000. *Domitila: A Cinderella Tale from the Mexican Tradition.* Fremont, CA: Shen's.

delaPaz, M. 2001. *Abadeha: The Philippine Cinderella.* Fremont, CA: Shen's.

dePaola, T. 1979. *Strega Nona.* New York: Aladdin.

———. 1981. *Fin M'Coul, the Giant of Knockmany Hill.* New York: Holiday House.

———. 1996. *The Legend of the Indian Paintbrush.* Reprint ed. New York: Paper Star.

———. 2002. *Adelita: A Mexican Cinderella Story.* New York: Grosset & Dunlap.

Ehlert, L. 1992. *Moon Rope/Un lazo a la luna.* New York: Harcourt Children's.

———. 1997. *Cuckoo: A Mexican Folktale.* New York. Harcourt Children's.

Hamilton, V. 2000. *The Girl Who Spun Gold.* New York: Blue Sky.

Heyer, M. 1989. *The Weaving of a Dream: A Chinese Folktale.* Reissue ed. New York: Puffin.

Howland, N. 2002. *The Matzah Man: A Passover Story.* New York: Clarion.

Jaffe, N. 1998. *The Way Meat Loves Salt: A Cinderella Tale from the Jewish Tradition.* New York: Holt.

Jiang, J. 2004. *The Magical Monkey King: Mischief in Heaven.* Fremont, CA: Shen's.

Kimmel, E. 1990. *Anansi and the Moss-Covered Rock.* New York: Holiday House.

———. 1998. *Hershel and the Hanukkah Goblins.* New York: Holiday House.

———. 2003. *The Runaway Tortilla.* Orlando, FL: Winslow Press.

Lowell, S. 1992. *The Three Little Javelinas.* Flagstaff, AZ: Northland.

McDermott, G. 1977. *Arrow to the Sun: A Pueblo Indian Tale.* New York: Puffin.

———. 1993. *Raven: A Trickster Tale from the Pacific Northwest.* New York: Harcourt.

———. 1996a. *Musicians of the Sun.* New York: Aladdin.

———. 1996b. *Zomo the Rabbit: A Trickster Tale from West Africa.* New York: Voyager.

Mehta, L. 2002. *Anklet for a Princess: A Cinderella Story from India.* Adapt. M. Brucker. Fremont, CA: Shen's.

Merril, J. 1997. *The Girl Who Loved Caterpillars: A Twelfth Century Tale from Japan.* Reprint ed. New York: Paper Star.

Nye, N. S. 1997. *Sitti's Secrets.* New York: Aladdin.

Paye, W. L., and M. H. Lippert. 2002. *Head, Body, Legs: A Story from Liberia.* New York: Holt.

Root, P. 2004. *Big Mama Makes the World.* Cambridge, MA: Walker.

Seeger, P. 1994. *Abiyoyo.* Reprint ed. New York: Aladdin.

Sierra, J. 2002. *Can You Guess My Name? Traditional Tales from Around the World.* New York: Clarion.

Steptoe, J. 1993. *Mufaro's Beautiful Daughters.* New York: HarperTrophy.

Tabak, S. 1999. *Joseph Had a Little Overcoat*. New York: Viking.

Vuong, L. 1992. *The Brocaded Slipper and Other Vietnamese Tales*. New York: HarperCollins.

Young, E. 1989. *Lon Po Po: A Red Riding Hood Story from China*. New York: Philomel.

Poetry and Songs

Ada, A. F. 2001. *Gathering the Sun: An Alphabet in Spanish and English*. Tarzana, CA: Rebound by Sagebrush.

Ada, A. F., and F. I. Campoy. 2005. *Mamá Goose: A Latino Nursery Treasury*. Bilingual ed. New York: Hyperion.

Alarcon, F. 2005. *Laughing Tomatoes and Other Spring Poems/Jitomates risueños y otros poemas de primavera*. San Francisco: Children's Book.

Bryan, A. 2001. *Ashley Bryan's ABC of African American Poetry*. Reprint ed. New York: Aladdin.

Cooling, R. ed. 2004. *Come to the Great World: Poems from Around the Globe*. New York: Holiday House.

Dulacre, L. 1992. *Arroz con leche: canciones y ritmos populares de América Latina* New York: Scholastic Paperbacks.

Griego, M. C., et al. 1988. *Tortillitas para mama*. Bilingual ed. New York: Henry Holt.

Hoberman, M. A. 1994. *My Song Is Beautiful: Poems and Pictures in Many Voices*. Boston: Little, Brown.

Pomerantz, C. 1993. *The Tamarindo Puppy and Other Poems*. Reprint ed. New York: Mulberry.

Steptoe, J. 2001. *In Daddy's Arms I Am Tall: African Americans Celebrating Their Fathers*. New York: Lee & Low.

Getting Along in America

Ada, A. F. 1996. *My Name Is María Isabel/Me llamo María Isabel*. New York: Aladdin.

Aliki. 1998. *Marianthe's Story: Painted Words, Spoken Memories*. New York: Greenwillow.

Altman, L. J. 1995. *Amelia's Road*. New York: Lee & Low.

Choi, Y. 2003. *The Name Jar*. New York: Dragonfly.

Cohen, B. 1998. *Molly's Pilgrim*. Revised ed. New York: HarperTrophy.

Levin, E. 1995. *I Hate English*. New York: Scholastic.

Park, F., and G. Park. 2002. *Good-Bye, 382 Shin Dang Dong*. New York: National Geographic.

Polacco, P. 1998. *Chicken Sunday*. Reprint ed. New York: Paper Star.

Pryor, B. 1996. *The Dream Jar*. New York: HarperCollins.

Recorvits, H. 2003. *My Name Is Yoon*. New York: Farrar, Straus and Giroux.

Surat, M. M. 1989. *Angel Child, Dragon Child*. New York: Scholastic Paperbacks.

Wahl, J. 2004. *Candy Shop*. Watertown, MA: Charlesbridge.

Sampling of Picture Books Representing a Variety of Cultures

Ada, A. F. 2004. *I Love Saturdays y domingos*. Reprint ed. New York: Aladdin.

Ancona, G. 1994. *El piñatero/The Piñata Maker*. New York: Harcourt.

Andrews-Goebel, N. 2002. *The Pot That Juan Built*. New York: Lee & Low.

Baker, K. 1997. *The Magic Fan*. Reprint ed. New York: Voyager.

Bryan, A. 2003. *Beautiful Blackbird*. New York: Atheneum.

Cisneros, S. 1997. *Hairs/Pelitos*. New York: Dragonfly.

Cohn, D. 2002. *Dream Carver*. San Francisco: Chronicle.

Dillon, D. 2002. *Rap a Tap Tap*. New York: Blue Sky.

Dorros, A. 1997. *Abuela*. New York: Puffin.

———. 2005. *Julio's Magic*. New York: HarperCollins.

Garza, C. L. 1990. *Family Pictures/Cuadros de familia*. San Francisco: Children's Book.

———. 2000. *In My Family/En mi familia*. San Francisco: Children's Book.

Gollub, M. 2004. *The Twenty-Five Mixtec Cats*. Santa Rosa, CA: Tortuga.

Guback, G. 1994. *Luka's Quilt*. New York: Greenwillow.

Hest, A. 2003. *When Jessie Came Across the Sea*. Cambridge, MA: Candlewick.

Hopkinson, D. 1995. *Sweet Clara and the Freedom Quilt*. New York: Dragonfly.

Lee, M. 2002. *Nim and the War Effort*. New York: Farrar, Straus and Giroux.

Mendez, P. 1991. *The Black Snowman*. Reprint ed. New York: Scholastic.

Mitchell, M. K. 1998. *Uncle Jed's Barbershop*. Reprint ed. New York: Aladdin.

Mochizuki, K. 1995. *Baseball Saved Us*. Reprint ed. New York: Lee & Low.

Mora, P. 1994. *Pablo's Tree*. New York: Simon & Schuster.

———. 2000. *Tomas and the Library Lady*. New York: Dragonfly.

Nolen, J. 2003. *Thunder Rose*. New York: Silver Whistle/Harcourt.

Orozco, J. L. 1997. *Diez deditos: Ten Little Fingers and Other Play Rhymes and Action Songs from Latin America*. New York: Dutton.

Perdomo, W. 2002. *Visiting Langston*. New York: Henry Holt.

Ringgold, F. 1996. *Tar Beach*. Reprint ed. New York: Dragonfly.

Soto, G. 1996. *Too Many Tamales*. New York: Putnam.

Thong, R. 2004. *The Wishing Tree*. Fremont, CA: Shen's.

Whitford, A. P. 2004. *Mañana, Iguana*. Bilingual ed. New York: Holiday House.

Williams, K. L. 1991. *Galimoto*. Reprint ed. New York: Mulberry.

Winter, J. 1994. *Diego Rivera*. Reprint ed. New York: Dragonfly.

———. 2002. *Frieda*. New York: Arthur A. Levine.